HIGHLAND LIBRARY

W9-BTL-245

BRAVOS AND APPLAUSE FOR
A SONG FOR MARY

"Atmospheric . . . a touching tribute."
— *New York Times*

"A poignant and honest work."
— *New York Daily News*

"Daring stuff, wonderful stuff . . . a New York past rescued."
— *New York Observer*

"A memoir as rich as his family was poor . . . poignant."
— *Chicago Sun-Times*

"Loving . . . riveting . . . poignantly re-creates life in the tenements . . . will make you feel good a million times over."
— *Newport News Daily Press* (VA)

"A moving memoir of growing up in the tenements of New York City . . . also the record of an astonishing spiritual journey."
— *Modern Maturity*

"In this life-affirming reminiscence, the author thanks, through beautiful words, his mother for all her sacrifice."
— *Publishers Weekly*

"Captivating . . . a funny but heartbreaking picture . . . a 'song' that's worth singing."
— *Albany Times Union* (NY)

"A clear, wry, entertaining voice."
— *Roanoke Times* (VA)

more . . .

HIGHLAND LAKES
LIBRARY

"The deftly told saga of what led Dennis Smith up to the big red doors of his now-famous Engine Co. 82."
— Tom Wolfe, author of *A Man in Full*

"Richly detailed, lovingly told memoir . . . vividly re-creates the pains and joys of an impoverished Irish-American boyhood."
— *Kirkus Reviews*

"A soft look at a tough world . . . simply and lovingly told . . . a meaningful book."
— William Kennedy, author of *Ironweed*

"Tough, tender . . . heartfelt . . . genuine and memorable."
— *Irish Voice*

"Readers will have a hard time putting this down . . . highly recommended."
— *Library Journal*

"Clear, vivid, evocative. . . . The portrait of Dennis's mother, Mary, is at once unaffected and complex. An honest and admirable book."
— Thomas Flanagan, author of *The Year of the French*

"Moving. . . . Smith's good-natured storytelling makes this book worthwhile."
— *Greensboro News & Record* (NC)

"Told with elegant simplicity . . . another resonating memoir from the club of New York Irishmen called the Nine First Fridays, of whom Frank McCourt and Dennis Smith are stars."
— Thomas Keneally, author of *Schindler's List*

"Tough . . . inspiring."
— *Firehouse* magazine

"Magical . . . what all memoirs should aspire to—images poignant and sharp; memories painful and vivid. . . . If there was a crown jewel for memoirs, it would surely rest here, with this book."
— Lorenzo Carcaterra, author of *Sleepers and Apaches*

A SONG
FOR MARY

Also by Dennis Smith

Report from Engine Co. 82
The Final Fire
Glitter and Ash
Firehouse
Dennis Smith's History of Firefighting in America
The Aran Islands: A Personal Journey
Steely Blue
The Little Fire Engine that Saved the City (for children)
Firefighters: Their Lives in Their Own Words

DENNIS SMITH

A SONG FOR MARY

AN IRISH-AMERICAN MEMORY

WARNER BOOKS

A Time Warner Company

AUTHOR'S NOTE

This book is not a novel.

The persons, places, and situations are real, and the dialogue is reconstructed as best as I can remember it actually occurring. I have changed just a few of the names because I am sensitive to the right of privacy within families.

If you purchase this book without a cover you should be aware that this book may have been stolen property and reported as "unsold and destroyed" to the publisher. In such case neither the author nor the publisher has received any payment for this "stripped book."

Copyright © 1999 by Dennis Smith
Reading Group Guide copyright © 2000 by Dennis Smith and Warner Books, Inc.
All rights reserved.

Warner Books, Inc., 1271 Avenue of the Americas, New York, NY 10020

Visit our Web site at www.twbookmark.com

w A Time Warner Company

Printed in the United States of America
Originally published in hardcover by Warner Books, Inc.
First Trade Printing: March 2000
10 9 8 7 6 5 4 3 2 1

The Library of Congress has cataloged the hardcover edition as follows:
Smith, Dennis, 1940–
    A song for Mary : an Irish-American memory / Dennis Smith.
        p. cm.
    ISBN 0-446-52447-6
    1. Smith, Dennis, 1940–   —Childhood and youth. 2. Irish Americans—New York
(State)—New York—Social life and customs. 3. Catholics—New York (State)—New York—
Social life and customs. 4. Irish American families—New York (State)—New York.
5. Novelists, American—20th century—Biography. 6. Firefighters—United States—
Biography. I. Title.
PS3569.M523Z47 1999
813'.54—dc21
    [b]   98-22786
ISBN 0-446-67568-7 (pbk.)   CIP

Cover design and illustration by Honi Werner

For my brother Bill
with love and admiration
and for Carlin and Henry Patrick
the coming generation

Prologue

Sitting with my brother in the first pew of Queen of Angels Church I can hear the beeping horns and speeding cars and trucks on Queens Boulevard, and I wish it were quieter. I look around the church and into the faces of my five children and my brother's four, searching for some sign of grief. Do they miss her? I keep asking myself.

Do they know anything about her?

There are no flags or draperies on her casket, no brass or silver ornaments. Just a small bouquet of mixed flowers sitting on top, about where her folded hands would be. The casket looks strong and modest, words that apply to her like colors on a drab canvas.

These sons and daughters and nieces and nephews of mine have had privileged upbringings and little has been missed for the wanting. But they are the grandchildren of a tough New York life. I study them now as the priest goes through the Mass, all of them young adults, each with a life of his or her own, each with a unique set of problems and confrontations, needs and desires. Sure, they loved her, but I wonder if any of them have found time in their busy and complicated lives to touch themselves with her life, to be anointed with a memory that might protect them or help them or make them more complete.

Why didn't I think of it beforehand? There will never be another opportunity like this. I could have written something, the priest could have introduced an oration. But she wouldn't have approved of that kind of singling out, even at the funeral. No, keep it modest, she would advise. Remember that railroad tracks are plain and ordinary, but they'll get you where you're going.

Still, I want them to remember this moment, for it should be a monument moment.

The priest is at the communion, and I go to the altar.

"I want to say something," I whisper.

The priest is shocked out of the usual.

"Who are you?" he asks.

The children are lined up behind to receive.

"Their father," I say, gesturing toward them.

I stand to the side until the communion is finished, but the priest goes past me as if I am invisible. He busies himself at the altar, paying me no mind, but I stand my ground. I'll have my say in or out of his agenda.

Finally, he looks up to the small group, and says, "A family member wants to say something."

I look at the small casket enveloping what has become no more than ninety pounds of skin and bones. There is not a cough or a sneeze or a shuffle in the church. The traffic sounds have momentarily disappeared, and it is perfectly quiet. "Just one thing," I say, "that I want to ask you to think about as we're all gathered here trying to commemorate a life. The true epitaph is not the message epitomizing a person that is etched into a headstone, but the memory that resides in the swelling of the heart. Each of you might have hundreds of memories, but you have to make sure you find the right one, the one that speeds the blood. Sometimes, you have to search long and deep within yourself to find that particular memory, and when you find it you'll know, for this is the epitaph that will stand your test of time. So I ask you to remember Mary like this, and like anything in your life that is worthwhile, there is no time like now to start."

Chapter One

I am seven years old and I know the difference between right and wrong.

It's been my job for more than a month to take the erasers out to the school yard at ten minutes to three each day and clap them against the brick wall so they'll be nice and clean for Sister Maureen in the morning. But today, when we were standing for our afternoon prayers, Peter Shalleski knuckled me in the back of the head. We were in the middle of the Hail Holy Queen. It's too bad that Sister Maureen didn't see that. She only saw that I took Shalleski's ear right after O Clement O Loving O Sweet Virgin Mary and twisted it so that it nearly came off. I should have bopped him right there in front of everyone, in the middle of the Hail Holy Queen, but I know he is tougher than anyone in the class, and I know as sure as Charlie McCarthy has a wooden head that Shalleski is going to get even with me later for the twisted ear.

I don't care.

My head is hurting from where he knuckled me, but I know it is going to hurt even more as Sister is about to give me a whack with the pointer across the back of my pants. I wish I had corduroy pants instead of these thin gabardines. Here I am standing on the bare wood-slat floor, eyes closed, biting my teeth together as hard as they will go, my hands flat against the chalky blackboard, leaning over for all the class to see, as the thin pointer comes swishing down and goes *shwitt* across my shiny pants.

The sting goes through my body as I knew it would. I want to scream out, but I can't. None of the boys ever screams out, even if Sister gives three whacks, which is the most she gives. It is like it has been all thought out and in some rule book tucked in a corner somewhere in the sacristy of the church. The girls never get it, and even if they did it wouldn't hurt so much, because there is so much material in their blue uniform dresses.

I can feel the sting now as it is running up and down my body and all the way across my face, and I feel my face becoming red as I turn to the class and try to straighten up.

"Sit in the back of the class until three o'clock," Sister said.

"But what about the erasers?"

"Never mind the erasers. There'll be no more erasers for you."

It is the first job I ever had, the first time I am doing something the others do not do, something different. She gave me the job because my marks led the class on the vocabulary tests, and to lose it now because Sister didn't see Shalleski slide a knuckle across the back of my head makes me want to cry.

But I know you can't cry in front of a whole class of boys and girls. It would be like screaming out when Sister whacked you with the pointer. They would start to call you Phil the Faucet, or blubber baby, or some stupid thing, and take out their snotty handkerchiefs every time you passed them in the hallway.

And so I just raise my voice a little bit.

"Shalleski hit me first, Sister, and I don't see why I should get punished because of what Shalleski did."

"Don't raise your voice to me, young man," Sister scolded.

Mommy is always saying this, too, calling me "young man" in a voice that means being a young man is not so good, and that it gets you in trouble. Maybe Mommy and Sister are related, long-lost cousins or something.

Sister waits for a few seconds before she answers me.

"If Shalleski jumped off the Brooklyn Bridge, would you?"

"So?"

"So next time don't hit back. Turn the other cheek. Think about what Jesus said in the Sermon on the Mount, and pray for anyone who you think is mean."

I am not so sure about this turn-the-other-cheek thing, because I know Shalleski, and, just as I am praying for him, you know what Shalleski will do? Shalleski will clout the other cheek, too.

Chapter Two

I think about telling my mother all the way up the four flights of stairs at 337 East 56th Street. I count the gum blotches on the twelve marble steps of each flight to keep from crying. No one ever told me about how to keep from crying, but I figured out that if you just thought about something else, concentrated on it, the tears wouldn't come. Thirty-one gum blobs, each a square inch or so, mopped over a couple of hundred times so that the edge of the gum looks like it's blended into the marble.

There is an *O'Dwyer for Mayor* sticker on the windowpane at the fourth-floor landing, and I begin to peel it off. I want to wait for another while before I see my mother, to relax a little. I always tell her everything, and I want to get it right about Sister Maureen, about being put up in the front of the class and getting it with the pointer. I can feel my eyes begin to get tight, and I stretch them wide open.

One of the doors at the front opens and Mr. Gentile comes out to walk his dog. There are two apartments in the front, richer people than us, because they have a view of the street, and everybody knows the apartments cost more to rent, probably more than thirty dollars a month. Mr. Gentile must have money in the bank, because he talks to himself and never smiles. Mommy told me that people with money in the bank never smile and they talk to themselves. The dog barks, and Mr. Gentile raises his hand toward me, and I flinch backward.

"Leave that alone before I give you one."

I feel stupid and embarrassed to let him make me flinch like that. I want to curse at him, but I know that I will meet him again in the hall and, like Shalleski, he will want to get even. So I run the length of the long dark corridor back to apartment 26.

"Goddamn kid," I hear him say as he pulls the dog down the stairs.

Chapter Three

"Mr. Gentile cursed at me."

"Don't pay any attention to him."

She pours a bit of Karo syrup onto a piece of white bread and places it in front of me. The table has a piece of red linoleum across the top, and the linoleum is cracked and splitting apart. The wood below is rotting out.

"Why shouldn't I pay attention to him?"

I am now picking at the linoleum.

"He's just one of those guineas who don't know nothing," Mommy says as she slaps my hand away from the linoleum.

"Sister Maureen must be a guinea, then."

"Why do you say that? What happened?"

Mommy can always tell when something is a little off, not quite right.

I again begin to feel a tug of the skin around my eyes, and I want to stretch my eyes out to get rid of the tug, and so I begin to make the dreaded face as I tell Mommy the story, pulling my chin down and stretching my eyes upward. It feels good. It gets rid of the tug.

"Stop making faces."

I do it again because I can't help it, and my mother reaches for the strap. I freeze, because I know I can't run. The three rooms are each not more than eight feet long, and the kitchen is about five. Not much space to run.

"Mommy, no."

The strap comes across my shoulder, stinging. But I don't flinch. Flinching from Mommy is like running. It gets you nowhere.

The strap is a piece of belt an inch wide and a little more than a foot long. It has a slit at the end which opens to fit over the back rung of the kitchen chair.

The faces are hard to control if I think about them, and so I put all my energy into the story about Shalleski, but before I can get through it I begin to feel the tears building up in my eyes, and my nose begins to run. I don't want to cry. I am not supposed to cry about such things, but I can now feel the tears on my cheeks. I put my head on the table and let my shoulders heave up and down.

"It is so unfair, so mean of her to take the erasers away from me."

"She was right to punish you," Mommy answers. "Stop the crying, alligator tears. Sister Maureen was right."

"She wasn't. And, anyway, I don't know what alligator tears are, except that they're phony, and I'm not being phony."

"Don't correct me. You have no control. You have to learn to control yourself or you'll never get out of trouble."

Chapter Four

I love the way Mommy always finds a way to the back end of a situation. If there is something on her mind, and she does not know how to speak it head-on, she goes around it to get where she wants to be. And so she begins to tell a story that I suppose is about Sister Maureen, but I know she isn't going to mention her by name.

"When you were fourteen months old—this was just before your father went to the hospital—you were sitting in your stroller. Your father was holding Billy in his arms. You leaned forward and the stroller tipped over, and as you fell you put your little arm out to block your fall. Well, your little hand went out, and the stroller handle hit your little thumb, and then your little thumbnail just popped off your finger."

I want to tell her that since I was just a baby my arm and my hand and my thumb and my thumbnail would have had to be little.

"Oh, how you howled, even after we bandaged it all up. You must have howled for three days. I felt so bad, because I guess I just wasn't paying attention, but it does show you how you have to watch out for yourself in this world, and don't ever rely on someone taking care of you. So if you lost the eraser job, there is not much you can do but find some other way that might bring you the joy and satisfaction that came from the erasers. You have to take care of yourself, Dennis."

She is a pretty woman, Mommy is. I know because the guys on the street sometimes whistle to tease her. The sun is bouncing off the window box where we keep the milk in winter so that we do not have to buy ice to keep the milk cold. And her teeth are sparkling as she speaks. She reminds me of the pictures the nuns are always showing us of the saints and the Virgin and the Divine Trinity, where their heads are always in halos and shining, except for the Holy Ghost, who looks like a bird, and God, who looks like Moses. She wraps her arms around me now. She is always wrapping her arms around me and kissing me on the head.

Her voice sounds as if she is singing.

"I just let my eye wander for a moment, and there you were on the ground. Your own mother let you down. And now you have to find something to replace the erasers."

"Are there any bottles?"

"Look under the tub, and I think you'll find some. But change your shirt first."

"What's wrong with my shirt?"

She is always making me into a quick-change artist.

"Look at the collar. It's dirty. Just remember that you'll always think about yourself the way you feel you're dressed. Do you feel dirty?"

"No."

"Well, you should feel dirty, because you don't have a clean shirt on."

"If I'm dressed like a circus clown, I'll feel like a circus clown?"

"Yes."

"If I have big fireman's boots on, I'll feel like a fireman?"

"Maybe you need more than boots, because the boots alone might make you feel like a fisherman, but right now I want you to feel like a young man who is going out in the streets with a clean shirt."

I want to ask her how I would feel if I was wearing Sue Flanagan's clothes, because I would do anything to be that close to Sue Flanagan, but I know that she'll just say that I'm being silly, and that Sue Flanagan is ten years older and I shouldn't be thinking about her. But it's like the faces. I can't help it.

The bathtub is in the kitchen, next to the kitchen sink, and is topped by a shiny metal cover. It is too high for me to get into, and I have to use a kitchen chair to step into it when I have to take a bath. Taking a bath is something I have to do, like saying night prayers or doing homework. Sometimes Billy is doing homework at the kitchen table when I am taking a bath, and I flick water onto his page, which is always a mistake. If there was no place to run in the apartment, there was really no place to run in the bathtub, and he would give me knuckles until my mother came from the living room and reached for the belt. I don't mind the belt so much when it stops Billy from giving me knuckles.

I study the three Rheingold bottles. They are in the shadow under the tub, and I can barely see them. They are worth six cents, but they are also pretty risky, I know. I can't just pick them up, and so I put my hand in toward the bottles slowly, carefully, and shake one. I make as much noise as I possibly can, hoping that if there are any roaches there they will scurry away. I take the bottles out from under the tub, one by one, by the neck and with two fingers, and lay them side by side on the floor, rolling them over and over to make certain they are clear of the roaches.

Mommy told me that the builders put the roaches in the walls when they built the place because they had a grudge against the Irish and the Italians. There are fifty roaches in the walls for every one you see, and sometimes I think, when I am lying on the top bunk at night, that the walls are shaking with all the roaches running around behind the plaster. There are more roaches in my building than there are fish in all the five oceans, and I think that I could get used to just about anything, but I can never get used to roaches. Some nights I just can't go to sleep thinking about the shaking walls.

Taking back the empties before my brother gets to them is always a special treat, and six cents is a penny more than we put in the collection basket at church. The sacrifice, my mother calls the collection. It could take a half hour at Abbie's candy store on First Avenue to spend six cents, because it isn't easy to decide between the candy corn, the dots on the sheet, the banana marshmallows, the juju fruits, the caps that I can bang with a rock on the pavement. All two-for-a-penny treats, and you have to fight through a crowd to get to them, for the boys in the neighborhood are always trying to create excitement in Abbie's so that the old Jew doesn't see them stuffing their pockets. The bottles are a chance-in-a-lifetime opportunity, and they come two or three times a week if my brother doesn't get to them first. They are like an allowance. Anyway, the only kind of allowance I have.

But the bottles do not come without the risk. I once put an empty to my mouth and had to spit out a cockroach. If you do that once, you will never do it again, and so I turn the bottles upside down over the sink to drain them and then shove them into a paper bag.

At Rossi's grocery I wait in line until Mrs. O'Bannon gets her roast pork sandwich, the guinea hero I dream about. Almost a foot long and oozing from the sides with mayonnaise sprayed with salt and pepper and topped with lettuce leaves, the roast pork is the most expensive one you can get at Rossi's, except for the roast beef at sixty cents. We hardly ever get sandwiches, and when we do, it's just salami or cheese, but I had the roast pork guinea hero once when Mr. Dempsey from the delicatessen on First Avenue gave me a half dollar for sweeping up, and Mommy said I could keep all of it.

The nickel and the penny chime together in my hand as I walk down the First Avenue hill in the shadow of St. John the Evangelist Church. My church. The traffic light changes as I am about to cross 55th Street, and I have to wait for a few moments for the cars to pass through from Sutton Place. I look next to me, at the twelve steps of the church, and decide to pay my Uncle Tommy a visit. A navigator, he went down with six others in a B-29. In a fog. In Bayonne, New Jersey, searching for an airport on their return from Germany. He had been on forty missions in the war, and so St. John's put a plaque up just for him in the back of the church.

Forty missions in Germany and lost in Bayonne. My Uncle Pat says it is like winning the Kentucky Derby and then getting killed by your horse in the stall.

I genuflect at the back end of the center aisle and eye the red sanctuary lamp which signifies that Christ is present in the tabernacle. It is burning at the side of the altar. He was always there, I found out from Sister Maureen, except for the time between the three hours' devotion on Good Friday and the first Mass on Easter Sunday, and I think that they would save a lot of candles if they just burned the red lamp when he wasn't there.

The church is huge and beautiful, with paintings on the ceiling from one end to the other, and great big columns going down either side, maybe twenty or more of them. I walk up to the shrine of the Immaculate Conception at the small altar to the right and kneel before it. I always do this because the Virgin, her hands spread far apart, smiles at me in return for any kind of a request. She lived for requests and applications, Mommy says.

I know that I have to say a prayer, and so I begin the Hail Mary. I know all my prayers. Even the Hail Holy Queen, which took a long time to put into memory. The Hail Mary is easy, and you get to say a lot of them because that is what the priest always gives you for penance when you go to confession. Five Hail Marys and two Our Fathers is what I always get.

Confession is great, because if you did anything wrong you can just say it in confession and then forget about it. You don't have to carry it around with you like a bag of bad apples over your shoulder.

I look up at the Immaculate Heart of Mary and wait for her to smile.

"Hail Mary, full of grace! The Lord is with thee, blessed art thou amongst women, and blessed is the fruit of thy wound, Jesus."

I always think about this wound of Jesus, and what wound it is, and what kind of fruit they are talking about. I suppose it is the bloody gaping hole in his side where the soldiers put in a big spear, and I am thinking that the fruit might be bananas and oranges because I don't think they grow apples in Bethlehem, which is the neighborhood Jesus comes from.

Today I ask the Immaculate Conception to make my father better, and she says she will and smiles at me. She doesn't actually talk but gives me a message. I always close my eyes and think that I am swimming in the bottom of a deep well, and looking up I see just a small circle of light in the middle of the blackness, and there in the light is the Blessed Virgin.

Maybe, too, you can make sure that Uncle Tommy is in good shape up there. That he doesn't need much.

Now it is time for the deal. What am I going to do in return for any favors? Last time I promised to wash the kitchen floor for Mommy, and so now I look up at the Virgin and promise to wear a clean shirt whenever I can remember. She seems to think that is a square deal, and so she smiles at me.

I return to the back of the church, which is really the front, and pass the big plaques with the names of all the St. John's men who were in the wars. The first one and the Second World War. Uncle Tommy has his own plaque, a small one.

I never knew him, my Uncle Tommy, never even saw a picture of him, but whenever I look at his plaque, I invent his face, and I put words in his mouth, just like I do with my father. Sometimes I put my father and Uncle Tommy together in a room, and they always argue about what ball game they want to take me to, for I think my father likes DiMaggio and the Yankee Stadium and Uncle Tommy likes Pee Wee Reese and Ebbets Field.

And so I stand before the plaque and talk for a few minutes to my dead uncle, kiss my fingers, and touch the cold bronze of his name. Just next to him is the heavy wrought-iron poor box screwed to the wall, and I separate the penny from the nickel. For a second, I hold the penny up like an offering, and then I reluctantly drop it into the poor box and bless myself with the sign of the cross. I do not want to give the penny up, but I picture my mother saying that if you forget the poor of the world, the world will someday forget you. It is what I remember each time I pass the poor box. So there is no choice.

That is two rolls of caps, the poor-box sacrifice, but I still have the nickel for Abbie's candy store, and a nickel will go a long way.

On the church steps, though, holding tight onto the black-painted handrail, I stop to think about the poor. Where were they? I don't know any poor except those in Ireland that my grandfather talks about. He lives with my Aunt Kitty in Sunnyside, and he is always talking. I can hardly make out what he is saying, what with his brogue.

"D'poor wuz dare, a always be dare. Dey was ten o' us ind a room an' dare was a lot less meat dare den dare wuz some music and a bit a da song."

He sounds like this, and he is always talking about music and being poor.

"You're not poor if you don't miss a meal, Pop," my mother tells him.

Uncle Tommy would have laughed at that if he heard it. And my father.

There's a family of coloreds that lives down on 54th Street, the only ones in the neighborhood. The father is the super there, and they don't look like they're as poor as colored people are supposed to be. They are all pretty fat. Like Mommy says, they don't look like they miss many meals. But their clothes are always dirty, and they go to public school.

There are so many things I don't know, like when people are poor and when they're not, or what this decimal point is that Sister Maureen keeps talking about, or why my father can't get better and come home.

And then there are so many other questions, like what is the story about the front of the church? Here I am standing on the steps of the church, and I know that, without an argument, this is the front of the church, but as soon as I walk into the church I am in the back of the church and have to walk all the way down the center aisle if I want to be in the front of the church again. So I guess there are two fronts of the church, but only one back.

Chapter Five

"C'mon already," Abbie is saying, "there are things to do instead of waiting for you to make up your mind. What's your name?"

"Moniker," I say, because I might be seven but I know it means a different name. My Uncle Tracy always says that his name is Tracy, but his moniker is Your Lord Worship Tracy.

"Monica is a girl's name," Abbie says. "What's your name?"

Abbie is always rushing you. If you have the nickel for an egg cream, he stands in front of you until you drink it, saying, "C'mon already." And he always asks your name, so that if he catches you stealing, he can tell the cops if you squirm out of his grip. A lot of the guys in the neighborhood steal every time they go into Abbie's.

"Just an old Jew," the guys say, "that gots lots of dough. He'll never miss a little candy."

I guess everybody thinks that stealing candy from Abbie is like stealing a pair of leather gloves from Bloomingdale's or a million dollars from the Rockefellers. There is a lot more where it came from, money and stuff, or Abbie's candy, and it will never be missed.

So it's probably a venial sin, and you'll get a few Hail Marys in confession, and it will be over.

But if you steal a nickel from an old widow woman that's on pension, you are sure to go to hell. Because that kind of sin is worse. No one ever said why.

Mommy says that if you steal from somebody one day, the next day you'll lie to somebody else, and your life will be worth nothing, because nobody loves a liar. If you're a liar, you'll never have a true friend, and what's the point of being alive if you don't have true friends?

I have red wagon wheels in one pocket, and licorice in the other, and a bagful of Good & Plenty. It is like a miracle what a few beer bottles will do. Abbie is now helping someone who wants an egg cream, and I could put a hundred wagon wheels in my pocket. But I guess Abbie paid for that candy, and if everyone stole some, Abbie would wonder what he paid for when he looks at the empty tray.

Kips Bay Boys Club is just around the corner on 52nd Street, and I am going there to have a game of Ping-Pong, and maybe pool if the big boys ever left a table free. Near the corner, I see Peter Shalleski and his brother Harry, who is my brother Billy's age. I know that I should put my Good & Plenty in a pocket as soon as I see Shalleski, but he is on me before I can take another step, punching like he was wound by a twisted rubber band. The bag of miniature white and pink logs goes out of my hand, and the candy spills everywhere, across the sidewalk, into the gutter, all over First Avenue. I am so mad that Shalleski does this. I want to fight back, but Shalleski has me by my shirt collar, screaming about his twisted ear, and how I got him into trouble with Sister Maureen.

What is the matter with me? I am frozen with something. I am not afraid. It's a kind of mixed-up feeling. I'm getting smashed and I can't help thinking that Shalleski shouldn't be doing this. Why does Shalleski have to punch and knuckle people all the time?

Shalleski is just a little bigger than me, not much. I could dodge him, and floor him with a roundhouse on the blind side, like I heard on the radio at the Joe Louis fight. Why don't I know how to hit him, instead of just putting my hands up to protect myself?

Shalleski is yelling with every punch. "Take that, you sonofabitch," he is saying.

Stop, stop, stop, I am thinking as I press my arms into my face.

Finally, Shalleski stops, I guess because I am not fighting back.

No one says anything, not another word. The two brothers just walk away, and I look at my candy all over the ground.

Could I kiss it up to God? Is there any of it that isn't too dirty to pick up? No, I am thinking. I don't want it because it's now dirty like the devil's ashes. Shalleski did that, and someday I will make him pay for it.

Both my ears hurt, and I feel the blood at my nose. I put my fingers to the top of my lip. It's not dripping too much, and so I throw my head back as I walk down 52nd Street.

Archie is standing at the top of the stairs at Kips. He is always there if he isn't playing dodgeball in the lower gym.

"Where's your club card?" Archie asks.

"Come on, Archie," I say, "you know me."

"Doesn't matter if I'm your brother or something, you have to have the card."

I have the black "midgets' card," the youngest age group. Midgets can just go to the lower gym to play school yard games, but the intermediates, like Billy, can use their gray card to play full-court basketball on the third floor.

I know that Billy will be in the upper gym. He's always playing basketball, or baseball, or reading. Mommy goes to the library every week to get the books, and Billy always reads them.

I have lived with Billy all my lifetime, and when you live with someone, you don't think a lot about them. They are just there like the kitchen sink. But, recently, I've been thinking that Billy has been pretty good with me, making sure I learn things that he has found out, like how to play rummy.

A few weeks ago he took me to Kips to teach me how to play Ping-Pong. We were hanging around 56th Street, doing nothing, and he just grabbed me by the neck, and like that we walked to Kips. All the while he was telling me that to get good at any sport where there is a ball, you just have to keep your eye on it, maybe just a little bit of your eye, but never take your eye off the ball completely for even half a second because someone was sure to do something just right then that you don't expect.

Since he took me to Kips for that Ping-Pong game, I have been playing as much as I can, and now I am getting pretty good at it.

Maybe, I am thinking now, he can do the same for boxing.

There is a lot of noise in the locker room because some of the boys are having a towel fight, snapping the towels at their crotches. I run past them to the gym and see Billy taking a foul shot.

"What are you doing after the game?" I call to him.

"I don't know," he yells back. "Going home?"

"Could you take a little bit of time with me?"

"What do you want? Ping-Pong?"

"To learn how to fight."

Billy looks at me like I am asking him for a loan of twenty dollars. He stops shooting the ball and comes over to me.

"You don't learn how to fight," he says at the sideline. "You just do it."

"No," I answer, "I gotta learn, 'cause I fell outta the stroller and lost my thumbnail, and I have to beat the brains outta Peter Shalleski. I have to plan it."

"What?" my brother says, a little confused. "Meet me in the weight room after the game."

The weight room is below the swimming pool and has a punching bag hanging by a chain from the ceiling and a few pairs of old boxing gloves around the room. There is also a pair of black punching bag gloves on the floor, three sizes too big for me, but I put them on and begin to punch the bag.

As I punch away I am beginning to remember the dancing lessons in the church basement, just before the Christmas Pageant. They made me dance with Peggy Sheehy. Or, maybe they made Peggy Sheehy dance with me. I remember the rules of dancing that the nuns taught us. Keep your head up straight, your chin out. Don't stiffen your knees, keep them buckled just a bit. Bring your shoulders back. Control the change of your weight from one foot to the other.

Maybe these rules are connected to boxing, I think. Maybe a good fight is like a good dance.

I am now bouncing around, jabbing at the punching bag, keeping my head straight and my knees buckled a little, and I am making it swing with each jab. Then I weave and bob, up and down, always throwing the jabs. Hit the bag, hit the bag, hit Shalleski the ratski. Swing the roundhouse. Keep the chin up.

Billy comes into the room and watches me some.

"You're doing pretty good," he says.

"Yeah, I know."

"You want to box?" He begins to pick up a pair of gloves.

I don't want to fight with my brother, even if the gloves are ten times bigger than my fists.

"No," I say, taking one last hard punch at the bag, pleased that I beat the bag to a pulp. "Let's go home."

Chapter Six

*B*illy puts his arm around my shoulder as we walk up Second Avenue, past Gasnik's Hardware, past Moe's Diner, past the newsstand. He's only nine, but he knows how to do everything. He's the basketball champ, the baseball champ, and he's never in fights, because nobody wants to tangle with somebody that moves as fast as Billy. And he is always good with lessons, no matter if it's history or boxing. "Just don't take any crap from people," he is saying. "Shalleski may give you some lumps every time, but he'll begin to respect you."

"I don't want his respect," I say, trying to walk in step with my brother. "I just want him to stop bothering me and maybe kick the crap outta him. Like kick the can."

Billy laughs.

"Maybe you hafta get madder," he says. "Maybe you're not mad enough to hurt him."

"I could kill him."

"You could? Paddy Gilligan has a zip gun."

That was something I didn't think about. Not only could I say I could kill Shalleski, but I really could kill him. I only had to talk Paddy Gilligan into loanding me his zip gun. But there is a problem. Paddy Gilligan is the toughest guy in St. John's, and he is in the eighth grade, and he would never talk to me.

"Maybe I just wanna break his nose, give him a nose like Dick Tracy."

We walk past Speece's drugstore and over the Second Avenue cobblestone at 55th Street where they didn't finish the new street paving. We turn at 56th Street, and when we pass the Hotel Sutton, we cross to the other side of the street. It is late in the afternoon, but we had just put the clocks forward and it is still light.

It is only at the stoop that my brother takes his arm from around my shoulder. He takes a good look at me and gives me a small smack at the back of my head, and laughs. I guess he sees the dried blood at the end of my nose, but he doesn't mention it.

A few women are sitting there, newspapers shoved under them to protect their skirts. One is drinking out of a cardboard container of beer which she got at Billy's Bar and Grill on the corner. It is the only place in the neighborhood that still sells beer in containers. This is Sue Flanagan's mother. Sue Flanagan is sitting there, too. I love her, even though she is ten years older than me and in nursing school. She always pretends to want to kiss me, and she laughs when she squeezes me. She doesn't know that I love her. Usually, I like to pretend that I don't like to be squeezed, because I know that makes her squeeze me harder and longer, but now I just want to get home. If there is any blood showing on me, I don't want her to see it, and so I whiz by before she catches my eye.

My mother sees the blood before I get a chance to wash it off. She is dishing out the tripe. The tripe is like the inside of a dead sponge, and she puts it beside a few carrots and peas. It looks limp, like it died just a minute ago. I hate the tripe, because it is like eating the cardboard from inside my shoe. It smells like that, too.

"What's with the bloody nose?" Mommy asks.

"Dodgeball at Kips," I say, sitting down.

I know I am risking all my future friends by lying, but she will strap me for sure if she finds out I was fighting in the street, even if you could call protecting yourself fighting.

"Go wash your face."

I go to the sink in the middle of the kitchen and open the medicine cabinet above it. I take the soap from the shelf and wash the blood from under my nose as Mommy continues to talk.

"Don't they have people there to make sure you don't get hurt?"

"Archie was there."

"Archie is always there," my brother pipes in.

"What does Archie do?"

"He hits you with the dodgeball," I answer.

"He just plays the game," Billy says. "Archie is the greatest."

The tripe is making me sick. This happened before, and it made me sick then, too. About a month ago.

"I can't eat this, Mommy," I say. Billy kicks me under the table.

"Eat it and shut up," Mommy says, dishing out some peas.

"Isn't peanut butter and jelly good enough?" I say. "I like that."

"Sure, it's like eating sugar. You need the vitamins of this, so I don't want to hear another word about it."

When Mommy says she doesn't want to hear another word, she means it, and so I don't know what to do. I can't eat this tripe, but I know I can't say anything again. I feel like crawling up in my bed and closing my eyes. I know I have to think of something to take my mind off the tripe.

"Tell me about Daddy in the hospital."

I notice my brother squirm a little in his chair.

"Daddy is fine," Mommy says.

"When did you see him?"

"I saw him last week when you went to Aunt Kitty's to play with your cousins."

"You didn't tell me."

"I forgot."

"Why can't I go?"

"I told you a million times that they don't let kids in."

"Not even a son?"

"No, not even a son."

The tripe was getting cold. I knew it would be even worse if it got cold, if that's possible.

"Tell me again about the accident," I say.

"C'mon. Just eat your dinner."

"How did he fall off of the truck?"

"He just fell, is all."

"So why are his legs so bad?"

"Because he can't move them is why. You're not touching anything."

"So why can't he use crutches or a chair with wheels or something?"

"They don't want him to," Mommy says, getting upset with me. "And you are going to be in trouble, young man, if you don't begin to put your fork in."

I notice Billy cutting the tripe into teeny pieces and mashing it into his peas before he puts it into his mouth. He doesn't say anything. He never says anything when we are talking about Daddy.

"Mommy," I say, "if we didn't put the nickel into the sacrifice box on Sunday, would we have enough money to buy different food?"

This makes her mad, I could see, for she reaches for the strap behind her.

She puts the strap across her lap.

"I don't want to hear another word."

I am getting sick from the smell of the tripe, and I feel the tugging at the corner of my eyes. So I stretch my eyes upward and my chin down, and before I know it the strap has gone across my neck.

"Stop the faces and put the fork in."

The sting at the side of the neck feels like it is glowing, like the saints glow in the picture books. I want to curse and I want to cry, but to keep my mind off everything, I begin to cut the tripe into bitsy pieces and mash it into the peas and the carrots. I make little balls the color of green and orange and a kind of tan that looks like an old baseball glove. And I hold my breath so that it hurts more than the sting at my neck, and I chew one of the balls as quickly as I can before I blow up, and I swallow.

It works. If I hold my breath long enough.

My brother even knows how to eat the tripe without getting into trouble.

"Run the water for a bath," Mommy says.

I look at Billy, who is putting his plate in the sink. He disappears into the bedroom.

"Run the water for a bath."

There is no one but me and Mommy in the kitchen.

"I can't get the tub top off," I say.

"You did it before, so just run the water."

I don't want to take the tub top off because I know there will be the roaches there, standing upside down under the tub top. Sometimes there are ten or twenty of them and I am afraid that one of them will get on my arm, or worse, into my shirt. I could get Paddy Gilligan's zip gun and kill myself if one of them got into my shirt.

I pretend to try to take the top off the tub.

"It's too heavy, Mommy."

"For goodness' sake. Billy, get in here."

When my brother comes into the kitchen, I go into the bedroom. I don't want to see Billy open the tub top, because I know the roaches don't scare him the way they do me, and he could pick one up and throw it at me. Billy just does things without complaining, that's what everybody says, and he gets all hundreds on his tests.

Aunt Anna came over one day not long ago to have tea with Mommy, and Mommy was telling her about Billy getting such good grades and all. Mommy had Billy and me in new shirts sitting there in the kitchen with Aunt Anna, because Aunt Anna is the manager at the Wanamaker's store on 42nd Street. She is my mother's aunt, really, and the only rich person in our family. I know she is rich, because Mommy says so, and she lives in a house in Queens where you have to wait for the buzzer to buzz you in, and the floors are made of marble.

Mommy told us to be on our best behavior, and to be especially nice to Aunt Anna, because she said she was going to pay for Billy to go to camp this summer, some special camp where they read a lot of books and play tennis. No one on 56th Street plays tennis.

This is the first time I have ever seen Aunt Anna at our house. Billy and I are happy to be with her because she has brought us a box of chocolates, the kind where you don't know what it is until you bite into it, and we are just chewing away as Mommy gives her a cup of tea. Aunt Anna is sitting next to the icebox, and her arm is just a couple of inches away from it, and as she thanks Mommy for the tea, I can see just behind her that a small roach is walking slowly up the green enamel side of the icebox.

I get suddenly afraid, as afraid as if someone has broken into the house with a gun and is going to mow us all down. This is so terrible, so unlucky for Mommy.

Oh, Mommy, I am thinking, what will happen to us all if Aunt Anna hates roaches the way I hate roaches and sees that roach and begins to scream? Oh, Mommy, isn't there some way we can get that roach to turn around and go back where he came from? Oh, Mommy, why do these things happen to us, why aren't we living in a house where they have to buzz the buzzer to let you in?

Aunt Anna is just talking away as the roach gets higher and higher on the side of the icebox. I can see that Mommy and Billy now have their eyes on the roach, too, and Mommy is trying to smile, and I know she is hoping that Billy doesn't get up to give it a good swat, and that she is praying that the roach will change its mind. But the roach just stays on its course, and it will soon be high enough and over enough so that Aunt Anna will be sure to see it, and she will run out of the house and we'll never see Aunt Anna again in our lives.

"You know, boys," Mommy says, "I think that Aunt Anna will be more comfortable sitting in the living room, so why don't you go in there and fluff up the pillows on the couch for her?"

I am so glad to get out of the kitchen, and I go right to the couch. I have never before fluffed up the pillows on the couch because they are hard pillows and have springs pushing up on the tops, but I try to fluff them up as Mommy asked, and Mommy finally comes in and gives me a kiss on the side of the cheek and tells us that we can change clothes and go out now.

Oh, Mommy, I am thinking as I button my flannel shirt and open the kitchen door, watching the roach now planted on the top of the icebox, I wish I didn't have to leave you alone to worry about things like Aunt Anna seeing roaches in our house.

I am now sitting on the windowsill waiting for the water to get high enough to get into the tub. It is dark, because the room is so small and the window is at a corner of the courtyard where there is hardly any light. The room is just large enough for the small bunk beds and a four-drawer dresser edging the window. There are some pants and jackets hung on the back of the door on a nail. It is a crowded room, and I have to squeeze between the bunk beds and the wall to get to the dresser and the windowsill. Suddenly, I hear a great thump, like somebody threw an elephant from the roof. And then I hear a great scream coming from the apartment next door.

The window in our bedroom cannot be opened, because it has been painted over a hundred times, and so I run into the kitchen.

"It's the guineas again," Mommy says.

I look out of the kitchen window into the back courtyard, and I see Mrs. Giambetta next door at her window screaming her head off. My mother looks over my shoulder and then pulls me away from the window.

But just before she does I can see crazy Mario sprawled and splattered across the yard concrete five stories below. Crazy Mario is Mrs. Giambetta's son.

"Just stay away from the window."

"I want to see," Billy says.

"There's nothing to see," Mommy says, blocking Billy's path to the window. "Go take a bath."

"Crazy Mario jumped outta the window," I say to Billy.

"Shut up, and take a bath, both of you."

Mommy turns away from us. It looks like she is looking for the strap, but I can see her shoulders going up and down, and her body vibrating like the radiator when the steam comes up. She goes into her room and she tries to shut the door, but it can't shut because there is no closet in Mommy's room and all the clothes are hung on the back of the door and the doorknob.

I go in and see her on the bed. She is thin, and the bed takes up almost all of the room. The bed looks so much bigger than she is. Her face is pressed against a pink spread, and she is crying. I never knew she cared about crazy Mario.

"I'm sorry, Mommy," I say to her.

She turns to me and catches her breath. Her eyes are so pretty, and it makes me sad to see them so red and swollen.

"Oh," she says, trying to smile, "it doesn't have anything to do with you. Tenement tears, you know? It's just that everything is so hard for everybody . . . especially mothers . . . Poor Mrs. Giambetta."

"She's still screaming, Mommy. Do you hear her?"

Mommy gets up and sits on the side of the bed. There is just enough room for her legs to fit between the wall and the bed. "Sure," she says, "I hear her. I just wish we could move out of midtown, maybe to a housing project in Queens, or maybe back to Brooklyn."

It seems she is talking to me, but not talking to me, because she is looking out the window at the fire escape and the back of the buildings on 57th Street.

She takes a deep breath and looks at me. She smiles, and gets up and pats my fanny. "If I could only get off this welfare, we could get a better place. Someday."

I never think much about being on the welfare, because Mommy told us to never tell anyone about it. I know she doesn't like it, though. She keeps saying if only me and Billy were older, she could leave us at home and go out and get a real job instead of running to all these Sutton Place apartments to do the cleaning and then hide the money from the welfare. The welfare is like some disease that you can't talk about, and I guess it's something you don't really want.

"Why don't you like the welfare, Mommy?" I ask as we move into the living room.

She chuckles a little. "You know how in the morning," she says, "when you try to pour the sugar in buckets on top of your farina?"

"Yeah," I say, "and you always grab the sugar bowl and take it off the table."

"Well," she says, "welfare is like a bowl of sugar. It makes things taste better, but it can make you fat in the long run, and if you're fat it's hard to move around."

"Can it kill you?"

"Kill is pretty final, Dennis. New York City has been good to us with the welfare, and God knows where we would be without it. It's just, if you can get away without any sugar in your life, then you're better off. But you never know about anything. Mrs. Giambetta was never on welfare and look what is happening in her family."

"Poor Mario is dead, huh?" I ask.

"I guess so," Mommy says. "I never knew him, except I saw him sitting on the stoop like he was hypnotized."

That's why they call him crazy Mario, I am thinking as I lie in the top bunk, thinking about the day. He just sat around staring at the cracks in the sidewalk. He made no response if you talked to him, even if you said "Excuse me" when you passed him in the hall or if you held the vestibule door for him. He was old enough to be in college, but, I am thinking, if all he does is stare at the sidewalks, he probably doesn't know how to read. I wonder what he stared at in his apartment. Did he have a certain part of the wallpaper that he liked more than the other? I knew they had wallpaper because I saw it once when I passed down the hall and their door was open, a million little flowers. Wallpaper was expensive, like a phonograph or one of those big radios that got Chicago, and you didn't have such things unless somebody gave them to you. I wondered what it was like to have no life at all, and to have wallpaper and just stare out in front of you like some statue, and to have no voice to say nothing to no one. It's like being dead, not talking to anyone, or not knowing if anyone was around you. And Mario is probably better off being dead, but I wonder where he is. Up or down? Heaven or hell? Did he do a lot of sinning behind those eyes that just stared out? Did he see Sue Flanagan's thighs when she crossed her legs on the stoop? That would give him a sin. And now he is dead, plopped like a pancake in my backyard, and I hope he is in heaven because in heaven your eyes are opened and you see everything, and Mario could have his voice back and he could say hello to everybody. But can you go to heaven if you jump out the window? I wonder who can answer that for me.

Chapter Seven

We are in a big hall, a Democratic club up on Third Avenue and 59th Street. When the trains aren't going by outside on the Third Avenue El, we can hear the fiddle music. I am counting, seven, seven, seven, and then three and three. This is an Irish reel, and it is not so hard to do, but there are so many kids in the room we are tripping over each other. The music never stops. It just goes on and on, the fiddle player at the front of the room with a cigarette curving out of his mouth looking out of the window as he plays, watching the trains go by, or seeing who is walking into Bloomingdale's across the street.

I hate it here, everyone crowded in this big room, sweating, jumping up and down like we were crushing grapes. I could be at Kips Bay in the swimming pool, but I am here because of my grandfather.

Mommy takes me here twice a month—Billy, too—to learn how to do the dances of the old country. The old country is not my old country. America is my old country. I've been in this country for seven years, since the day I was born in the Jewish hospital in the town of Bedford-Stuyvesant in the state of Brooklyn, and so it is old to me.

Mr. Mulvehill is doing the teaching, and he just goes on and on like the fiddle player, counting the numbers aloud like a cash register taking a bagful of pennies, ". . . and a one two three four five six seven

and a one two three four five six seven and a . . ." He goes on and on
until he yells at somebody for not listening to the music, but I wonder
what a miracle it would be to hear the music over the screeching of the
trains on the Third Avenue El and Mr. Mulvehill's countless numbers.

The lessons are free, and that is why Mommy drags us up here.
We used to go in the back room of Breffney's Bar on 58th Street, but
the crowd of kids got too big and they had to move it to this place.
Some Irish society, I don't know which one, pays Mr. Mulvehill to
teach us the reels and the jigs and the Stack of Barley and the Siege of
Venice, which I think is a place in Italy that I guess the Irish captured
in a war. The Irish have wars the way the French have girlfriends, my
grandfather says, a new one every week or so. I don't understand my
grandfather very much, because he comes from Cork, which besides
being the top of a bottle is also a town in Ireland where they talk so
fast that they say ten words for every one of ours. I am guessing that
the fact that my grandfather came from Cork is the reason we have to
do the dances of the old country. Why couldn't my grandfather come
from some nice place like Mexico, so that instead of learning the
dances we could learn how to take a nap after lunch?

Mr. Mulvehill gives other lessons for money, but there are not too
many kids in those classes. Those that go to the paid classes are mostly
girls. I don't know why we have to come here for our free lessons, except that Mommy has told us that in America the Irish have to keep
their dances and their songs, or they will be in danger of getting the
jobs in the banks and becoming milquetoasts, which is a toast as white
as milk and a complete failure as toast. And, anyway, there's not much
for free in our neighborhood except for Saturday confessions at church
and the Ping-Pong game at Kips Bay Boys Club.

Mr. Mulvehill calls everyone "you dare," and then he ends every
sentence with "got it?"

I have my count going pretty good, and I can see between my
hops and three steps that Mr. Mulvehill is coming over to me. Oh-oh,
I am thinking, because Mr. Mulvehill hardly has anything good to say
except a yell.

"You dare," he says to me, "listen to the music dare, an' keep your
eyes dare on your nose an' keep your head straight dare, got it? An'
hands down like fists glued against your sides, got it?"

"Yes, Mr. Mulvehill," I say, bopping away from him in my sevens.

He says this to everyone, but I don't know why I should let him yell at me like this. I think everybody in the room is looking at me, and I think he should yell at somebody else, because I have all my sevens and threes memorized. The kick steps are coming in another month, and we're going to have to remember much more than the sevens and threes, and Mr. Mulvehill will just go on yelling at everybody, anyway.

The music breaks and I look around for my mother through the crowd of forty or so kids who are still bopping up and down just for the fun of it.

Mommy is sitting on a wooden seat at the side wall, and I go over to her.

"Get back in line," she says. I can hardly hear her in the clack of the bopping kids.

"I am tired of dancing, Mommy."

"You are not tired."

"I am, and I don't like it."

"Dancing is good for you, it makes you stand up straight."

"You told me that milk is good for my teeth, too, but how come I get so many toothaches? And don't say it's growing pains."

"Don't argue with me, Dennis, until you gain another hundred pounds."

I guess she means that I can argue with her when I get bigger, but somehow I know that she won't let me argue with her even if I'm in high school.

I go back to the line when the music starts, and I start counting my sevens. How long, I am thinking, before I can argue with my mother, before I will be able to not do something that I don't want to do? Some kids have been coming here for years, from kindergarten all the way up to the eighth grade. So many dances to know, and so many numbers to count. And I'll be here, too, until I'm an old man. All because of my grandfather.

Billy took an old wooden liquor box and made a stable for Christmas. Mommy put a bunch of straw in it and a few figures she bought at the five-and-ten, and we made a little Christ child out of some cotton and a piece of old sheet. She bought a baby Jesus with the other figures, but the one we made looked like the real McCoy and not like a doll. Billy cut a hole in the back of the box for a tree light, and when it was all lit up, it looked like there really was a baby God in the stable.

There were lots of good gifts under the tree: flannel shirts, pajamas, socks, a football game that runs on batteries, a bunch of coloring books, and a paint box with watercolors, made in occupied Japan.

Now it's two days after Christmas, and we still don't have the batteries for the football, and Mommy gives us the money to buy them at the candy store across the street next to the Hotel Sutton.

Billy is racing me down the stairs two by two to go to the candy store, and when we get to the vestibule, something happens that is so different from anything I have ever seen that I can only think about what fun I am going to have.

All we can see before us is a wall of white. The snow is up and over the stoop and almost up to the top of the front door, tons and tons of snow. It must have come down from the sky like a falling mountain, even bigger than the Alps. I am now wishing and wishing, feeling my eyes getting bigger and bigger, that I got a sled for Christmas instead of the electric football. What fun we could have today with a sled. Maybe someone on the block has one and will let us take a ride.

A bunch of neighbors are in the hall and talking about how everything is closed for the day: banks, grocery stores, churches, everything.

We run up and tell Mommy that the candy store is closed and that there is the biggest amount of snow on the ground that ever fell. But Mommy doesn't seem so happy. In fact, she looks sad and disappointed.

"I saw the snow on the windowsill," she says, "but I didn't think it was this bad, and I have to go to Mr. Austin's."

"But," Billy says, "everything's closed."

"Mr. Austin isn't closed, and he wants me there today."

"The snow is higher than the door," I say.

"You guys will have to come with me," Mommy says. "I just have to get there."

"No, Mommy, we have to play in the snow."

"Later, maybe," Mommy says, "but you'll have to come with me."

*   *   *

Now Billy is making a path with a shovel he borrowed from Mr. Bopp, the super. People all over the block are digging away to make pathways, and there is a big path in the middle of the street, with snow so high on both sides that you think you're in a tunnel without a roof.

We reach the middle path, and we make our way down to Sutton Place, and then Billy and I have to dig our way out of the middle path and into one of the buildings on York Avenue, where we meet a doorman who is digging a path of his own.

Mommy talks to him for a minute, and he tells her that she can't go into the main entrance.

"I'm sorry, lady," I hear him say, "but the rules are the rules."

It is a warm day, and there is no smoke coming out from anyone's mouth when they talk.

We make our way in the middle path again and go around to 57th Street. There we have to dig out of the middle path again with the shovel and our hands, Mommy and me acting like steam shovels scooping up the snow, until we get to the iron gates of the service entrance. The service elevator man takes us up to the tenth floor, the four of us crowded into the elevator with a big burlap bag of garbage.

Mr. Austin has a marble floor when you go into his apartment, and he tells Mommy that the marble floor has a lot of stains on it and that it has to be clean for a party he is having tonight.

"Who will ever come out in this snow?" Mommy says, and she laughs a little.

Mr. Austin doesn't think this is so funny, and he sort of scolds Mommy.

"Well," he says, "whoever comes will walk on a clean floor, anyway."

Billy looks at me, and I know that he wants to hit Mr. Austin over the head with the shovel. Mommy brings us into the kitchen, where we sit on the windowsill and watch her fill a pail with soap and water. We don't say anything as we watch her because we know that she is embarrassed. I feel pretty bad that she is upset.

"Okay," she says finally as she throws a brush into the pail, "so he is not a very nice man, but we need the money. I can't wait around for sunny days to get some work, you know."

Chapter Eight

*B*illy is ten years old, and he shouldn't have done it.

I am putting my tie on, getting ready for school, and Mommy has been going through Billy's homework book, checking his lessons, and she has just seen what he has written on a back page. And she is yelling at the top of her lungs.

"This is so disgusting," Mommy is saying, "and you should know better than to say this. To write this vile thing. Filthy, gutter mouth. How did you get to be so repulsive? Your father would never use language like this, and your grandfather, either."

I hear Billy running, and Mommy is running after him. She has a wooden hanger in her hand.

"Your grandfather is a gentleman, and he cares about keeping his mouth as clean as his shirt. But you . . ."

Billy is now through the kitchen. I hate it when Mommy goes on and on like this. She gets something in her mind and it is there forever, and she never gets off it.

"You," she is yelling, "you make me sick."

Billy runs into our little room and jumps into a corner of the bottom bunk bed, trying to hide. Mommy is right behind him.

"Detestable piece of work," she yells. "I'll fix you, young man."

She is now swinging the wooden hanger, and the hanger goes off

Billy's leg and it breaks in half, but Mommy is still swinging, and the broken part of the wood goes into Billy's leg, and Billy's skin rips and he is bleeding all over the bottom bunk, and Billy yells, but just once.

I run out into the kitchen, and I see Billy's notebook open on the top of the kitchen table, and I pick it up and read the words. I can see why Billy should have known better, for he is ten years old, and should know that if you have to write, in large block letters, PAULIE FRYDE IS AN ASS-SUCKING FAGGOT, you should write it on a piece of paper that isn't in a notebook where your mother can read it.

Mommy comes into the kitchen, and I drop the book, and she opens the medicine cabinet above the kitchen sink and pulls out a box of Band-Aids. But there is only one Band-Aid, and Billy will need a much bigger bandage to stop the bleeding, and so Mommy takes a kitchen towel and tears it in half and runs back into Billy, who is as silent as a lamb under a shady tree.

Billy limps a little, but it is not too bad, and Mommy says that the cut won't need any stitches. She taped the kitchen towel around his leg, and we are going off to school now. Mommy is at the door, and she has Billy's homework book in her hand. Her bright green eyes are all watery. She kisses Billy and gives him the book.

"Tear that page out," Mommy says, "and throw it in the garbage under the front stairs."

"All right, Mommy," Billy answers.

"And we won't talk about it again."

"All right, Mommy."

Billy has to walk down the stairs one step at a time, and as we limp down together he makes me promise that I won't tell anyone at school what happened, I guess because Paulie Fryde will have a good laugh if he found out that Billy got beat because he wrote that Paulie Fryde was a faggot.

I promise, easily, because there is no way I would ever tell anyone, anyway.

St. John's school yard, just across from us on 56th Street, is filled with running and shouting children, the girls all in blue jumpers and white blouses, the boys in white shirts and blue ties. Billy and I get there just as Sister Regina, the principal, rings the big brass handbell. It is almost like watching a movie go into slow motion to see what happens when Sister Regina rings the bell, for all the running and shouting stops immediately and everyone walks quietly to their class line and gets lined up, like boxes on a drugstore shelf.

Sister Stella looks very old to me, older than Mommy, and her face is always in shadows and just barely sticks out from her bonnet, like it would stick out from a small cave. Sometimes I expect to see bats flying out from Sister Stella's bonnet. On the first day of class she wrote on the blackboard, "Be happy and you will learn." She is the only nun I ever heard of who talks about being happy. Petey Poscullo says she probably takes opium.

But she told us that her favorite saint is Saint John Bosco of a long time ago, who was a teacher like her and who said that the teacher has to love the students or else nothing happens. So she is always talking about love and being happy.

There are twenty-one of us in the classroom, and I am sitting in the front row, next to Marilyn Rolleri. Marilyn is a quiet girl, one of those girls who you never know is there except that she has the right answer to every question that is ever asked. And Marilyn has the thinnest legs, so thin that I wonder how they hold her body up. She wears white socks which she folds over neatly, and when I have nothing to do in class, I look at her legs against the old, gray wooden slats of the floor and think about touching them, maybe playing Trust Me, where you keep inching your hand up a girl's uniform saying trust me until she says I don't trust you anymore. Then you have to stop. I have never done this, but Joey Jurgensen told me he did it with Jenny Gilmore before she transferred to public school. Joey got lucky there, but I know that he never got to kiss her. It is not easy to kiss a girl in our neighborhood.

There are three tall windows that shine light into the classroom like it was a movie set. I am doing my penmanship lesson, practicing the capital letters as Sister Stella has written them on the board. It is the Palmer Method of writing, and it works out pretty good if you remember to use the Sunday cane at the front of the *H, K, M, N, U, V, W, Y,* and *Z*.

"More than a third of the alphabet," Sister Stella told us, "depends on the straightness of the Sunday cane."

I think I am doing them all right, but Sister Stella is now behind me and hits my knuckles with a ruler. It doesn't hurt. Sister Stella wouldn't hurt anyone because it would interfere with them being happy, and if you are not happy, you can't learn.

"Your Sunday canes," Sister says, "are wiggly, and you could make them a lot straighter."

The problem is that I can't get Billy out of my mind. I never saw Billy being a wise guy, or a tough guy, and I wonder why he would write curse words in his notebook. Mommy has a small sign on a piece of cardboard that she tacked up on the wall next to the icebox in the kitchen. *Let your speech,* it goes, *be like apples of silver set in pictures of gold.* I think it's from the Bible, but it doesn't say. I only know that Mommy always wants us to use proper language, and cursing is not allowed.

I work on my Sunday canes, especially the starting lines on the *M*s and *N*s, making them perfect half-moons at the top and lines straight as a fire pole at the bottom. I do this, and I am happy, the way Sister wants us to be.

The art teacher arrives, and the class stands to greet her, singing, "Good morning, Mrs. Gray."

Mrs. Gray is a woman almost as wide as the blackboard, and she has hairs growing under her chin. She may not be pretty like Mommy, or happy like Sister Stella, but everyone in the class always likes to be with her. She has this way of drawing pictures on the easel she carries from class to class, and it is something like a magic show. She creates things so quickly. She can draw a boy catching a homer, or a girl running through a field, faster than a magician can pull a rabbit out of a hat. She makes outlines of figures first with a charcoal, and then she colors them in. I so wish I could do that, make something come to life with nothing more than a little piece of charcoal.

"Pastels," Mrs. Gray says. "Today we are going to learn how to use pastels. And I have a set of pastels here for each of you."

Petey Poscullo gives them out, and I open the box. There are six colors, like chalk, but square instead of round. I touch one and the color stains my finger with just the smallest touch. I have never had a box of real artist's colors, just the crayon box that Mommy always brings out when I am sick with a cold and in bed.

Mrs. Gray has put a large sheet of clean paper on her easel and begins to draw the outline of a house.

"What color should I use?" someone in the back calls out.

"Any color you like," Mrs. Gray answers. "We are going to draw a barn on the side of a hill in the countryside."

"Are there barns in Central Park?" Robert Reilly asks.

"I don't know," Mrs. Gray says. "But this one is in the country where there are cows and chickens and lots of trees. I am going to make my barn red, because that is the way I remember it, but you can make it anything you like."

"Even blue?" Barbara Cavazzine asks.

"Sure, blue would be nice."

"How about brown?" Diane Gillespie asks.

"A brown barn sounds exciting."

I am not so sure about the color of my barn, and so I begin to copy the shapes the way Mrs. Gray is doing on her easel. I begin to make my barn red, like hers. Only hers looks like a real barn, with boards going across the sides, and mine looks like a red box. But I can suddenly see how the colors are folding into one another, and the lines get thick or thin depending on how hard I press down on the pastel. I forget about everything as I fill in the greens of the trees and the field. It is so much fun, and I definitely fall into the category of happy learning as I make the picture look something like a real barn in a real field with real trees. I study the picture a little, take the yellow pastel stick in my hand, and dab at the side of the barn.

I look over at Marilyn Rolleri, and I see that she has made a swell picture, which looks a lot like Mrs. Gray's barn. She could be a great artist, I am thinking as I make wide stripes of yellow. A great artist with skinny legs.

I am in the middle of 56th Street now, and my yellow barn is rolled up and tied with a rubber band. I see Billy just in front of me, and I run to catch up with him. He is still limping a little.

"How are you?" I ask.

"All right."

"Why did you write those curses, anyway?"

"I didn't."

"You didn't?"

"No, Richie Gilmore did."

"Why didn't you tell Mommy that?"

We are on the stoop now, and Billy pushes the big, red, glass and wood door open. He holds it for me.

"Because," he says as I pass, "I let him write it there, and I didn't rip the page out. Why should I get him in trouble for something that I could have avoided in the first place?"

"But Richie Gilmore is a brizzer," I say, "and who cares if he gets in trouble?"

We are on the stairs now, taking them one by one, slowly. Billy laughs, and punches me lightly on the shoulder.

"That," he says, "is beside the point, Dennis."

It is much later now, and I am lying on the top bunk. It is dark, and I guess Mommy and Billy are asleep. I can hear two cats battling it out down in the backyards, and then all is quiet. I can think better in the quiet. I am still trying to figure out what it is that is beside the point.

Chapter Nine

*M*ommy is punishing me because I was ten minutes late for dinner yesterday, and so I cannot go to Kips this afternoon. I would have been on time, but Mr. Dempsey asked me to sweep the store again. I thought he would give me a quarter or even more, but I only got a dime. It wasn't worth a dime to be kept from going to Kips. Instead, I have to sit around Mrs. Grayson's apartment on Sutton Place while Mommy works the vacuum and washes Mrs. Grayson's clothes in the sink.

She puts on a housecoat over her skirt and sweater. It has so many flowers that it looks like wallpaper. As she buttons it up she tells me to sit in a kitchen chair and to read my book.

"I don't have a book," I say.

Mommy takes a book from her bag and hands it to me. It is a library book, *Hans Brinker,* a book about a person in another country where there is a lot of ice on the ground. It snows sometimes on 56th Street, but there is never any ice. Slush comes with the snow.

You can always tell a library book because the corners are usually popping out with frayed cardboard, and I think of a new book and new snow, and how quickly both get dirty. I don't think I have ever seen a new book, one that has never been read before. I take this book and begin to read it. I have read most of it before, and soon I am rooting for this Hans guy to win the ice skating race. All the time, I am watching Mommy out of the corner of my eye. She keeps running from room to room, whistling and carrying things. She is mopping, and dusting, and lifting photographs from the piano. I'd like to try the piano, but I know Mrs. Grayson wouldn't like that, because I once opened a bottle of Coke there and she made Mommy pay for it, and so anything of hers was not mine. That's what Mommy said.

In the kitchen Mommy puts the washboard in the sink and runs the water. There is a mound of clothes on the floor, blouses, pants, underwear. Mrs. Grayson is very old, and so I don't care much about her underwear. But the idea of underwear on the floor makes me think about Sue Flanagan. I know I would like the underwear if the underwear belonged to Sue Flanagan. Sue Flanagan always wears those sweaters that are so thin and tight you can see the complete outline of her brassiere, and I know I would like to see Sue Flanagan's brassiere.

I stood next to Mommy. She is sweating, and looks tired from so much running from room to room, and from the washing.

"Can I help you, Mommy?" I say, dropping the book on the table. "Could I wash those things for you?"

"Go read your book," Mommy says. "Boys don't do people's wash. Especially little boys. They read books if they know what's good for them."

I am always reading books, anyway, and so I don't know why she won't let me help her. Mommy is now scrubbing up and down the washboard, and her eyes are closed. Up and down, she goes, up and down, like she is exercising.

It is too bad that Daddy isn't better. It's too bad that he doesn't have the good legs so that he can go to work, and Mommy could go to one of the parks down by the river, like the other women on 56th Street. And Mommy could sit there and read magazines, and knit, and talk about the Italian kids who wear pegged pants and get away with murder by their parents, and the way everything at Rossi's store is so expensive. And Daddy could come home at night and talk about the actors in Hollywood like Ronald Reagan, who was complaining in the Congress house about communists in the movies, but I don't know what communists are except they are bad and we pray against them in school, and about Jimmy Stewart, who was always talking about feeding the poor starving children in Europe, but they never mention Ireland, only Italy and India and China, even though I know that China is not in Europe. And I could talk to Daddy about the Dodgers being in Cuba for spring training and how come the Dodgers couldn't just practice underneath the 59th Street Bridge the way we do at the Police Athletic League games.

"Mommy," I ask, "could you buy me a new book someday, a brand-new one without anybody's fingerprints all over it?"

"You mean," Mommy says, "*would* I buy you a new book, not *could*. And my answer is that there are so many books in the library you should read first. After you read all of the library books, we can think about a new book. Okay?"

"Okay, Mommy."

"Now," Mommy says, like she has just finished something. She is standing with her hands on her hips looking around the kitchen in Mrs. Grayson's house. "The kitchen floor once over, and we can go home."

"Mommy?"

"Yes, Dennis?"

"I think I read all the books in the library already."

"You're full of soup, Dennis. You haven't read all the books in the library."

"How many more do I have to go?"

Mommy's hands are still on her hips. She looks like a model in a magazine because she is thin and curvy. She's smiling now, and her long brown hair swings back on her shoulders.

"Do you know our building?"

"Yes. 337 East 56th Street."

"Right. How many floors?"

"We are on the fourth, and there is one more up and then another to the roof."

"Six stories high, and made of all bricks, right?"

"All bricks."

"How many bricks do you think?"

"Maybe a hundred?"

Mommy laughs out loud.

"No, Dennis," she says. "There are thousands and thousands.

And if you think of each brick representing maybe fifty books, then that's how many books are in the library. And do you know how many books you've read?"

"How many?"

"Maybe two bricks' worth," Mommy says, holding two fingers up. "So think about how exciting it is when you look at all the bricks in our building, that you have so many more books to read, and to have all that fun still before you."

"Yeah, and who is going to carry all those bricks home from the library, huh?"

She is bending over now in her laughter, a high giggle kind of laugh. She smiles a lot, but she hardly ever laughs, and to see her laughing makes me feel happier, too.

Mommy stops laughing and gets on her hands and knees. She looks around and begins to crawl across the floor, pulling a big bucket of steaming water next to her. She has a rag in one hand and a brush in the other.

I don't even like to carry groceries up the four flights of stairs, I am thinking as I watch her, never mind all these bricks she is talking about.

She is now crawling backward, the brush going back and forth like an out-of-control clock. Every once in a while she stops and wipes the sweat off her forehead with the rag.

It would be good if I could have just one book that was new, where the corners weren't tattered, and I don't have to worry about all those bricks up the four flights.

Suddenly, watching Mommy, I begin to think that I am just talking about myself, and it's so selfish to just think about what I want, new books or anything else. My mind goes weird, like it is on fire inside my head as I begin to think about her, watching her here on her hands and knees in Mrs. Grayson's kitchen. I don't know another kid whose mother does this anywhere, except in their own houses, and I am getting awfully sad awfully quick. And mad. I am mad about all this. Why is my mother the only mother I know who gets down on her hands and knees for all these people? This is not our house, this is not our floor she is cleaning.

No. We are in Mrs. Grayson's house on Sutton Place. And why

can't we live here? I mean, why can't Mommy be like Mrs. Grayson? I know she has no choice, but why can't it happen, anyway? My mind is racing around in circles. I am thinking all this even though Mommy says you should never wish you were somebody else. But I am getting madder and madder as I continue to think about it. Why couldn't Mommy be Mrs. Grayson, instead of the other way around?

And then maybe I could have a new book, and we could sit and read it together, even for just a day.

Chapter Ten

*I*t is Tuesday afternoon. I know it is Tuesday because there is altar boy practice every Tuesday, and Sister Stella let us out of class fifteen minutes early.

I'm on the altar holding a tall candlestick high up, as if I'm offering it up to God. It's not so easy to do this when you're only eight. It is made of gold, and it's heavy, and I am afraid of dropping it. I know that there are people in the church making visits, and Father O'Rourke is behind me giving us instructions on how to be good acolytes. I should be paying more attention, but there are big holes in my shoes. I had cardboard in them, but it rained and the cardboard went like soggy liverwurst. I forgot to put in new cardboard, and so there are holes in my socks, too, and I can picture the threads falling out of the holes and all the people in the church laughing, and Father O'Rourke, too. I know that I want to throw the back of my cassock over my shoes, but I can't hold up the candlestick with just one hand, and I pray to God to make Father O'Rourke get it over with. I don't even have the Latin memorized yet, and here he is giving us the instruction to serve at High Mass.

"Okay," Father says, "we are at the Consecration now, and the priest has the Host high in the air, so you're on, Delaney."

Richard Delaney is in charge of the bells, brass bells that look like three round upside-down bowls, and he hammers each bell so that it sounds like NBC on the radio. Delaney is a good bell ringer, and the sound goes around the church. It makes me think of the radio, NBC, sold American, look sharp, feel sharp, be sharp, the Shadow knows, Bobby Benson and the B bar B, Henry, Henry Aldrich, coming, mother, and I am thinking of these things to get my mind off the holes in my shoes, and to forget how my arms are hurting from holding this thing so high. And then my eyes tighten, and I make the faces, and I'm glad Mommy isn't here to see me.

Father Hamilton comes on the altar and the first thing you notice about him is his white socks. The boys in school can't wear white socks unless we have a note from home saying we have foot scurvy or the creeping crud or something. I wonder if Father has athlete's foot? He is a lot younger than Father O'Rourke, but he is completely bald, and has skin the color of Chinese apples, a sort of red and brown mixed together. He works with Father O'Rourke, and he grills us all the time. And if he's not asking us about the Latin, he wants to get the inside stuff about everybody's family.

We are all standing here, lined up like penguins.

"How is your mother, Dennis?" Father Hamilton asks me.

"Fine, Father," I answer, and wait for him to ask something more. He is always asking us where we went last weekend if we weren't at Mass, or where did you get that new coat, or is your grandfather still living out in Brooklyn? He once asked me if my mother was working, and I told him my mother is always working, and he asked if she had a real job, and I told him she goes from one job to another.

He turns away from me now.

"How is your father, Peter?" he asks Petey Poscullo.

"Fine, Father."

"Did he get a new job yet?"

"I don't know, Father."

"You don't know?"

"He don't talk to me about that."

"*Doesn't,* not *don't,*" Father says. "And you, Timmy. Is your sister still living on the farm upstate?"

"Yes, Father," Timmy Thompson answers.

I didn't even know that Thompson had a sister, but I guess when sisters go to farms upstate, they are in prison or something like that.

"Okay," Father Hamilton says to the whole group, "I am going to teach you how to pronounce the Latin of the Suscipiat."

Father Hamilton recites the Suscipiat slowly. It is the hardest prayer for any altar boy to memorize, and we all listen carefully because Latin doesn't always sound the same way it looks on a page.

"There are two words here," Father says, "that you have to practice, and if you don't get them right, you will never get on the bus for Coney Island."

Father knows that will get our attention because the only real reason we become altar boys is to get that extra day off from school and go on that trip to Coney Island every May.

"The words are *sacrificium* and *totiusque,* okay, and you will repeat them now as I say. *Sa-cra-fee-see-umm,* okay."

Someone is heard to say *sa-cra-fish-ium,* and Father makes us say the word ten times before we can get on to *totiusque.*

"*Toe-tea-us-quay,* okay," Father continues.

Someone says *toe-ta-as-quay,* and we have to do that word twenty times.

When Father Hamilton is finished, he looks over at me and sees that I have put my hands, cassock and all, into my back pockets, and he yells.

"Stand up straight, Smith," Father barks, "and put your hands at your side."

I jump as he yells. At first I am a little frightened, and then I get angry that he singled me out this way, embarrassing me. You would think that I was walking off with the tabernacle itself, the way he yelled. But I just stand straight and say nothing.

Father Hamilton goes on some more about the different Latin words, but I am not listening anymore. I am just standing with my hands at my side. I feel like telling Father Ford about him. Father Ford is the nicest priest I know, and he is the boss next to Monsignor O'Connor. He would tell Father Hamilton to let a kid put his hands in his back pockets if that's where he wants them.

Finally, it is over, and Father O'Rourke says we can go home. The next time, he says, we will get to the *mea culpa,* and we should read in our missals about the Offertory.

I love being in this church. It's such a big place, and the lighting is always perfect here, little candles throwing these big shadows that change whenever anyone walks around. I am always studying these gigantic paintings on the ceilings, and the ones on the walls that seem to move in the light, with the gold around the halos that flashes like it is part of a huge neon sign. And what I like, too, is that there is only one reason to be here, to be in this light and the quiet, and that is to talk more directly to God. I mean, you can talk to God anywhere—in your bathtub, at second base, anywhere—but it is better here somehow. And, here, you can see how many of the statues you can make smile. I think it's an honor, too, being an altar boy, because it makes you different from all the other boys in class, even if you didn't get an extra day off and got to get on the bus for the annual outing to Steeplechase Park in Coney Island.

Father Hamilton is just being a pain, I am thinking as I walk up First Avenue, and it's not so bad. I shouldn't let him rile me up. Mommy says that we should be careful about what people we let rile us up, because most of the time it is just a waste of a good rile. I have a lot to feel good about. I am the youngest in the altar boy class. I got in the class even though I'm only in the third grade, because of the high marks I got in vocabulary. So they made an exception. Usually, you have to be nine.

I see Mr. Dempsey standing outside of his delicatessen when I get to the corner of 56th Street. He waves to me and calls out.

"Hey, kiddo," he says, "do you want to earn fifty cents and sweep the store out?"

It would take me just a little while, I am thinking, and I would be a little late for dinner, but he said fifty cents this time. At least it wouldn't be a dime. I wouldn't risk being late again for a dime and spend the whole time after school tomorrow with Mommy at Mrs. Grayson's apartment on Sutton Place.

Mr. Dempsey gives me a broom and asks me to start in the back of the store, where there are a million boxes waiting to be unpacked. There is a customer in the store, and I start to move the boxes around and sweep behind them. The boxes are like mountains, stacked very high, and I feel very little in front of them. As I sweep, I am thinking about the eraser job that Sister Maureen took away from me. She should have known just how careful I was to get every last speck of chalk dust out of those erasers, so that she would be glad that she asked me of all the boys in the class to do the job. And here I am, being as careful as I can to get to all the corners and sweep them clean.

Mr. Dempsey is saying goodbye to the customer at the front door. I am thinking that I never saw him walk a customer to the front door before, and I wonder why he is doing it. I see him from way back in the storeroom corner. He turns the lock and turns the OPEN sign over. It is so early to be closing the store, I am thinking, and I begin to sweep a little faster so that I can be through before he closes the store. And Mr. Dempsey comes to the back of the store and says he wants to show me something, and he picks me up and puts me on one of the small boxes, and he is holding my wrist, and I don't like that he is doing that, and he is unbuttoning his pants, and then he takes himself out of his pants and I begin to get very frightened, and I don't know why he is doing this, and I wish Mommy was here to see me make a face, and to tell me to stop, and to tell him to stop. He pulls my wrist over so that my little hand is near to himself, and I pull away, but his grip on my wrist is so strong, and I want to run, anywhere, and to tell somebody that I am only eight years old, and Mr. Dempsey has me a prisoner in the storeroom of his delicatessen, and he pulls my little hand a little harder until it is nearly on top of himself, and I want to get away, but he is pulling, and I think of my brother Billy and of how quick he is in everything, and so I begin to yell at the top of my lungs and wriggle as quickly as I can, jumping down from the box, screaming, trying to free myself from his strong grip, jumping fast from foot to foot, pulling away on one side and then on the other, beginning to punch at Mr. Dempsey with my free hand, saving all my strength for one big tug away from him, and then he looses his grip, finally, as I charge away and I run to the front of the store, but the front door is locked, and I am screaming now as loud as I have ever screamed, and Mr. Dempsey looks afraid, and he is yelling for me to shut up, shut up, and he opens the lock, and I never look at him, but run out of the store as fast as I've ever done anything, and I run to my stoop where there are some women sitting on newspapers, and I thank God that Sue Flanagan is not there because I can feel the red in my face and the tears in my eyes, and I feel so embarrassed, like I did something very bad and people were pointing at me and saying there is Dennis, the little kid who will do anything for fifty cents, and so I jump up the steps of the stoop and run right past them, into the hall and up the stairs, not a word or a squeak out of me.

Then I am on the fourth floor, and I am out of breath. I remember now that I never started to cry, and that makes me feel a little better, and I think it is because there is nothing that I did wrong and I wish I could make everything go away and just go back to church and Father O'Rourke and the bells. And I would even listen to Father Hamilton. I am not in the mood to cry. Instead, I am in the mood to get a zip gun and shoot Mr. Dempsey. And I think, too, that I am too mad to go into the house, and I don't want Mommy to see me like this because she will ask a hundred questions like Sam Spade. I try to calm down by counting to one hundred in sevens, and I get to ninety-eight, and I try to think of something else to think of. I am having a hard time breathing, I guess from running so fast up the stairs, and I am making the faces.

Calm down, I tell myself, calm down or you'll never be able to go home. What am I going to say to Mommy? I can't say anything. I can't even tell Billy because I know Billy will go around and throw bricks through all of Mr. Dempsey's windows, and the police will come, and Billy will tell them everything, and then I'll go to jail, too, because I told Billy and so I started it all.

Elephants, I think. I'll count the elephants clumping through the jungle, stepping on trees and making them fall over so that the other elephants have a path, and in my mind I can see these animals in slow motion, one by one, each holding the other's tail, each helping to keep the line straight so that they will all get to where they are going in one piece. One, two, three, four, and they are moving so slowly I wish I could make them gallop, but they just plod ahead like turtles.

I notice now that I am breathing better, and I begin to walk down the long, dark hall to apartment 26. At the apartment door I pick up a corner of the linoleum at my feet, grab the key, and open the door.

Billy and Mommy are at the kitchen table.

"Boy oh boy," Mommy says, "are you lucky. One more minute and you would be in your bed without your dinner."

I bless myself as I sit, and look at the plate that Mommy has put before me. It is ravioli, soft ravioli, the kind from the can. They are like marshmallows. I once had real ravioli at Dante Vescovi's house, and it didn't taste anything like this. It was scrunchy. I can't talk, and so I just yes and no everything to death, and try to be anything but suspicious. I can't eat, either, but I force myself. The raviolis don't taste so bad, but they are as hard to eat as the tripe because my stomach is beating time with my heart, and I keep thinking that all I want to do is lie down and go to sleep.

God, I don't want Mommy to find out about this.

Chapter Eleven

*E*veryone in the third grade except for Greta Schmidt is lined up for the bus that will take us to the Guggenheim Dental Clinic on 72nd Street. Greta's father is Dr. Schmidt, and we go to him for school examinations. The welfare doctor does not do regular exams, just the emergency ones. The Schmidts have their own house on 53rd Street, and so they are rich. Dr. Schmidt would not sign the release form to send Greta to the dentist with us, and Greta does not know why. And so I feel a little sorry for Greta because she has to sit in Sister Urban's class all day, and nobody likes Sister Urban. Not even the priests, and they like everyone. Father O'Rourke and Father Hamilton never seem to talk to her at our assemblies, but they talk to all the other nuns. I'll have to go to Sister Urban in the fifth grade, and Billy told me it is like going to reform school, only she beats you worse than the prison guards. Maybe she'll get diphtheria or something before I get there, and she'll have to recuperate for ten years. Billy had diphtheria last year and almost died. He had to stay in the hospital for a month, down in Bellevue, and Mommy cried a lot every night. I made her tea. It always cheered her up when I made her tea.

We were doing sentence diagrams all morning, and I hate that. I hate grammar the way I hate tripe. It is not necessary, because if you are going to tell someone a story, it will be a good story or it won't, and how you diagram the sentences of the story won't help. If I am late for dinner, and Mommy is rip-roaring mad at me, the last thing in the world I would think of is diagramming the sentences of my excuse.

My favorite sentence is one I made up, which says, "Me and Billy are going to Abbie's candy store because Abbie is giving away free egg creams." I know it's wrong to write it that way, but I only care about the egg cream part.

School has been a lot of trouble to me this year, and I don't know why.

I haven't been memorizing hardly anything, like the dates for the discoverers I have to know for the tests, and the rivers in Brazil. You have to know these things to be promoted, but I just don't care about being promoted, or even knowing that Hannibal crossed the Alps because he happened to have a lot of elephants. It's not that I want to do anything different, either. I just feel that school is as important to me right now as swimming in the East River in the wintertime.

I have tried to study my lessons every night, but after ten minutes or so I begin to get fidgety, and so I quit and listen to the radio. Sister Stella yells at me every day for not doing my homework, and then she puts her arms around me like she is sorry for yelling at me.

I keep thinking that if my father was with us and he had a job, everything would be a lot different. Mommy wouldn't have to spend all that time on her hands and knees, and we could go places, and buy things, and Mommy could have time to have a lot of friends.

Mommy knows that my school grades are not as good as they used to be, and she keeps asking if Sister Stella is spending enough time with me and helping me. She thinks Sister Stella doesn't pay much attention to me. But I keep telling her that Sister Stella loves all the students because of Saint John Bosco, and she is always being nice to everybody. How do I know if she's spending enough time with me? She's always there in the class, anyway.

All the kids like Sister Stella because she never hits anyone and no one ever gets into trouble in her class. Except for Raymond Rabbitscabbage, whose real name is Rasakavitch, and who calls things out in the middle of her lessons and then gets sent to stand in the coat closet with the door closed.

But Sister Stella always hugs him when he comes out.

The bus stops in front of a building that looks to me like a Con Edison plant, for there are high windows that are wired to keep the crooks out. We go in, the twenty of us, two by two, and sit on long metal benches. Sister Stella is there watching over us, and so it is easy for us and we don't have to keep absolutely still. Some nuns will clout you good if they catch you talking when you're supposed to be quiet, but not Sister Stella. If she catches you talking, she just clips you under the chin with her bent finger a couple of times. That makes most of us laugh, and then Sister Stella laughs with us.

Each of us has a list with the capitals of the countries in South America.

"Memorize the list," Sister said to us when we sat, "and we will have a test tomorrow."

I start with the first five, Lima, Montevideo, Caracas, Bogotá, and Rio something. Maybe the dentist will know.

I am one of the first to be called, and a nurse takes me into a small cubicle. I am told to sit in a large stuffy chair, like the one at Freddy's, the barber on 58th Street. A young guy comes into the room, wearing a white jacket with two pencils in the handkerchief pocket. He looks a little like crazy Mario, and he is carrying a small pick and a round mirror. He tells me to hold the mirror up so that I can look into my mouth, and he picks at my teeth. He goes right to a tooth that hurts, and I yell. It is up top and way in the back, and my jaw begins to sting. My teeth never hurt like that unless I let cold water go on them.

"That's one," he says as he goes to the next tooth and jabs at it. "Ahh, here's another. It is the next-door tooth."

I yell again as he picks at it.

Another man comes in. This one is also in a white jacket. He has hairs sticking way out from his nose. The guy steps back and the man looks into my mouth and then reads a paper that the young guy shows him.

"Okay," he says, looking at me, and then they both leave.

In a minute the young guy comes back with a nurse who is carrying a tray of silver tools.

They give me something to drink, a small paper cup of orange syrup. It makes me a little dizzy, and after a while the nurse comes behind me and holds my shoulders as the young guy shoves a pair of pliers in my mouth. He begins to tug at my tooth, and I can feel the tooth moving. I realize he is pulling my tooth out, and it comes out easily. It hardly hurts at all. He holds the tooth out in front of me so that I can take a good look. And then he throws it in the garbage can.

As he goes in for the next one I realize that this one hurts the moment he touches it, and I wince and try to shift out from the nurse's grip. This tooth, though, is like a mule, and it won't come out, and he pulls so hard I think that my mouth is leaving my body. The nurse's hands are practically going through the skin of my shoulders as I shake and squirm, and she never loses her grip.

"Take it easy," the young guy says, "take it easy."

I am yelling bloody murder now, trying to figure out why they would let such a young guy do this in a clinic, and the guy keeps saying, "Take it easy, don't make it hard on me."

In all of this time, he has one hand pressed down hard on my nose, and I don't know now if my nose hurts more than my mouth.

"It's coming," the guy says. "Don't make it hard on me."

I don't know how he could be thinking that it is hard on him when I am being picked apart like this.

When the jackass of a tooth finally does come out, it comes out suddenly, and the pliers jerk from my mouth and slam into my lower lip. The lip begins to bleed, and the nurse is getting upset. She doesn't have any gauze, and she runs to get some.

The young guy throws this tooth into the garbage can, too.

When the nurse returns, she has a big wad of cotton that looks like it has been soaked in monkey grease. She puts it into my mouth and tells me to bite down hard. It feels funny in there, like the whole side of my mouth is missing. She then presses gauze on my lower lip until it stops bleeding. After a while, the nose-hair man comes in again and looks into my mouth. He takes the cotton out and throws it into the garbage can with my teeth.

"Good, good," the man says. "All right."

When he leaves, the nurse smiles at me and then fills my mouth again with the cotton. She is close to me, and I can see how the material of her uniform is being stretched at her breasts. I wonder if Sue Flanagan has ever been in this clinic with her nurse's uniform, and if she leans in close to people like this. I can smell the nurse's hair, she is so close, and it smells like applesauce. I think it is so funny that they have tortured me here and left the Grand Canyon in my mouth, and still I am thinking about Sue Flanagan and applesauce.

In the bus, going back to school, I sit next to Ann Kovak, a tall blond girl who could be the prettiest girl in school if she wasn't so quiet and shy. She sees I have my hand pressing against my mouth, and she leans over and pats my other hand.

She says, "It will be okay tomorrow, Dennis."

Most of the rest on the bus are quiet, except for Dante Vescovi, who is bragging that he doesn't have any cavities.

"How about the cavity on top of your shoulders?" Raymond Rabbitscabbage says.

"Maybe they missed a cavity," I say. It is hard to talk with all the cotton in my mouth, and it hurts as I move my jaw up and down. "They can miss things at the clinic, you know."

The bus hits a bump, and the bump goes right to the empty space in my mouth. I don't want to yell because no one else on the bus is yelling. Sister Stella is knitting something in the front seat. She doesn't look at the knitting as she does it. She is looking out the window, watching the buildings go by.

"That's no clinic," Dante says to me. "That's a school for jerk-offs."

A school for jerk-offs. It's no wonder Dr. Schmidt wouldn't let Greta go.

I think about this all the way back to school.

The next day at school, Sister Stella gives each of us a pamphlet about a girl named Maria Goretti who died a long time ago, even before my mother was born.

I like it when they give things out at school, like scapulars and holy pictures and miraculous medals. Usually, we just take these things home, but today Sister gives us the pamphlet and then makes us read it out loud. I like to read out loud, but today is not the day to do it. Ann Kovak was wrong, because my mouth is still so sore from the dentist that I can't really talk.

The class is reading like they are singing a song or saying the pledge of allegiance, and Sister sees that I am not doing it with them. She quietly comes down the aisle and knuckles me under the chin a few times. She does this to everyone, and no one ever seems to mind, but now my mouth is hurting like she poured boiling water inside of it.

"Oww," I say, and the class shuts up like there was a fire alarm or something.

Sister Stella looks so surprised, because everyone knows she wouldn't hurt a fly.

"My teeth hurt," I say to her. "I have a teethache."

The class laughs at this, and I am laughing to myself, too, because there aren't even any teeth there anymore where it hurts.

Sister puts her arms around me and smiles at me. She tells me that I don't have to read with the others, and then she starts them up again.

Soon I forget all about the pain in my mouth because this Maria girl got me so interested in her life. She is called Blessed, which is not like when you bless yourself. But Bless-ed, which is kind of a title, and it is something that you have to get to be before they can make you a saint.

This Blessed Maria had a very hard life in Italy. It was just around the time the automobile was invented, and the radio, but before the First World War. We are now getting all those dates right in class, and I guess that is why Sister is making everyone read this.

Her father dies when she is a little kid, so she has no father, and her mother is very poor, so poor that they don't have any food at all, and they look for scraps of food around the town. But Blessed Maria just smiles at everybody and always tries to make people happy, until one day a guy comes in and tries to rip her clothes off. She is only eleven years old, and she tells the guy that she would rather die than be impure, but the guy is crazy and he has a knife with him. He threatens her, but she tells him that she belongs to God. She is just eleven, and she stands up to this guy and tells him that she is with God—something, I think, that takes a lot of courage.

This poor girl, I am thinking. She must have gone through so much more than what they are telling us in the pamphlet.

"This is a very beautiful story," Sister Stella says when the class finishes the pamphlet.

And I guess it is, too, except that it is so sad when the guy kills her with the knife. They then sent him to prison for twenty-seven years, and the first thing he did when he got out of jail, because he talked to Blessed Maria one night in a dream, was to go to her mother and ask for her forgiveness.

I don't know if Blessed Maria's mother ever forgave him. I guess she did, but the pamphlet didn't say. I don't think my mother would forgive someone if I was killed like that. Maybe she would if he became a priest or did a lot of penance, but she would have to say a lot of prayers first to get her in the mood.

Chapter Twelve

Mommy has made me put on a tie, and Billy, too. We don't have a real suit to wear, either of us, but we have on our best clothes, each in a white shirt, tie, school pants, which are the light gabardines, and a plaid lumberman's jacket. I am wearing my old Klein's-on-the-Square shoes which Mommy glued together when the sole fell off completely, but she keeps talking about going to Thom McAn's to get new ones. Sometime soon, she says. I hope it is soon because the holes are getting to be dollar holes, and I have to change the cardboard every night. Billy and I never care much about the dime-sized holes, or the penny holes, the nickel holes, or the quarter holes, but when the holes get to be half dollars or silver dollars, it is hard to make the cardboard work right, and if it rains, it is like walking barefoot in the bathtub.

Mike Shurtliff did not pay Mommy any money for washing and ironing his shirts for a long time, because he works in show business and hasn't had a job. But he is our next-door neighbor and Mommy told him that she would do his shirts, anyway, and he could pay her sometime when he got the money. And today was the big day—that's what Mommy said—the big payoff, because Mike gave her twice as much money as he owed her for the shirts. He got a good job on Broadway with a play about the death of a salesman. Mommy said we should celebrate Mr. Shurtliff's good works, and so she is taking us out to dinner.

I am nine years old, but I feel as excited as a little kid because this is the first time I have ever gone to a restaurant. Well, I've been to Riker's for a Coke and a doughnut, and to Nedick's for a hot dog, and a couple of times to Emiliano's for pizza pie.

But this time, Mommy told us, it will be so different. There will be linen napkins and flowers on the tables.

It is cold, and Mommy and Billy walk so fast that I have to run to keep up with them, and our breaths make enough smoke for a steam engine to go to Canada. It is dark on Second Avenue, and there is hardly anyone on 57th Street, which is usually crowded. We race to Third Avenue and then up to 58th Street. Every once in a while I look at Mommy. Her head is very erect, and her shoulders are back, and her hair is blowing way out behind her. She reminds me of one of those women you see on the front of an old sailing ship, sailing through the New York wind as if she were sailing across the ocean.

Mommy points, and I can see the big sign surrounded by lights. It says JOE'S ORIGINAL RESTAURANT. I have never been to a play on Broadway, or to the movie palace in Radio City, which is a whole city not far from here, but I cannot think that it would be more exciting than going into a restaurant where there are napkins and flowers on the tables. The restaurant is big, but I cannot see in because all the windows are steamed up and dripping. There's something very exciting about a steamy room on a cold night.

I laugh for a minute because it reminds me of my grandfather. "Dare wuz ne'er enough turf," he said to my mother just last week, "an so we mostly froze in da County Cork." My mother laughed then, and said, "It's a lot easier to be poor, Pop, when there's steam heat."

Mommy holds the door for us, and I see as we go inside that the floor is made of marble, and there are many small tables covered with white cloth. I see the little vase of flowers on every one of the tables, and they are all different colors. There are so many flowers, it reminds me of the altar at church.

A man in a short black jacket and a bow tie asks Mommy what she wants.

"A table," Mommy says, "a table for three."

She is smiling, and I am glad to see her so happy.

"Do you have a reservation?" the man asks. He does not smile back at Mommy.

"We don't even have a telephone," I whisper to Billy.

"I don't know," Mommy says, looking down at us. "Did you make reservations?"

I shrug my shoulders, and Billy looks dumb. Billy hardly ever looks dumb, but that's how he looks as he puts his hands out, palms up.

"I guess we don't have a reservation," Mommy says, "but we've been planning this for some time."

"How long?" the man asks.

"A lifetime," Mommy says.

She smiles at Billy and then at the man.

He takes us to a table in the very back end of the restaurant, near two big double doors. Mommy stops in her tracks.

"Oh," Mommy says. "Do you have another table, maybe where it's quieter?"

It seems pretty quiet to me, except for the doors that are swinging open and shut like a fan.

"This is what we have, lady," the man says.

"What about those?" Mommy asks, pointing at some empty tables we passed by.

"They are reserved," the man says.

"What for?" Billy asks.

"For people," the man says.

"I'm people," Billy says.

The man spreads his arms out. "This is all," he says. "You can have it or not, I don't care."

"Sure," Mommy says as she sits. I think Billy is going to argue with the man, but Mommy grabs his hand, and she never stops smiling. She is so happy to be here. As happy as I am.

Another man comes over and asks what we want. I am thinking that I would like an English muffin.

Mommy picks up a menu from the three menus the waiter has put down on the table. She reads it a minute.

"Oh," Mommy says again. She looks surprised, like she saw a beer can in the collection plate or something.

"Well," the waiter says, beating a bass drum with his foot.

"Could you give us a minute?" Mommy says. She is still smiling as she watches the man leave, putting a pencil behind his ear.

"Boys," Mommy says, "I was here once, but they have changed the menu since. It costs more than I thought, so we'll have a light touch, huh? I will have a salad to begin."

"To begin what?" I ask.

"You always begin with something in a restaurant, but we can only get one thing, so we will have a salad and then I can share it with you."

"Do they have any English muffins?"

"Maybe, but the salad is better for you."

"I want an English muffin."

"You don't know what's good for you."

"But I know what I want."

"No you don't," Mommy says. She stops her smile for the first time, and I know she means business.

"You always say 'You don't know what's good for you' even when you make me eat tripe and black beans and noodles."

Mommy begins to smile again.

"Tonight," she says, "I will tell you what's good for you, and you will be thankful that you have something that is good for you."

"Not if it's not an English muffin," I say as I look at the menu and try to read it. A lot of the words are in a foreign language.

"Look," Billy says, "a shrimp cocktail. What's that?"

"It's too expensive is what it is," Mommy says.

"How about a steak?" Billy asks.

"Also."

"How about pork chops?"

"Too much."

"Hot dogs?"

"Maybe."

"Probably," I say, "they give the tripe away for free here."

Mommy laughs at this.

"What's a Salisbury steak?" Billy asks.

"It's good for you," Mommy says.

"That means we can afford it, I guess," Billy says.

"It means it is very good for you," Mommy answers. "They put onions and a gravy over a steak that is chopped up."

"Chopped up how," Billy asks, "like a hamburger?"

"Better than a hamburger."

"How?"

"Bigger, better, you'll like it."

I can see that Mommy is pushing the Salisbury steak, and I am thinking I'll be glad to get it with the flowers and the linen napkins.

"Forget the English muffin," I say, holding a knife and a fork in each hand. "I'll take the bigger and better you'll-like-it hamburger."

The man comes back, and Mommy asks him for a couple of the Salisbury steaks, a salad, and something called a knockwurst. All the names in this restaurant are strange and new, and I can imagine coming here every day and ordering something that I don't know how to pronounce or recognize when I see it. There is something on the menu called escargot, which Mommy said is a snail in a shell, and I can't think of anything that is more disgusting. I'm glad Mommy didn't tell us that escargot is good for us.

We just sit there and talk as the food comes.

"They are starting up dances at Kips Bay," Billy says, "just for the teenagers, and it won't be long before I can go."

"Yeah," I say. "It's good that we took the Irish dancing because at least you know how to dance alone."

"Wise guy," Billy says. "I can get all the girls I want to dance with me."

"You better bring a camera," I say, "because nobody will believe you without a picture."

"Do you know," Mommy says, "they just invented a new camera that develops the film inside the camera while you wait?"

"That's what Billy needs," I say.

"Uncle Andy said he is going to buy one to take pictures of your cousins."

"Could we get one?" Billy asks.

"Sure," Mommy says, "when we win the Irish sweepstakes."

The Salisbury steak comes, and it's a big football of a hamburger, covered with gravy and surrounded by mashed potatoes. Mixed together it's the best hamburger I ever had, and if my fork could lift it,

I would eat the bottom of the plate with a little more gravy. The man comes back after some other guy takes our plates away, and he asks what we will have for dessert.

Mommy gives him one of her smiles. "Could you come back in another minute?"

The waiter leaves, and Mommy turns to us, saying, "I have a great idea."

Billy and I smile, too, and I can see my brother's eyes light up a little.

"Why not," Mommy says, "pick up some of the good and expensive Bryer's ice cream on the way home, from the French place on Second Avenue? It's not the packaged ice cream, but the really expensive stuff, and they pack it in by hand there."

"Okay," Billy says.

"Better than anything," I say.

Expensive or not, it would be nice to get something that is better than anything, anyway.

Mommy is holding the ice cream as we are walking home. Billy is holding her one arm, and I am holding on to the other as we walk into the wind.

"The ice cream," Mommy says, "will never melt in this weather."

I feel proud of my family as we walk together like this, just coming home from a restaurant, as good as anyone else in the neighborhood, as good as the Scarry family, who go out to eat once a week anyways, because the father is a bartender and gets a lot of big tips from the drunks on First Avenue. I know we shouldn't envy anyone, and we shouldn't want anyone to envy us, but I can't help feeling good and special that we have been to Joe's Original Restaurant tonight.

A few days later Billy takes me to Lexington Avenue and 49th Street. It is a short, cold walk, and when we get there, there is a line of people going around the block.

"We'll have to wait in the line," Billy says.

"It's too cold," I say. "Let's just go to Kips."

"This Motorama will be worth it," Billy says, "just you wait and see. Archie gave me the passes, and we don't want to insult him, you understand?"

We stand on a subway grating, and the heat rises up and keeps our feet warm, anyway. We are there for almost an hour before the line starts to move, and in no time at all we are in the ballroom of the Waldorf-Astoria hotel.

I've never seen anything like this in my life, I am thinking as I look around the huge room. There are about a hundred cars all around us, each on its own platform, each more unbelievable than the one next to it, each car like something they made only for the future, each one looking like it came from Mars, all of them shaped like gargantuan bullets and bombs, with high wings coming out of the back fenders, all in these fantastic colors with seats of the softest leather made to wrap right around your body—oh, oh, if I could just go for a ride in one of these cars.

"Billy," I say, "do you think we could get Archie to get us a ride in one of these things?"

Billy laughs. "No," he says, "but I think we can sneak up on one of the platforms and sit in one until they catch us."

We walk around until we see a long and low car, shining like the sun, looking like it is made of pure silver, and it has one big light in the middle of the front, and other lights all around it, its two doors spread wide open like wings that are almost scraping the floor, and a top that is half up and half down, and the man in charge is off to one side talking to a bunch of people, and Billy boosts me up on the platform, and then he climbs up, and we crawl real fast, him on one side of the car, me on the other, and we creep into the car, me behind the steering wheel, and I sit way back and grab the steering wheel, and I try to look out but I can't see over the wheel, and Billy says to honk the horn, but I press down on everything and nothing honks, and I ask Billy where he wants to go, and he says he wants to go to Riker's on 53rd Street where all his friends will see us, and I turn the wheel like crazy, laughing, smiling, happier than I have ever been.

The man in charge sees us, and he comes over, but he doesn't say anything. He just has his arms folded, and stands there, watching, and then he throws his head back and he lets out a big laugh.

Oh, it's better than Coney Island here at the Motorama.

Chapter Thirteen

There is always a line outside of Kips Bay Boys Club on Saturdays. Sometimes it goes down 52nd Street and around Second Avenue. Two boys come out, two boys go in. Everyone wants to be inside, and not just because everyone else is in there. The place is hopping with things to do for kids. Boys are playing pool or Ping-Pong, swimming in the downstairs pool, making wooden lamps or pottery bowls or jewelry out of copper in the shops, or they are in the main gym, or the small gym on the roof, or, if you are little like me, you go to the lower gym in the basement. Midget mayhem, Archie calls the lower gym, but I don't know what mayhem is, and I forgot to look it up. I could go to the club's library and look in the dictionary, a book almost heavier than I am.

I am just a couple of boys from the entrance, and Archie sees me. He's got this way of whistling and then putting his hand in front of his face and pointing at you. He then curls his finger and yells out, "Hey, son." That means he wants you to stop something, like cursing, running, fighting, and the other things you're not allowed to do at the Boys Club. Sometimes, like now, when Archie whistles at you, it means he wants to see you.

*   *   *

Archie brings me to his office, a small cubicle with some filing cabinets and a paper-covered desk, and then he leaves, saying, "I'll be right back."

I've never been in this office before, and I am wondering, what is the story here? Archie Mangini is the second banana at Kips Bay Boys Club, but he is the one you see every day. Mr. McNiven is the club boss, but he is always out trying to get money from people on Sutton Place. That's what I heard, anyways.

I look around the office and eye the beat-up brass bugle Archie sometimes plays in the halls for fun. "Keep active," Archie is always saying, "keep excited, and if you don't have a trumpet to blow like I do, then just yell a little." And so we do a lot of yelling at Kips Bay.

I begin to read the brass plates on all the trophies Archie has on his desk and on top of the filing cabinets—swimming trophies, basketball trophies, one for debating. I don't know how old he is, but he is out of college, someone told me. Maybe he's twenty-five, maybe a little more, but it looks like Archie gets trophies for everything the way Jackie Robinson gets homers. It must come natural.

I think Archie is the kind of man boys wished they had for a father, especially if they didn't like their own fathers too much. I've heard guys say they wished Archie was their father because he's fun. He will kick you out of the club in a flat second if you curse or spit or something like that, but if he's not being a pain, he's making you laugh.

I would rather have my own father, though, no matter what kind of a solid man Archie is. I think about this for a minute as I sit down in a hard wooden armchair, the kind that will dump you out if you lean back too fast.

I know so little about my own father. I wonder if he ever got any trophies. I saw a photograph of him in Mommy's drawer where he is standing in an empty lot, wearing a baseball glove. Maybe he got a baseball trophy. Who knows?

It's funny the amount of things I don't know about my father, like would he want to go to the nine o'clock Mass with Mommy? Or would he go to the twelve-fifteen like so many of the fathers I know, like Mr. Walsh and Mr. Scarry? And I wonder if he would wear a suit, like Mr. Walsh. I never saw Mr. Scarry in a suit, but he is always in a shirt and tie with a sweater or a windbreaker. And I wonder if my father uses hair tonic in his hair. And would he make us eat tripe and beef liver, or would he buy us a dog so we could feed it the bad stuff under the table? Would he throw the ball around with us in the 59th Street park, even with his crutches? I bet he was a good ballplayer. I wonder if he would take us up to the balcony in the RKO 58th Street, or brush his teeth after every meal the way Mommy tries to make us do, or give us a good beating the way Mr. DeLisi gave to Bobby DeLisi when he caught him with dirty pictures.

I know so much more about my friends' fathers, and it is hard to try to figure out what my own father would want me to do. Would he want me to be a doorman, or a bartender, or a construction worker? Would he get me a job, maybe, when I get big? Maybe a job on the railroad like Uncle Andy and Mr. Walsh. Maybe on the Railway Express truck with him if they give him his job back. Jeez, there are so many things to know, and I don't know any of it at all.

Archie comes into the office and he closes the door behind him, a wide door covered with wire glass. He throws a pile of folders down on his desk. A couple of kids are out in the hall, and they press their hands against the door, like they were on a ship and looking for land. Archie gives them the heave-ho sign with his thumb as he sits behind his desk, and they disappear.

"You know what these are?" he asks, holding up one of the folders.

"How should I know?" I answer. I have no idea what Archie wants me in his office for.

Archie looks at me for a minute. I guess he thinks I am being a snotty wise guy, and he just keeps looking at me.

"These are reports," he says finally, "that I have to send to the city youth agency about certain kids who have gotten in a lot of trouble."

"So?" Why do I want to know this? I ask myself.

"So, Dennis," he says, "the reason kids get into trouble is that they begin to not care about things—their family, school, homework—and then you find out they don't even care about their future."

I know if he is calling me Dennis, and not calling me "son," that he means business here. Somebody from school must have talked to him. God. Maybe even my mother. She's been harping a lot about doing better in school.

"So?" I ask, looking down.

"So," Archie says, "I met Father O'Rourke on the street yesterday, and he told me that you were having a hard time at school."

"I am not," I say. I don't like people talking behind my back, I am thinking, even if it is true. "Father O'Rourke has a big mouth, anyway."

"He didn't say you were in trouble or anything, but only that your brother gets such good grades in everything, and you are not doing so good. Are you?"

"What does Billy's marks have to do with me?"

"I guess everybody expects more of you. You're in the fifth grade, and you should be doing things the right way by now. Is it too much to ask that you pay better attention to your schoolwork?"

I don't know why, I am thinking, I should have to do as good as my brother in anything. He gets all the good marks, and he is great at all the sports, and what has that done for anybody? He spends all of his time reading about history and religion and my mother is still over there every day on her hands and knees going from one end of Sutton Place to the other, nobody caring about her, nobody doing anything for her, and it's all such a rotten full-a-crap business, anyway. Nobody cares if she has a good and decent day in her life, and she does everything right. So why should I have to learn to do things the right way?

My hands are sweaty, and I feel myself squirming in my seat, but I don't say anything.

"You can do so much better, Dennis," Archie says. "And you know it."

All the statues in Archie's office are shining with the light that is shooting in from 52nd Street. They are like golden treasures. Billy has a couple of trophies, but all I ever got is a silver medal for coming in second when I swam the breaststroke at the all-city swim meet at Madison Square Boys Club.

"I don't give a shit, Archie," I say, still looking down.

"Watch your language, pal," Archie says. "Don't be like that with me."

"I just want people to mind their own business," I say, looking up at him.

"Business, Dennis, can be all of life, caring about everything. That's the way it is at Kips Bay. If you're a part of this boys' club, we're going to care about you."

"But," I say, getting up from my chair, "there's nothing wrong with me, and, anyway, I don't care who cares."

I know I don't have to talk about it to Archie or to anyone if I don't want. It's a free country, and I can do what I want and when I want.

I go to the door, thinking that if I could just get outside I wouldn't have sweaty palms. I don't need Archie, and I don't need Kips Bay. There are a lot of things to do on 56th Street, and I can hang out with guys who never come to Kips Bay.

I turn the doorknob and pull, but nothing happens. The door doesn't budge. I yank at it with all my might, and it is like it is riveted shut. I turn and look at Archie.

He is smiling.

"I can't get out," I say to him.

Archie gets up and walks to the door. He grabs the doorknob and kicks the bottom of the door.

It opens like a garden gate.

"There's a certain way of doing everything, Dennis," he says, winking at me. "Running away from me now, here, is just not the right way."

Archie puts a hand on my shoulder and leads me back to the chair.

"We just want to give you a boost up," he says.

All right, I am thinking. I'll have to sit now, and tell Archie that I'll do better in school. It won't take long.

I am kicking a can all the way home, thinking that with every kick I am telling everybody to leave me alone. I don't care what any of them think. School is not the greatest place in the world, anyway, and if I wanted a trophy, I would practice my breaststroke. If I wanted good grades, I'd spend more time with my homework. Everyone always says you can do so much better. They sound like a record.

I give the can one last, mighty kick, and I can see the small crowd of women in front of my building. My mother says that women who just sit on stoops envy the rich and judge the poor, but I never see many rich people on 56th Street, unless they are walking down to Sutton Place. I guess there are women in the world who don't do anything at all. They don't work or take care of children or even play sports. They just sit around with their friends, like they were royalty. My mother keeps to herself. She never sits around with the women of the building, on the stoop or anywhere, and she never tells anybody anything. She doesn't want us to tell anybody anything, either. What they don't know won't hurt them, she always says.

Sue Flanagan is sitting on the top step of the stoop with her mother. She has her student nurse's uniform on, and a blue jacket that is open so that you can see her name written on the side of her white dress. The dress is like silk, shiny and hugging her tightly. She gets up and throws her arms out as I walk up the three steps of the stoop.

"Here's my little Dapper Dan," Sue says. She always calls me Dapper Dan because my mother makes me wear a clean shirt every day, and I have to have it tucked tightly into my trousers.

I have a feeling Sue will hug me.

"Hello." This is all I can say, but I am thinking that I could kiss her if she would let me.

How do you kiss? I am wondering. I mean, kiss a real girl, and not someone who is an aunt or your big cousin or your mother. I am ten years old and I've never been near a real kiss.

Sue puts her arms around me and squeezes hard. I am pressed up against her shiny uniform and what's under it. My ear is right on one of her bazooms, and I feel the skin around my eyes tightening. And now Sue begins to move back and forth like she is dancing with me, and the dancing is like swimming in water. I can smell her perfume, which smells like a procession of girls in white dresses with garlands of roses. She is dancing with me and I can smell her perfume, and the dancing and the smell make me want to close my eyes and dream.

Oh, will I ever get old enough to kiss her?

Chapter Fourteen

My mother is sitting at the kitchen table, going over the little notebook where she writes down all the money she spends. The sun is shining through the kitchen window, and her hair looks very soft falling over her shoulders, like little waves of melted butter. She has a pencil in her hand. There are just three things she has to have money for all the time. She has to pay the bill at Rossi's grocery store or we won't be able to get milk and bread. We don't get milk and bread every day, but we always have it. My mother is always saving milk, and when she pours it into a cereal bowl, she never covers the cereal with the milk. She pours it an inch from the top and tells me to mix it up. Do this every day for a week, she says, and you have saved a whole quart.

I love breakfast, and my mother makes sure it is out at a quarter to eight every morning. Billy is always on time for breakfast because he loves breakfast even more than I do. If we are more than five minutes late, there is no breakfast, and she pours the cereal back into the box, and sometimes I have to punch Billy away from the kitchen sink so that I can wash my face and brush my teeth. My mother is very strict about time. "How will you ever go to work on time," she says, "if you can't be on time for breakfast?"

Billy has a job, but I don't have one yet.

Another thing my mother has to pay is the man that comes from the landlord every month, and if you don't give him the money, they take your furniture and put it out on the street, like they did to Mrs. McClusky next door. I felt sorry for her then. She was sitting on her furniture in the middle of the sidewalk, holding a cat in her hands, and an hour later she was gone. I never saw her again, and that is what happens if you don't pay the rent. You disappear from the face of the earth, that's what my mother says.

Also there is Mr. Karp, the insurance man, and he comes every week to get twenty-five cents from us. Mom has to sign his book each time, and he has to sign a piece of paper that she has. He must be very rich because he gets twenty-five cents from almost everybody in the building, and in all the buildings on the block. My mother says she has to pay the insurance because if she dies without insurance, they will just throw her in the river, and the tide will take her to Africa or somewhere she doesn't want to go.

"If the tide would take me to Ireland," I remember her telling the insurance man one day, "I wouldn't have the insurance at all, but I'd put my bathing suit on and hope to die."

My mother has never been to Ireland, but her mother and father were born there, and told her that it was more beautiful than heaven. I believe it. Everyone is always saying how beautiful Ireland is, and I wonder why they left it at all.

Now she stops writing in her little book and stares off for a minute.

"Dennis," she says, "I think you should get a job. Every little bit that we can put together would help. And now that you are ten, you are getting old enough to have a real job. Working, you know, is the second key to heaven."

I never thought about heaven having a lock on the door.

"What's the first key?" I ask.

She laughs, saying, "Obeying your mother."

"I had a job, Mom," I say, "but you told me to quit it."

I worked for two Saturdays at the drugstore on 49th Street and First Avenue. It was a delivery job, and the doctor there paid me ten cents a delivery, which I thought was pretty good. The only thing was that, after dusting every bottle and box on every shelf in the store, and washing the floor in the back, and cleaning the glass in the cases with the perfume, there were only two deliveries all day, and the doctor gave me twenty cents.

After the next week when there was only one delivery, and I did the floors and the cases and the bottles, my mother went down to the drugstore and showed the doctor the ten cents and told him he should be ashamed of himself. I was very embarrassed and kept my eyes down all the time. My mother gets on her high horse sometimes, and she would tell off the queen of England if she wanted to.

I wish I could have kept the job, but my mother told the doctor that she wouldn't let me go to his drugstore again, even if I was dying with the consumption and he was giving away cough syrup. She then left the dime on the counter, and she held my hand as we walked out of the store.

I would never tell my mother that I wish she didn't do something, but I did think about that dime as we passed Abbie's candy store on 53rd Street, and of the new Yo-Yos that he just put out for a dime.

"You have to be careful about people," my mother said as we walked up First Avenue, "because you'll meet some who are never sorry for their sins."

"And I do want a job, Mom," I say, "and I'd even go back to the drugstore."

"I know, honey," she says, "but that was not such a real job, and maybe a different kind of job would be better. Maybe Billy can help you find something."

I wish I could find a good job because every time I hear someone talk about somebody being rich they say he has a good job. I don't know where you get these good jobs, but I am going to ask Billy to help me.

Chapter Fifteen

It is Saturday morning, and I am playing off-the-point with Bobby Walsh down by the tennis courts on 55th Street. I am wearing a brand-new pair of dungarees my mother just bought me, and I'm feeling like I could win at anything today. Usually, I get Billy's old dungarees, or worse, his old corduroys, but these were a surprise, and fit just right.

We are playing games of eleven, and I am a little behind, but I know I can beat him if I put my mind to it. But I'm a little tired. I started the paper delivery job this morning, and I had to get up at five-thirty to carry all those *New York Times* and *Daily News* through the hallways of Sutton Place.

Before me is a brick wall about ten feet high that goes all around the tennis courts on York Avenue, and the wall has a brick edge that goes across the bottom and another edge about three feet up from the sidewalk. I am trying to hit the spaldeen hard enough off the top edge so that it will land just about in the middle of a parked car across the street. I stop to make a big yawn, but then I concentrate on what I am doing. I pinpoint myself. That is what my mother always says, pinpoint yourself to something and you will get it done. So I am pinpointing the point of the tennis court wall, and the ball is coming closer and closer with every try.

Now Bobby is sprawled across the fender of the car. He missed the catch, and so it is my game, third in a row.

We go to the cellar of 25 Sutton Place South where there is a Pepsi machine. We are pretty quiet because we know that the service elevator guy will try to give us a kick in the seat if he sees us here. The soda machine costs a nickel, and Bobby has fifteen cents of his thirty cents' allowance with him. The Walshes have some money because his father works for the railroad and plays the Irish fiddle in the Third Avenue gin mills for extra cash.

Bobby puts a nickel in the machine, and we share the bottle of Pepsi, though he drinks most of it. He gives me about two inches in the bottom of the bottle to finish off.

And as Bobby heads up the stairs to the street, I stand there and drink the bottom of the soda, and then I shove the bottle back up into the machine.

I should have some money soon, too, because Billy got me the job. It's not a good job, but it will help. I am getting twenty cents an hour for delivering the papers. Fat Walter who runs the candy store on 57th Street and First Avenue says that he pays for one week the week after. Billy told me that Walter does this so that the kids will come back again to deliver the papers. It takes about an hour and fifteen minutes to take the papers from building to building, up the service elevators, and through the hallways, but they only pay for an hour. "If you go fast," Fat Walter says, "you can do it in an hour."

Next week I'll have my own thirty cents to spend. I told my mother that I will give the rest to her.

We quit the elevens after three more games, and we are sweating good now.

"I'll race you to the Pepsi machine," Bobby says, "and I'll buy another soda."

"Great," I say, and we take off like Olympic sprinters to the basement of 25 Sutton.

We race as hard as we can until we get to the bottom of the stairs, and then we run quietly like we are ballet dancers. Bobby puts the nickel in and pulls down on the handle. I hear the bottle drop. Bobby sticks his hand in the machine, and he pulls out the empty bottle I had left there an hour before. His chin drops to his chest, and he looks as if someone told him he was really adopted.

I am disappointed, too, because I want some soda.

"What's this?" Bobby says.

"Damn, Bobby," I say, "I don't know. What's that?"

"It's a friggin' empty bottle is what it is," he cries.

"What are you gonna do?" I ask.

I am doing everything I can to keep from laughing, especially since I am really thirsty and want some Pepsi.

Bobby sinks into his pocket and pulls out another nickel, his last one. This time the machine gives him a whole deal, and we return to the street, Bobby sucking down the bottle as we go up the stairs. When there is an inch left, he hands the bottle to me. I take my shirt out and wipe the top. This is going to taste good, and there is nothing like a cold soda after sweating it up. Even if there is just an inch.

As I raise the bottle to my lips I see out of the corner of my eye that Shalleski and his brother are coming toward us.

"Hey," Bobby says to them.

"What are you guys doing?" Shalleski's brother says. Harry is a tall and skinny boy, two years older than Shalleski and a little nicer.

"Off-the-point," Bobby says.

"Give me some of that," Shalleski says to me, reaching for the bottle.

"No," I say.

I stare at him, but I know I am not going to stare him down.

"Give me that bottle," Shalleski says, "or I'll kick your ass in."

"No," I answer, "it's mine."

I can feel my body beginning to shake. I know this will lead to a fight. You just know these things, the way you know the guy in the movie will rip your ticket in half when you give it to him. One action leads to another.

I am afraid, and I know that he can see I am afraid, but I remember what Billy said, too. It is hard to talk, I am so nervous. The skin around my eyes begins to tighten, and I make the face, but I know I am not going to let Shalleski get this bottle. There is only one thing for me to do, and I know I am going to get hurt doing it, but I know, too, that I have to be quick, quick like my brother. So I hand the bottle to Bobby. As soon as Bobby takes the bottle I have a free hand, and I feel myself squeezing my fingers hard into my palm so that my fist is as tight as it can be, like a piece of hard wood, and I swing it around as hard as I can and punch Shalleski across the side of his face. I guess I could have hit him in the mouth, but I didn't really want to hurt him or knock his teeth out. I am hoping that a punch like this, an easy one, will keep him from getting too mad at me.

I just know I have to do this.

Shalleski begins to yell as he falls back.

"You fuck, you fuck," he is screaming as he recovers, and lunges at me. He grabs me around the waist and pulls me to the ground and begins to punch wildly at me. I am on the ground, but I don't punch him back. I don't want to be in this fight, but I know I have to be here. I just try to cover my head and face so that his punches go off the side of my arm. He is strong, and I can feel the muscles in his body tighten as he grabs me around the neck.

I could fight back easily enough if I wanted to, but I just want him to know that he'll have to fight me every time he gives me a bad time. I don't care about winning or losing, but Shalleski has to know he is going to have to go after someone else the next time.

God, I am thinking as I take a good punch to my head, I have to take care of myself. So I begin to move around quickly, knowing that I don't want to be like a statue. A statue is too good a good target. I feel myself getting out of his grip, and I know I could punch him right in his teeth if I wanted, but something is holding me back.

He has his arm around my neck, but I have one arm under his neck, and the other arm is free. I could bust him a good one now, if I wanted.

Then, suddenly, Shalleski is saying, "You give? You give?"

It is easy to stop it now, even though I have a free fist to bop him one. I just have to say "Give," and it will be all over.

When someone says "Give," you have to stop. That is the way it is on the east side. I could say it in a second, but I have to think what I want to do with my free fist. Should I crack him hard?

My heart is not in this fight. I know that.

I don't like Shalleski, but I don't want to hurt him, either.

I am here on the ground rolling around with Shalleski in my new dungarees, and I am still remembering what he did to me back there on First Avenue a few years ago. I so wanted to get even with him then, but now it doesn't matter so much. It doesn't matter that he sent all my candy flying across First Avenue.

And there have been plenty of other times, too, that Shalleski has acted like a pain and bullied me. Little things, like punching me hard in the middle of the back in the school yard basketball games. But, still, I don't want to hurt him, even if I could kick the shit outta him. I don't know why. It just doesn't seem worth it.

Passing through my mind now, but just for a second, is Sister Maureen in the second grade talking about turning the other cheek, and giving somebody your coat, too, if he asks you for your shirt. I remember that she also said it was easy to say this, but much harder to do, and I think now that I don't want to give Shalleski anything. I don't want to take anything from him, either. I just want us to be equal, if that could be in the cards.

Finally, after thinking about all this, I say the famous word. "Okay," I say as he is choking me, "I give."

But Shalleski starts to punch at me again. It figures that he wouldn't be fair, and I should have known better.

And now Shalleski's brother pulls him off.

"He says he gives," Harry says, "so break it up."

Shalleski gets up, and he and his brother move on up the street, and they don't look back. I turn to Bobby, and he hands me back the bottle of soda. There is still a little left in the bottle, and I take it to the curb and pour it out.

"Hey," Bobby yells out, "what the hell are you doing?"

"The soda doesn't matter," I say. "This is not why I punched him."

"You coulda gave it to me."

"It don't matter," I answer.

"Maybe you coulda beat him," Bobby says.

I am laughing now, and I can't wait to tell my brother Billy.

"Ahh, Bobby," I say, "maybe and ten cents gets you on the subway."

I guess you have to make one point at a time, I think.

Walking up First Avenue to 56th Street, I am scraping a stick along the block-long fence that goes around the church and school of St. John's. It makes a clattering sound, like a drummer in the St. Patrick's Day parade.

Suddenly, Walsh begins to laugh out loud. He is pointing at the knee of my dungarees.

"Hey, Dennis," he says, "you got a hole in your pants."

"Holy shit," I say.

"Now," Walsh says, "you got a hole in your pants, a hole in your shoes, and a hole in your head."

God, I am thinking, my mother will kill me.

I should have hit that Shalleski when I had the chance.

Chapter Sixteen

Sister Urban is looking over the class with that funny look she has every time she wants to lash out at someone. Raymond Rabbitscabbage farted, just a little noise. But it gives me an idea, and I put my hand in my shirt, cup it under my arm, and squeeze down. I am good at this, and it makes a terrific fart noise. Petey Poscullo laughs out loud. Raymond Rabbitscabbage farts again, and this time Petey Poscullo can't stop laughing. I know that Sister Urban is out for a farter, and Petey knows that she will settle for a laugher if she can't find a farter. So Petey is now pointing at me, and Sister Urban is flying down the aisle. Her wide black habit knocks the books off of Gilda Galli's desk, and she doesn't stop to help pick them up for Gilda. She tears toward me, and I feel like running.

"It wasn't me, Sister," I cry out, "I swear."

But that doesn't stop her. She grabs me. She pulls me by the arm, and I can see her hand go way back before she swings it around and slaps me hard across the face as she pulls me from the seat. I am stunned that she does this, and I yell.

"Shit," I say, "I didn't do nothing that bad."

She pushes me to the back of the room and has me standing with my nose one inch from the brown wall. She puts her mouth next to my ear and yells at me.

"If you ever curse in this room again," she screams, "I will have you thrown out of this school as fast as you can blink."

Raymond Rasakavitch is now as silent as a guardian angel, and Petey has stopped laughing. Ann Kovak, who is always so sweet and friendly, looks like she is going to cry. She is so shy anyway, and now her eyes look so sad, and her lips are pursed up. The rest of them, too, look scared and caring. I know that everyone in the class is feeling sorry for me, and I will let them know that I would beat the crap out of Poscullo if he wasn't two years older than me because he was left back twice. Poscullo's going to have a mustache when he graduates.

Here, with my nose against the wall, I listen to everyone in the class talking again about Blessed Maria Goretti. You can't get away from the saints in my school, and Blessed Maria comes up like clock-work every term. She fought her attacker off until she died, protecting herself from sin.

I think that she must have been a frightened little girl, but my nose is against the wall, and I can't say anything. And so I close my eyes and think of Blessed Maria Goretti, and of the fight she must have put up to keep from committing a sin.

Suddenly, I am thinking of Mr. Dempsey, and what would have happened if I didn't get away from him that afternoon in the deli-catessen. I wonder if Mr. Dempsey would become a priest if he killed me.

I guess once something like that happens to you, you can never forget it, and I still think about why people like Mr. Dempsey don't get arrested, or why God doesn't find some way to stop them from hurting little kids. And how come God lets a nun cream a kid like this in front of everyone?

My face is burning, and I try to rub it a little to make the burn-ing go away. But Sister Urban sees me and calls out from the front of the room.

"You just put your hands at your side," she says, "or I'll tie them behind your back."

Whenever I go to church, I always ask God to help make every-thing better for everyone. I know that I'm ten years old, and it's 1950, and I have a job, and I'm supposed to act older and not care about God or church, because everybody now is getting a television set and watching it is the big thing. But I love talking to God because I know He cares about me. Just like my mother does. But I worry that He has too many people talking to Him at the same time, and doesn't have time to get to me.

Chapter Seventeen

My mother holds my face in her hands.

"Look at this," she says. "What happened?"

There is no mirror in our bathroom. The bathroom is just a little square not much bigger than the bowl itself. There isn't even a light, because there is just room enough for your knees if you are sitting, and you can hold the door open a little to let some of the kitchen light in. So my mother pulls me in front of the mirror above the kitchen sink.

"Just look," she says, pointing.

I can see Sister Urban's handprint in red across the side of my face. Now I guess I have to tell her about what happened, but she hates it if I have been bad in school. Or anywhere. She can get the strap on me to add to the punishment if I did something bad. But, I am thinking, I didn't do anything that bad. And so I sit down in a kitchen chair and tell her about Rabbitscabbage and Petey Poscullo, and even Gilda's books, and Ann's sad eyes, and how Sister Urban ran down the aisle.

"You just made a crack underneath your arm?"

"That's all I did, and Petey . . ."

"It is kid stuff," she whispers, "just kid stuff. Put your jacket on."

Now I am in the dark corridor of the second floor of St. John the Evangelist school, and we are looking for Sister Urban. I don't want to be here because no matter what happens I know that I am going to be a problem for Sister Urban for the rest of the school year.

I am hoping against hope that Sister Urban is not to be found, but there she is, sitting at her desk reading papers. I never have the luck.

"You wait here," my mother says.

I don't think I have ever seen her this mad.

The door is wide open, and I listen to what my mother has to say. She doesn't give Sister Urban a moment to say anything back, and she is talking like a Gatling gun.

"I just want to tell you," she says, "that my son has a red mark across his face the exact size of your hand, and I don't give a fiddler's anything what he has done, you are never to touch him again, and you can come to see me and I will do all the punishing, but if you ever put your hand on my child again, I swear on all that is holy and good that I will come across the street to this school, and I will find you, and before everybody I will tear the hood off your head and put a match to it."

Sister Urban is as stunned as I was when she whacked me, and in less than a second my mother has me by the hand, and we are walking out of the school, across the street, and back up the stoop on 56th Street.

"She is going to hate me, Mom," I say as we walk up the gum-stained marble steps of the hallway.

"She'll do no such thing," my mother says. "She'll respect you."

I guess my mother is right. I know she wouldn't do anything to get me in trouble. But I'm glad about one thing, anyway: that there were no kids in the class when my mother got there.

Chapter Eighteen

My mother has been seeing this guy named Tommy Quigley. Billy says that Quigley is a queer name, and not a name to make you like someone. But she goes out with this Quigley sometimes, probably too much if you ask me. Quigley comes over and has dinner with us at the kitchen table. My mother makes fish sticks or something good like that when he comes.

"He is just a friend," she said one day when Billy asked her why he comes around.

I think of Daddy every time I see this Quigley guy, but Billy says that I shouldn't worry about it, that she has to have friends. She only has Aunt Kitty and Aunt Helen to make her laugh.

Sometimes I feel so sorry for my mother. She doesn't have time to make a lot of friends because she is always running from one apartment to the other trying to get together more money than the welfare will give her, just so she can buy things for the house and for me and Billy.

"Don't tell anyone that he comes here," she told me and Billy.

She always wants to keep everything a secret. I guess she feels bad that this guy comes here when she already has a husband up in the hospital. I don't even know how she met him, and she wouldn't tell me, anyway. She never talks much about herself, except when she tells us how hard it was for her mother and father when they came here from Ireland. I don't even know the name of the high school she went to, or if she had a best friend, or what her first job was. And if I ask her things, she usually says, "Oh, it's not important" or "We just got by."

One day, though, I got her talking, and she told me about growing up beside a firehouse in Brooklyn, and that she loved the firemen who would send her to the store for sandwiches when she was a little girl because they couldn't leave the firehouse, and then they always gave her a big tip. That's as much as I know about the way she grew up.

Billy told me he thinks her big secrets come from her being poor when she was little, that she didn't want to think about it anymore. I don't know what it's like to be poor like that, but I remember her saying that you are only poor if you miss a meal when you want one. And I remember, too, when she told Pop that it was easier to be poor when you have steam heat. I don't know what it could have been like for her.

Quigley works in a delicatessen somewhere, and I don't like people who work in delicatessens, ever since Mr. Dempsey. I don't even go into delicatessens anymore. I wouldn't go into a delicatessen if they were giving away potato chips for free.

My mother went out with Quigley tonight, but she came home earlier than she said she would. She said she'd be home at nine-thirty, but she came back at eight. Billy was still listening to the radio in the living room, and I was on a kitchen chair reading about Heidi. I don't know why my mother gets me these books about people in other countries. I'm in the sixth grade now, and should be reading mystery stories like Scarry does.

She didn't say anything much when she came in. She just put her robe on and read a magazine, the way she does most nights.

Now it is the middle of the night. I have just eased out of my sleep. I didn't put my pajamas on when I went to bed tonight. I don't know why. I was lying on the top bunk, thinking about putting my pajamas on, but Billy came in and turned off the light.

And when the light went out, I stopped thinking about anything but Marilyn Rolleri. I fell asleep thinking about her, and now I am awake again thinking about her. It is funny about being in the dark, for when the lights are out, I can be completely alone, just alone to think about my life. In the dark you can make things happen, things you never speak of. I can take Marilyn Rolleri and walk with her anywhere, say anything to her, do anything. A separate world can begin when the lights go out, and I put myself into Marilyn Rolleri's life, and now in the darkness of my room I am sitting with Marilyn Rolleri on a park bench down by the Pepsi-Cola sign.

I don't know what it is I like about Marilyn Rolleri because she hardly ever says hello to me. Still, she doesn't have skinny legs anymore, and she has the biggest breasts in the class. I am wishing that I sat across from her like I did in the third and fourth grades, so I could watch her breasts moving up and down as she breathes. Maybe I could watch them grow, too, a little more each day.

Some of the guys in the class are always talking about getting boners, and I am wondering why I never can get one except when I am sleeping, even now when I am thinking about Marilyn's breasts, thinking about moving my hand into her blouse on the park bench, wondering what they look like naked, what size are the nipples, what color?

Jeez, when will I ever be old enough to have a boner?

I now begin to put my hand down inside my underwear, thinking that I can make it work, that I can have all that fun the guys talk about. I think about holding myself, but I suddenly stop. I can feel my face glowing red in the darkness because I know that I shouldn't be doing this. Boys shouldn't do this at eleven years old, or even at sixteen. It's a sin, I know that, and that I can go to hell if I get hit by a car tomorrow.

I know I'll have to go to confession. Some of the guys go to St. Agnes where the priests are from foreign countries and hardly speak English, and confession is a breeze. If you say that you copped a feel in the back row of the RKO, or you Mary-palmed it twice this week, or you murdered the mayor, it's all the same with them: three Hail Marys and two Our Fathers. But to me, confession probably works better with God if you get a priest who speaks your language, at least if you want it to do any good.

Jeez, I can't get away from thinking about religion in everything I do. Religion and Jesus and the Blessed Virgin are such a part of my life, like my name or even my legs. Everything I ever learned about

God and the saints begins now to pass through a kind of veil that is before my eyes, and I suddenly see Blessed Maria Goretti, that young girl in a plain dark dress on a dirt road, just standing there, minding her own business, like in the photograph of her I saw in school. Even though she had no father and her mother had to slave for bits of food, she did everything she could to make her life decent, so that God would say that her life is okay. And now I see Marilyn Rolleri, sitting with me on a park bench, in a tight skirt and a blouse that is half open, and then I see my guardian angel right there next to me, shaking his head, saying that God would never think that this is okay, and I'm realizing that I don't want to do this because my mother and Billy and Father Ford and even Sister Urban would not like it if they thought I did something like this, and so I tell myself to think about the DiMaggio brothers or the Marx Brothers or the Brothers Grimm and all those stories, and to think about me and Billy going off to Kips for a Ping-Pong game, anything but this famous boner that everyone talks about. And I think about Ping-Pong and a good slice shot until my eyes are so heavy that I forget where I am.

I don't know how long I have been sleeping before I hear an explosion.

Bang.

It is frightening, and I jump up out of my sleep, and I can see Billy is out of bed completely in his underwear.

"What is it?" I ask.

"Somebody has kicked the door," Billy says.

"Why?" I say. "Why would somebody do that?"

I was feeling my stomach turning. Where was my mother? Were we all going to get killed?

Bang, the crash comes again.

I can feel my body beginning to shake, the way I felt before I punched Shalleski. I wish there was someone here to take care of us, but I know that we are alone. We have to stop whatever is going on, we have to get someone here, some big person. My mother is now up, and she turns on the kitchen light.

Bang pow.

Another loud kick at the door, and this time I can see that the wood at the bottom of the door is caving in. I know now that the door is going to be kicked in, and I jump down from the bed, and Billy and I are standing here, both of us shivering in our underwear, staring at our mother, wondering what she will do, afraid to say anything to her.

My mother reaches for the key to Mike Shurtliff's apartment, the one across the hall. Besides doing his shirts, she now also cleans the apartment for him once in a while, and she has the key in her hand, and she tiptoes over to us and whispers to me as she hands me the key.

"I am going to open the door," she says as quietly as she can, her voice cracking, "and he will rush in, maybe, I don't know."

"Who is it, Mom?" Billy asks. His hand is on her arm, and it looks so small there even though he is thirteen.

"It's Quigley," my mother says, still whispering. "But, Dennis, you have to go into the apartment across the hall. The lock is easy, just turn it and push. There is a phone in Mike's living room. Call the operator. You understand? Call the operator, and tell her to send the police here, give her the address. Can you do that?"

Oh, God, I never had to do anything so important as this. I want to get it right.

"Go in," I repeat, "and say to the operator to bring the police to 337 East 56th Street, apartment 26."

"Yes," she says, "just do it fast, as fast as you can."

"What about Billy?" I ask. "I want Billy to come with me."

"I need Billy here with me," she says, pushing me close to the door.

"Can I get dressed?" I ask.

"No," she says. "There isn't time."

Bang. Pow. Bang.

More kicks to the door, and this time the door is cracked open, and I can see what I just know is Quigley's brown shoe.

"Go away!" my mother screams. She is yelling at the top of her lungs. "Go away, Tommy, the police are coming."

There is another kick, and this time his foot comes all the way through the door, and the foot is sticking in the kitchen. And then he kicks more and his foot gets higher and higher. The door is getting a hole in it that is getting bigger.

My mother pushes me to where she wants me to stand, and she

puts Billy behind her. She gives me a wild sort of look, and her eyes seem like they are on fire. She then opens the door in one sudden jerk, and Quigley begins to push his way into the apartment. He is grabbing my mother, and I don't know if I should try to stop him, to hit him with something, or what I should do. I am eleven, and I should be able to beat this Quigley up.

"Go, Dennis," my mother screams. "Fast."

I push past them and scrape my arm against the side of the doorway. I can see it start to bleed. I run to the door across the hall and try to push the key into it. But my hand is shaking too much. Christ, I am thinking, help my hand put this key in the lock. Finally, it falls into the lock hole.

I go into the living room and search for the phone, but I can't find the light. Oh, God, turn on the light for me. I go back into the kitchen and feel around for the string that I know is hanging from the ceiling. I have seen it, and I know it is there, but I cannot find it, and my body is shaking much worse now. At last, I find the string and pull it, and the light shines right on the telephone, and I dial "zero" and tell the operator to send the police because someone is killing my mother. She asks me for the address three times, and she won't let me off of the telephone.

"I have to go," I say. "I have to see what is happening."

"You just stay here on the phone," the operator says, "until I make a connection."

"What connection?" I say. "I have to go."

"Stay on the phone, dammit." She is yelling at me. My mother is being killed and this operator is yelling at me.

A man comes on the phone now, a policeman, I guess.

"What is the address?" he asks.

"I already told the operator," I say. "The operator knows the address."

"What is the address?" he asks again.

God.

"337 East 56th Street," I say, "apartment 26, fourth floor."

"What is the matter?" he is now asking.

"What is the matter?" I repeat. "My mother is being killed by

Quigley, that is what is the matter. *He's killing her, don't you under-stand?"*

I want to hang up the phone, but the policeman on the line won't let me say goodbye. He keeps asking me why all this is happening, and I tell him that I was just sleeping, and how should I know any of this? How should I know why any of this is happening? I am eleven, and this policeman thinks I am a reporter.

I am still on the telephone when I hear the police. They are right outside. They are running down the hall. I can see them pass by Mike's door, and I can hear them wrestling with Quigley.

I apologize to the man on the phone. I don't want to hang up on him, but I have to go. I drop the phone and run. At Mike's door, I see Quigley being dragged by. He is cursing, and the policemen are punching him as they drag him. All the neighbors have opened their doors, and I know that my mother will be mortified to know that all the neighbors were woken up.

Where is she? I wonder. I begin to panic. I don't care about the neighbors, and I don't care if they see me running through the hallway in my underwear. I just want to see my mother. I want to see if she is okay.

Chapter Nineteen

My mother is holding me in her arms. I am eleven years old and my mother is holding me in her arms like I was two. She is sitting on a kitchen chair, and she is just staring at the hole in the kitchen door, and she is rocking. Billy is standing next to her, with his hand on her shoulder.

"I just have you guys," my mother says, wiping a tear off on the shoulder of my undershirt. "I just have you guys to help me."

Chapter Twenty

I don't know why kids have to die. I mean, we don't even know half of what we're supposed to know yet, and we haven't even done half the things we're supposed to do, and still, we can die. Just like that, your guardian angel looks away for just a split second, and then *pow*, you're gone.

I'm in line now with the rest of the class, walking quickly to Frank C. David's Funeral Home on 55th Street just off First Avenue. It is a warm day, and we have left our coats in the classroom. First Avenue seems very bright as we glide down the hill from 56th Street.

I feel so sorry for Ann Kovak. I think the whole class does, because no one says the smallest peep as we walk the avenue. She was so nice. She didn't just say hello in the morning the way everybody does. No, Ann always said, "Good morning, Dennis." She'd mention your name so that you felt you were a little important with her. And that was good because Ann was so pretty, quiet and pretty, with skin as white as a full moon, and a shy smile that my mother said was like a sweet song.

She sat between Mary Hanlon and Angela Gaffney in the second row, the three of them always with their hands folded on their desks when they weren't writing, heads and shoulders straight as boards, looking like they were dolls on a prize shelf at Coney Island, looking like you could pick them up whole with your hands. They never said anything they shouldn't, and they always had the right answers, like the angels were on their side.

But Ann died yesterday. She was so thin, and when she tripped on a curb on 57th Street and hurt her spine, she wasn't strong enough to take the pain. She just smiled and closed her eyes, they told us at school, and passed away.

And Harry Shalleski just died, too.

I didn't really know Harry, and even though I don't like his brother, I'm sorry he died. He's just another kid, like us.

I don't know what it is to die, and it is something I have never thought much about. I am thinking now, though, that I am feeling pretty spooky because I don't know what to expect. Not afraid, just sort of weird.

I suppose everyone in the class thinks it's weird, too, for there is not much going on, and everyone is so quiet, except for a few of the girls who are crying. I have never seen a dead person, except when Joey Jurgensen's mother died a couple of years ago, and the whole class came to Frank C. David's. I remember thinking then that her face seemed to be flat, that the air had gone out of her cheeks. But Mrs. Jurgensen had been sick for a long time before she died, and I guess Joey sort of expected it to happen. He didn't seem so sad, and he thanked the class for showing up.

But, here, this is not just a dead person. This is Ann, a kid, like us, and we are not supposed to think about an eleven-year-old in a dead condition. And so this visit to the funeral parlor is a lot different because everyone was Ann's friend and no one believes it's her in Frank C. David's Funeral Home.

And Harry was just a kid, too. He wasn't sick a day in his life, and he died from a mistake.

Harry Shalleski and Michael Harris were sneaking into the RKO up on 58th Street and Third Avenue. Just a few weeks ago. They climbed a fire escape next to the movie as far as they could go, which was five stories up. There they saw a catwalk, I guess a ledge on the side of the movie house, and if they could go along that ledge, they could reach the top exit door and fire escape of the movie house. I heard the catwalk was about four feet long or six. And there were two ropes there, hanging from the roof. Michael grabbed one rope and pulled himself along the ledge to the movie house fire escape. He told Harry to just grab the rope, but Harry made a mistake, and he grabbed the other rope. The other rope hanging from the roof wasn't tied to anything, and so Harry and the rope fell away from the catwalk, and Harry went down five stories.

Michael slid down his rope for the whole five stories, and his hands were burned and cut from the rope, but when he got to the yard, Harry was a bloody mess.

It is in the middle of the afternoon. People are crowded in little groups around the big room at Frank C. David's. Everyone is whispering. No one is laughing, or telling stories, or remembering good times. I guess you don't remember good times when a kid is dead like this. I'm straining my neck to see around the crowds, to see if I can see Ann, but I'm also thinking of Harry.

Harry was Billy's age. They weren't friends, but Billy was pretty upset when he told my mother all about it. We were eating spareribs boiled in sauerkraut. Mom made it specially for Billy because he likes the spareribs, which the butcher mostly throws out. But Billy couldn't eat anything that night. He said he just wanted to go to bed and to sleep because he didn't want to think about Harry any more that day.

"Harry was one of those guys," Billy said, "who you like but don't think much about. You don't look to hang around with him, or wait for him on the stoop, or ask him to go down to Kips with you. But now, after this, we'll never forget him."

I remember thinking that I don't want to die just to be never forgot.

Harry's family took him to Philadelphia to have a funeral, and none of Harry's friends on 55th Street got to say goodbye to him.

But now we're saying goodbye to Ann. We are lined up single file, and Sister Cyril is pushing us gently past the casket. The boys and girls aren't going fast enough and we are being jammed up like sardines. Suddenly, I see Ann. We were told by Sister to say a prayer for the repose of her soul as we walk past, but I can only think that she looks like she is just a pretty girl taking a nap in a white dress. I am stopped now in front of the casket, staring down at Ann. I want to pray and to ask God to make sure she's happy, but there is something else on my mind, something I don't like, and I can't say any prayers as I see her there, her skin more white than the moon, as white as snow, and looking as cold. That's what I don't like. She looks so cold lying there, puffs of white silk all around her, under her head, curving around her shoulders, down over the sides of her arms, and then across her waist. She is like a cold angel on these clouds of silk, and I want to make her warm.

We can't see her legs. It is like her upper body is lying in a pie plate surrounded with meringue. I wish that she looked warmer and happier, that she was taking one of Sister Stella's lessons where nothing matters unless you're happy, and I want to push her thin hand up to her pretty face and put a finger near her mouth, so that Father Hamilton would get angry when he comes with his white socks to say the prayers, and he would yell at Ann and tell her to stop biting her nails, and to put her hands by her sides, and Ann would wake up and laugh.

We pass by the family, and I see Ann's mother sitting on the edge of a long row of wooden seats. Her eyes are closed and she is clutching a pair of rosary beads. Tears are coming from her eyes like from a fire hydrant. These are the real tenement tears, I am thinking, tears that come from her insides, insides that must be ripped apart, and I wish the baby Jesus would come to her and sit on her lap, because only the baby Jesus will come to sit on the lap of a mother who is looking at the face of her dead daughter in a funeral parlor.

Sister Cyril ushers us to the back of the room, where we stand quietly. No one really knows what to say, anyway, and even if we did, we would be careful about speaking because all the mourners are whispering and Sister Cyril would be fast with a hard pinch if we talked.

You learn two things early with Sister Cyril, the first that she will get you with no exception if you act up in the line, and the second is that if you tense up all your muscles when she approaches, she won't get as much skin, and the pinching won't hurt as much. Some days I walk around the whole day long making muscles like Charles Atlas.

Father Hamilton enters the room and stands by Ann's coffin to say a silent prayer. Ann's hands are by her sides, so Father Hamilton doesn't yell at her, thank God, because I don't think Ann's mother could take Father Hamilton yelling at her coffined daughter.

Father Hamilton turns to us. I can see his white socks shining out beneath his cassock and I wonder if his feet itch. There is dead silence in the room. He turns his Chinese-apple face from side to side, I guess making notes in his mind about who is here, and what questions about their families he will ask when this is over.

"Please," Father Hamilton says, "kneel for the rosary."

I pull a pair of rosaries out of my pocket. I don't know why I call it a pair. Maybe because it has all the beads together with the crucifix, so that there are beads for the Hail Marys, and the crucifix to remember why you are saying the rosary to begin with.

But, wait a minute, there are also single beads that are used for either the Our Father or the Glory Be. So maybe it's not a pair. Maybe it's a set. A set of rosaries, but that doesn't sound right.

Most of the class is standing on a thick green rug, but I am off the rug and in a corner of the back of the room. Below me is a floor of hard wood, and I realize this as I kneel. I should have found a piece of the rug. And I realize, too, that my handkerchief is in my jacket pocket, which I left at school, so I don't even have anything to put under my knees.

"In the name of the Father the Son and the Holy Ghost," Father Hamilton says.

All the prayers, I am thinking as I bless myself, sound like one word when Father Hamilton says them. I don't think he likes the English language very much, because he only speaks slowly when he is saying Latin.

I am not kneeling for more than ten seconds when my knees begin to hurt.

"The first Sorrowful Mystery," Father continues, "the Agony in the Garden, OurFatherwhoartinheavenhollowedbethynamethykingdomcomethywillbedoneonearthasitisinheaven."

"Give us this day," I begin to mouth the words, thinking that this day is a day I want to forget, a sad day. Maybe if I fool around with the prayers, I could forget the funeral parlor and how sad we all are, "our daily bread," which I think could be a peanut butter and jelly sandwich, "and forgive us our trashpasses," except I never know why we are praying about passing trash, and do we pass it like a football or like the salt and pepper, "as we forgive those," and I think about Shalleski and forgiving him for punching me all the time now that his brother Harry died and went to Philadelphia, "who trashpass against us," all this garbage piled up against us like a wall, "and lead us not into Penn Station," but, I know it's temptation, though I always say Penn Station to see if anybody hears, and I think of the temptations in the world, like Sue Flanagan's hard-starched nurse's uniform and Marilyn Rolleri's tight skirt, "but deliver us from evil," folding and throwing, delivering the way we deliver the newspapers from the *Daily News* and the *Daily Mirror,* "Amen."

". . . HailMaryfullofgracetheLordiswiththeeblessedartthoua-monk'swomanandblessedisthefruitofthywoundJesus," Father goes on.

"Holy Mary," I say, thinking is this the monk's woman in the blessed-art-thou-a-monk's-woman, and I thought Joseph was a carpenter, but maybe he was a monk, too, and if he's not a monk, what's this other monk doing with Mary anyway, "Mother of God," and this fruit of the wound of Jesus, maybe instead of a wound where the Romans put a spear in him Jesus has a Chinese apple like Father Hamilton's face, there in the wound where he's supposed to have a Sacred Heart, "pray for us sinners," oh my knees are buckling out from under me, and there are so many sinners, almost everybody, I guess, and they expect me to kneel here with little glass needles in each knee, for the lights go out sometime in everybody's room and they are alone with the dark and the thoughts of going into anybody's life and doing what you want with them, and if that's not sinning I don't know what is, "now and at the hour of our death," and I guess we will all die together here if it is the same hour, and I will certainly die soon if I have to kneel here through a whole rosary, and I am so sorry that Ann is dead, because I will miss her very, very much, "Amen."

The "Amen" is like a chorus because everybody in the room says it.

We say the other five Sorrowful Mysteries, the Crowning with Thorns, the Scourging at the Pillar, the Carrying of the Cross, and the Nailing to the Cross, each mystery a decade of ten Hail Marys and an Our Father and a Glory Be. My knees can last maybe another thirty seconds, and I say a fast prayer to the baby Jesus asking him to make Father Hamilton stop here, and don't let him go into the Joyful and the Glorious Mysteries, too.

The prayer works, and Father Hamilton finishes the last Glory Be.

"GlorybetotheFatherandtotheSonandtotheHolyGhost."

"World without end," everybody answers but me, "Amen."

I am quiet, because I am now thinking about the Holy Ghost, and why does everybody, Billy and Betty Fallon down at the library of Kips Club and my mother, say that there aren't any ghosts except for this one exception, and I wonder if someday someone will tell me there isn't any Holy Ghost the way there isn't any Santa Claus. And I think, will they ever get their ghosts right?

And what will become of Ann?

I am in my kitchen and pouring Karo syrup over a piece of white bread before me. Mom has a big bagful of shirts on one of the four small kitchen chairs, the one where the leg won't stay in the socket. She is wetting each shirt and then rolling it up and piling it on the tub top, getting ready to iron them, I guess. I have never seen so many shirts, and they are so big that Billy and I could get in one of them together. There is an iron being heated on the stove, sitting on a hot plate.

There are no curtains on the kitchen window, and my mother has pulled the shade down most of the way so that Mrs. Gibson doesn't look over the alleyway and see the size of the shirts that are being ironed. People could see that these shirts were way too big for me or Billy. It's a secret that my mother does the ironing like this. And so it is pretty dark in the kitchen.

"Mom," I say, "if there are no ghosts in the world, how come we have a Holy Ghost?"

"Don't they teach you that at school?"

"No."

"Sure they do. Don't they teach you about the Holy Trinity?"

"Yes," I say, "the Father, the Son, and the Holy Ghost, but they don't tell us how come."

My mother is laughing.

"Well," she says, smiling, "maybe you just need to know that this is how it is, and believe that this is how it is."

"What about angels?"

"Same thing," she says. "There are angels. Everyone has a guardian angel, and there is an army of angels in heaven. It is just how it is."

"Is Ann an angel now, do you think?" This ghost thing has got me very confused, and I guess angels are the same thing with a different name.

"I don't know. I don't know what happens to little girls when they go to heaven."

Mom's pile of shirts is pretty high now, so she gets up to take the ironing board out from behind the door in my room.

"I hope," I say, "Ann has become an angel, because maybe she'll come down and rub off a little angel dust on my report card."

"It is very sad for that family," my mother says, "for that to happen to such a lovely little girl."

My mother puts the legs in the slot beneath the ironing board and stands it up, saying, "Maybe Ann will come down and rub off a little on you."

She pulls an old sheet over the ironing board and pins it at the bottom.

"I don't need an angel," I say, scraping my plate with the fork. "Just my report card."

"Everybody needs an angel, Dennis."

"So what's the difference between an angel and the Holy Ghost?"

I am now licking the plate with the Karo syrup, and my mother grabs the plate out of my hand and puts it in the sink.

"An angel," she says, "doesn't lick his plate, that's for sure. Not at your age."

"So what's the difference?"

My mother now sits down across from me and puts her chin in her hands.

"The way I learned it," she says, "is the way Saint Patrick told it to the Irish after he changed back into a person from being a stag."

"What's a stag?"

"A big deer. Some evil king . . ."

"Most kings are evil," I say. "You said that when you told us the story of Henry VIII."

"This one was worse, and he wanted to kill Saint Patrick for lighting a fire, and then Saint Patrick turned into a stag so they couldn't catch him. When he came back, he told all the Irish people that—"

"The snakes had to go?"

"No," she said, "that the Holy Trinity would always nourish them the way the clover nourished him when he was a stag, and he picked up a shamrock, and he showed that there was just one stem and three leaves, all the same size, and that was the way God was, the Father, the Son, and the Holy Ghost, all in the one thing."

"So the Holy Ghost is like God?"

"The Holy Ghost is God."

"And Jesus?"

"The last of the three leaves, maybe the one on the end, maybe the one in the middle, it doesn't matter except to know that this is what you believe."

"What do I believe?"

"That there are no ghosts in the world, but that there is a Holy Ghost, who is part of God just like the shamrock has three leaves in one stem."

"And a guardian angel."

"Yes, and a guardian angel, and I guess other angels, too."

"Oh."

My mother gets up from her chair, and grabs the iron. She sticks a finger on her tongue, and then slaps it against the iron. She puts the iron down again, and smiles at me.

"What," she says, "are you going to do?"

"I dunno. Go to Kips Club."

"C'mere, I'll give you a kiss."

"Ahh, c'mon," I say, squirming.

I'm eleven. I'm too old to be kissed like this.

Going down First Avenue, passing the church, I am thinking that I am still not sure about the Holy Ghost. But, I guess if you believe in God there is no great difference in believing in the Holy Ghost. And everyone believes in angels.

Chapter Twenty-one

*I*t's just a little more than twenty blocks up to the Metropolitan Museum, and so I am walking it. Sister Urban took us to the museum last year when I was in the fifth grade, and we came by bus then, a bus no different from the Second Avenue bus. Sister told us the museum sent it in a special deal to get us to come to the museum, and she reminded us that we were to be certain to thank the bus driver, who probably had better things to do than have thirty kids from St. John's cluttering up his bus.

Now I'm in the sixth grade, and I'm going back there today, because I remember this Monet guy and this certain picture. I was standing in front of it, very close to it, when Sister Urban came up behind me.

"You like this painting, Dennis?" Sister Urban asked me. She had been very nice to me since Mommy told her she was going to burn the bonnet right off her head.

"Yes," I said to her, not being able to take my eyes from it.

"What is it you like about it?" she said.

I had to think for a minute because I didn't really know what I liked. I just liked it.

"The colors and the shapes," I said to her.

"Do you know what it is?" she asked, and I looked at the words at the bottom of the frame.

"It says a ruined cathedral," I answered.

Sister chuckled, saying, "It says *Rouen Cathedral*. Monet painted many of them, and there's one in Boston, and one in Paris, France. You could go all around the world looking at paintings Monet did of this cathedral."

I then turned and looked at her, an old, skinny woman with a wrinkled face sticking out of the shadow of her black Sister of Charity hood. I remembered that she slapped me, and that my mother yelled at her good, but, somehow, that didn't matter as she then stood behind me. It was the first time I ever heard her talk normally to me, and so I didn't mind the correction. I thought it was French and I didn't know French. I still don't know French. I don't know anyone who knows French except Mrs. Chappelle, whose apartment on 57th Street my mother cleans, and I don't suppose I will ever know French.

"It looks kind of ruined," I said, "and out of shape."

"But, here," she said, pulling me by the shirtsleeve, "step back. See how it becomes so much more alive when you step back."

How can these nuns, I was thinking, be so nice sometimes, and so mean so many other times, slapping and yelling at us for the smallest things?

"Do you see?" she asked as we moved backward.

And I did see, too. I was stunned by how the thing changed before my eyes from all these colors and shapes into a sharp picture of a church with a big carved doorway.

"It is like magic," I said. I was gaping, and didn't want to leave.

"It is art," Sister said as she turned to the rest of the class, and led them away so fast that I had to run to catch up.

It was one of those days that I think I will always remember, seeing that picture turn from one thing to another.

I am hoping now as I walk up the twenty-eight wide, giant steps that they don't charge any money to go to this museum. If they charge money, I won't be able to go inside. Some museums do charge money for kids in school and I think it's a rotten shame they do. Kids should just go in and out of museums the way they do libraries. I will be very disappointed if they don't let me in, because this is the first stop of my trip around the world to see all these pictures of the cathedral that Sister Urban talked about.

I walk beneath these huge columns, so big I think I am going into the biggest church I've ever been in, bigger than St. Patrick's Cathedral. Everything is so big here, and I remember I am still only twelve-years-old tall. But, no matter how small I am, I feel that I am important, that coming here is important. I'm not sure why.

Once in the front door I look around. Good, I think, there is nobody asking for any money. I'd feel bad if they asked me. The front room is enormous, and there are many big statues, so big that I have to back up to look at the tops of them, and each time I back up I bump into another one. They are all naked, except for a few that have curtainlike dresses wrapped around them, or silver armor. I guess each one is supposed to be someone, but I don't know who. And there are no signs around. They must all be somebody who did something great and important. My mother says the only way to be great at something is to work hard. They should have a statue of her here, I am thinking, because she works as hard as anyone I know. Billy, too. They should have a statue of Billy doing his homework because some nights Billy does his homework for three or four hours.

I still hate homework, and I never spend more than ten minutes at it. I just take the punishment they give out at school.

There is another stairway before me, this one the biggest stairway I have ever seen, and I count the forty-six steps on the way up. There is a big list of names written into the stone at the sides of the stairs, and I stop to read the names. There is nobody from 56th Street on the list, and I wonder who they all are. Maybe the people who built the place, the construction workers who made it look so beautiful.

There are a hundred little statues of ballet dancers on the second floor, and I study them. They are made of a dark brown metal, and they look like they have been made by the same person, and maybe of the same dancer. It must have been a lot of work to make all these statues, but they are all too much the same. I wish they had some soldiers in this case to keep the dancers company. Maybe the soldiers and the ballet dancers could dance together.

The museum is such another world to me. Everywhere you look you see things that bring you to different places and different times, and there is nothing like it anywhere else.

I pass a huge painting, ten times taller than me, of people in a chariot, with hundreds of angels in the sky. I wish there was someone to tell me what it is all about.

My father could take me if he was out of the hospital. What's he doing in that hospital, anyway, for so long, and no visitors allowed? I wonder if he ever went to a museum in his life? I could ask Mom, but she never talks about my father anymore. Daddy. I have never said a sentence with the word *Daddy* in it, or even *Dad*. It is always *my father* when I talk about him, but I haven't talked about him to anyone for such a long time.

I could ask my mother, like I say, but I don't want to be a bother to her, to remind her about it. She would get sad, I know.

Walking through the museum, I try to be as quiet as I can. I don't want to bother anyone.

There is a guard who is looking at me funny, and I wonder if he wants to throw me out. I think you have to be older to come here alone. So I am standing close to this man and woman who are looking up at a big painting of a bunch of half-naked people. Their necks are cranked up like they were looking at the stars. I am guessing that the guard will think I am with them, and he will leave me alone. The woman sees me standing here, and she smiles.

"Do you like the Rubens?" she asks.

I just nod my head up and down, but I don't smile back or say anything, because ever since that time with Mr. Dempsey I just make it a habit to never talk to people I don't know pretty good.

I walk quickly away, in the other direction from the guard, and pass through a few more halls. If there is anything you should know about museums, it is that they have more halls than you know what to do with, and they are attached like dominoes so that you never know which way will bring you to the end or the beginning. Finally, I come to the little room I remember, and I go right up to the painting of the cathedral. I put my nose so close to it that the guard who is walking around in this room snaps his fingers. He motions for me to get back, and so I come away a little.

And now I can see why I wanted to come back to see this picture. Everything in it changes a little as I move away from it. It is so weird that the colors and shadows have no shape at all when you are close to it, but when you step back, there is this big wonderful church. And I wonder how he did this, or how he knew to do it. So I begin to go forward, and step back, and I do this about ten times, like I am practicing Irish dancing. Each time I do this I am more amazed, not so much that the church appears, but that when it appears, it is so beautiful.

I don't think I have ever seen anything that has interested me as much as this.

Not even the Motorama.

Chapter Twenty-two

The summer breeze is whipping my face, and it seems like we are going a hundred miles an hour. Billy has gone on a sleep-away trip with Kips Bay Boys Club to play a basketball game at some other boys' club in Connecticut. His junior varsity basketball team has won the finals in New York City, and now they are playing other states for the championship. Billy is beginning to collect more trophies than Archie has in his whole office down at Kips Club.

My mother has a new friend. His name is Artie, and I am sitting in the back of his brand-new car, a 1952 Chevrolet. It is a hot day, and all the windows are open. This is the first new car I have ever been in, except for the car that time on the platform in the Waldorf, and we are going along some highway, just taking a drive in the new car, and I put my head out of the window. The force of the breeze is like being on some ride in Coney Island, where the wind takes the breath out of you. It is so cool, I like the feeling of flying through the air like this.

Suddenly, I hear the sound of a siren, and I turn to see a policeman riding beside us on a motorcycle. He has a funny look on his face, like he just drank sour milk.

"Shit," Artie says.

The policeman tells Artie to stop, and we go up on the sidewalk of the highway. It is just like I have seen in the movies, and I watch closely as the policeman slowly gets off his motorcycle, and slowly takes his gloves off, and slowly walks over to Artie. It is like he practiced it a hundred times.

The policeman leans over into the window.

"You know how dangerous that is?" the policeman asks. His voice is pretty snotty.

"What is that, Officer?" Artie says. "I don't think I was speeding or anything."

"The boy," the officer says.

The policeman is now pointing at me, and as Artie turns to look at me I can feel myself shrinking up.

"You mean Dennis?" my mother says.

Artie is staring at me. "What did you do?" he says in a voice that is like he is yelling at me.

"I didn't do anything," I say.

Looking at them, I wonder if anyone is going to be on my side, and I begin to get the feeling that I might be like the last guy picked in a choose-up for a ballgame. No one ever really cares about the last guy picked in a choose-up.

They are all now staring at me, and I don't know what I've done.

"He had his head out the window," the policeman says.

"You had your head out the window?" Artie repeats.

"You should get an act together," I say. I don't like the way they are treating me.

"Don't be smart, young man," my mother says.

The "young man" stuff again, it always leads to trouble. And so I keep quiet.

The policeman gives Artie a warning to control the passengers in his car, and puts his gloves back on.

"I'm sorry, Officer," Artie says.

"I'm sorry, Artie," my mother says.

"I'm sorry, Mom," I say, even though I don't think I've done anything so bad. But I know it will make her feel better. People always feel better when you say you're sorry, and instead of saying *hello* to people, sometimes I think we should just say *I'm sorry* when we meet them.

There is a silence in the car as we drive forward. The car is hot. But I think the policeman scared Artie, and he made us close all the windows, except for the window by him. This window doesn't make too much noise because it's not open far enough to make noise, and it's not open far enough to cool us off, either.

"It's very dangerous to put your head out of the window," Artie says after a while. "Twelve years old, you should know better."

I don't say anything, but I am hoping he doesn't become like a record.

There is more silence. I know that Artie wants to say more, but he is waiting for my mother to say something. He has known her for just a short time. I know he doesn't want to make her upset, and so he waits for her to say something. He wants her to be on his side, I bet.

But my mother doesn't say anything.

Mom made me dress up to go for a ride in the car, and I am wearing a clean white shirt and a pair of corduroy pants, the same blue ones I wear to school. I take the end of my shirt out of my pants and wipe the sweat from my forehead.

I wish it was my father driving the car instead of Artie. Sometimes I feel so alone when I think about my father. I see other boys at church or going to the subway with their fathers, and I wish that I could do what they do, even if my father had to be on crutches or be in a wheelchair or something.

And it must be so lonely for him, too, because I don't think my mother has been up there to see him for more than a year. Maybe she is trying to forget him, I don't know.

How hard it must be for him to be lying in that hospital all the time, with no place to go. I imagine that he must be very patient to put up with that, just sitting in bed the way I do when I have a cold, listening to the radio, reading magazines, or drinking bowl after bowl of soup. You can only read so many magazines, listen to so much radio, or eat so much soup. After that, there is nothing to do. You have to be very tough to put up with being in a bed twenty-four hours a day.

I don't ever want to be cooped up like that, like here in this hot car, or like at school, pushed into lines all the time to go into rooms with closed door and windows, hands out of pockets, head straight up like there's a board stuck in your neck.

I can't talk to anyone about it. Even Billy. Sometimes I wonder what Billy thinks about it, about our father being so cooped up all the time, but I know that if I ever say anything, I will just get him pissed off that I brought it up. If he wanted to say something about it, he would just say it. I'm just the youngest in the family, and everybody expects me to keep my mouth shut, I think.

There is just this forget-all-about-it attitude that covers our lives like wallpaper.

But here is Mom with this Artie guy, and I don't know what to think about him. He is not such a bad guy, and at least he doesn't get drunk like Quigley did. But he has no right to yell at me, not for anything.

He's an Italian, and my mother never really talked so nice about the Italians on the block. She used to call them the *guineas,* but I haven't heard her say that since she met Artie.

Sometimes I think she should marry somebody like this Artie, and then she wouldn't have to work so hard cleaning all the apartments. She wouldn't have to hide the money she earns from the welfare, either.

I know, though, she could never get married again, because we are Catholic, and being a Catholic means that you only get married once. Maybe, if she was born someone else, a Protestant or a Jew maybe, she would have a better deal, but she says that it's bad luck to wish that you were someone else. You could change yourself, maybe, make yourself better, but you should do it with the body that God gave you. That's what she says. Maybe things will change for her someday. Maybe things will get better enough so that she can get up from her hands and knees on Sutton Place.

Damn. I love my mother so much, and I can't understand why God doesn't change things for her.

It is now very hot in the backseat, and I want to ask Artie to let me open the window so we can get some air. But I don't want to talk, not after he yelled at me.

Mom looks pretty hot, too, but she has been very quiet. Sometimes when she gets quiet, she can be quiet for days at a time.

Chapter Twenty-three

$\mathcal{I}$ am lying in my bed now, the top bunk. It is summer, hot and muggy, and I have a wet rag around my neck. I always wear a wet rag around my neck when I go to bed in the summertime, for it soaks up the sweat.

I am staring into our kitchen. The kitchen has just a little light, which comes from the apartment across the alleyway, and I am watching the shadows across the icebox change as Mr. Gibson or Mrs. Gibson across the alleyway moves around in their own kitchen. It is eerie to watch, for it is like our neighbors are in my kitchen and a part of our lives. I have been lying here, awake, for more than an hour, watching the shadows. A mouse runs across the floor, stops for a second to look around, and then runs under the icebox.

It's so quiet, but once in a while I can hear dishes or pots and pans being banged together, or maybe somebody's loud voice saying that they can't find something or other. I hear Mr. Gibson cursing, but about what I don't know.

But, suddenly, there is a weird grunting and slurping sound, and I strain my ears to hear where it is coming from. It can't be from the outside of my window, because we can't even get my bedroom window opened, what with the hundred coats of paint on it. No. It is right here, from inside, from the living room. It must be my mother and

Artie. They must be making out or something, that's where the sounds are coming from. But what are they doing? Are they kissing? Would they be doing anything else? Oh, no, my mother wouldn't do anything else. I don't think so. Not with our father in the hospital and everything. God, I don't think so.

All this makes me very nervous and twitchity, and I feel like getting up and walking around the apartment, but I know my mother wouldn't like that. She'd say I wasn't minding my own business. God. Why do we have to live like this? Why couldn't our father just have been killed when he fell off that truck, if that is the story, anyway. Maybe there is something else wrong with him, like maybe he is blind and my mother is afraid to tell us about it. Maybe his skin is falling off with some weird disease, or who knows?

But sometimes, like now, I don't really care about it at all. I only care about why we have to worry about these things all the time, about not having a father, about a nut like Quigley or this Artie guy in the living room with my mother. I just wish things would get different for her, so that we could stop all these worries, and she could get unmarried and get married and we could have a father in the house like everybody else.

I don't like what is going on, and I begin to think about saying my night prayers, thinking Blessed Maria Goretti could hear me way up in heaven if I whispered. But you don't even have to whisper to pray. You can do it in your mind and it is as good. I am still thinking about all these religious things, about praying, about getting everyone in heaven to help us out a little.

Blessed Maria would like me, I know, if she could hear me. She's a saint now—the Pope just made her one—and she must have great powers. I wonder if she does hear me. There is nothing wrong with taking a chance, though, and I begin to whisper. "I know it's tough, Blessed Maria Goretti," I am more mouthing the words than whispering, "and you had to go through a lot just to be with God in heaven, but could you take care of my mother so's I don't have to listen to all these sounds coming from the living room?"

Chapter Twenty-four

Sometimes, on Sundays, all the aunts and the uncles come over. They get together to sing or to talk politics. "Diddley-do and the General's through," that is what Uncle Bob sings, because he doesn't like Ike. It is always a day for Irish songs and the chances of the Democrats and some salami and bologna sandwiches and lots of pretzels.

Billy and I look forward to these days with my aunts and the uncles because the cousins are good stickball players, and we get a game going on 56th Street. There are about ten of them. They come from Brooklyn and Queens, the cousins, and coming into the city is a hotshot thing for them. City guys, they think, are somehow tougher, and the 56th Street girls are prettier. I don't care much about that because I still don't pay much attention to girls, except when I think about them, and except whenever I see Sue Flanagan or Marilyn Rolleri.

Billy and my cousin Bobby are fourteen and always after the girls, always making time with them, and sometimes I follow them down to the river where they go with the girls to watch the Pepsi-Cola sign blink on and off. The 51st park down by the river is always dark, because there are so many trees there, and they sit there, the two of them, with whatever girls they can get to watch the Pepsi-Cola sign with them, and they try to feel them up.

Once I was sitting down there in the park with Walsh and Jurgensen and we saw someone—it was so dark we couldn't tell who—unbutton the blouse of a girl and feel around her brassiere. I think about this a lot, but I can never get the chance or the courage to ask a girl to walk to the river with me.

I am only twelve, but I wish I was thirteen, because the girls don't mind walking down by the river with a teenager.

There is not much room in the kitchen, and the four kitchen chairs and the one from Mommy's room seemed squeezed. The women along with Mom's cousin Tim sit in the chairs, and the rest stand around, leaning on the stove or the icebox. Uncle Andy is sitting on the top of the bathtub right next to the kitchen sink.

I can tell when all the uncles are beginning to feel good. "Feeling good" is the way Mom says everyone is when the party is in the middle. It is a good time, I am thinking, as Uncle Bob pulls me aside and asks me how I am doing in school. I know I hate school, but I don't want to say this to anyone. It is like being on welfare, and you have to keep it a secret.

"Okay," I answer him, "I guess."

"That's the boy," Uncle Bob says, "the only way to go. Always do good in school. You could get to be a bishop and kiss all them nuns."

Uncle Bob is a bartender and makes fun of everything. He wouldn't talk about kissing nuns if he saw what Sister Urban looked like.

Uncle Bob then slips me a dollar bill, new and crunchy. It is not my birthday or my Confirmation day or anything. He just slips me the dollar, and I feel funny about it, almost like I was the guy in front of Bloomingdale's, the crippled guy, selling pencils and comic books for as much as you can give him. No price or anything, but you just know he needs the money.

"Thank you," I say.

I take the dollar to our little room and put it in my top drawer. Later on I can give it to my mother.

It is getting late, and the keg of beer that Uncle Andy plopped in the sink is almost empty, but Mom says it's okay because she has some bottles of Ballantine in the icebox.

They are all singing "At a Cottage Door" for the millionth time, and I know it by heart now, and "God Bless You and Keep You Mother Macree" and "Let Erin Remember."

I always sing "The Rose of Tralee" whenever anyone asks me. The first verse, anyway, and the chorus, because I never learned the second. It is my song, my party song, and everyone always has to do a party song.

"C'mon, Dennis," Aunt Kitty says, "give us a song."

Hardly anyone, I guess, has ever learned the second verse, and I think that's true for most Irish songs.

"Yeah," my cousin Eileen says, "belt it out, will ya?"

It doesn't take much encouragement to get me in the middle of the kitchen, though, even for the one verse. My left hand is on the keg of beer in the sink, my right on the end of the kitchen table that is filled from one end to the other with glasses and bowls of potato chips and thin pretzels. The aunts and uncles all around, and the cousins, Arlene and Helene and Bobby and Freddy and Johnny and Larry and Ronnie and Eileen and Brian and Rosie and Joey and Billy, and my brother Billy, too. All standing in this kitchen where you wouldn't think more than three people could stand.

I have a high, clear, choirboy's voice, and I sing away at "The Rose of Tralee" the way I sing away at the Gloria or the Kyrie at the eleven o'clock High Mass. I get through the first verse easy enough, and then I get to the chorus, which I know my mother loves. I try to make every word count.

> She was lovely and fair
> As the rose in the summer,
> But t'was not her beauty alone that won me.
> Oh, no, t'was the truth in her eyes ever dawning
> That made me love Mary
> The Rose of Tralee.

It is my favorite because it always makes me wonder how someone can know when they see the truth in someone's eyes. Most people I know have eyes that make you want to hide, stern eyes, like all the nuns except Sister Stella, who is always laughing. I guess my mother's

eyes have the truth in them, especially when they shine with the wetness of a tear or two. Maybe that is why she cries when sad things happen, or when she gets fed up with something, these tenement tears that
she says are not really important, but that just come with the territory.

They all clap and cheer when I am done, and Uncle Bob tries to
give me a cigar, but I laugh it off as Aunt Kitty gives me a kiss. It all
makes me feel good, like I have done something that no one else can
do.

"That Dennis," Aunt Helen says, "I wonder who his Rose of
Tralee is."

She grabs me and begins to give me a kiss. I try to be friendly, but
I think I'm too old to be getting kissed like this by everyone.

I look at my mother, and she's got her hands together as if she's
praying.

"It's my mother's song," I say. "She's the Rose of Tralee."

Everyone laughs, and my mother says, "Blarney."

But I look at her as she says this. She's beaming. It's like I just gave
her a Christmas present.

Everyone sings in the family. Uncle Bill sings "Phil the Fluter's
Ball," and everyone tries to sing along as he slaps his knee and stamps
his foot. Mom sings "Paddy McGinty's Goat," because it is the one
song her own mother taught her as a kid. It's longer than a sermon in
church. I like listening to her voice. She only sings when she is with
the family like this. She never sings around the house. But she whistles
sometimes.

"God, Mary," Uncle Bob asks, "how do you remember all them
verses?"

"Nothing else to do, maybe," Mom answers.

Uncle Andy sings "Danny Boy."

When he is finished, Aunt Kitty complains.

"It is such a sad song," she says, "leaving flowers on the grave and
all. Let's just sing about the good times."

"Are there good times really?" Mom says. "Sometimes I think
there's just different times, maybe a little good, maybe a little not so
good, but I don't know if there are real good times, like in a long pe-
riod, the times of Christ or the times of Henry VIII."

"Oh, come on, Mary," Aunt Helen says. "There's lots of good times. We are all here, and that's something."

"Well," Mom replies, "good or bad, you still have to get through the day, don't you?"

"Yeah, sure," Aunt Helen says, "and the queen of England has to get through the day, too. But I bet we are having a better time of it."

Mom's cousin Tim is drunk and falls out of his chair. He must have had half the keg. He is a big man, and there is a commotion as my uncles try to lift him back into the chair.

My cousin Johnny grabs my wrist and pulls me into the hallway.

"Let's go Peeping Tom," Johnny says.

"You mean spying?" I ask.

"Yeah," Johnny says, "and it's dark now. Ya gotta do it when it's dark, up on the roof. You can see lots of things."

"Like what?"

"Like girls, stupid," he says, shoving me down the hallway.

We are on the roof, and the sign on the door going out to the roof is in big letters: NO ONE ALLOWED ON ROOF. It looks like it means business.

I never come up on the roof, except a couple of times, very hot nights when I slept there on a blanket with Mommy and Billy.

The door squeaks when we open it. It is so dark that it is hard to cross from one roof to the other along the six buildings that are all the same in our row on 56th Street. There is a small wall, less than two feet high, separating each building, and I trip over the first one and cry out.

"Shhsh," Johnny whispers. "You have to be quiet."

I squint my eyes until they get used to the darkness. It is about nine o'clock, and I am thinking that there is school tomorrow. Maybe I can stay out for another half an hour and my mother won't notice.

The Hotel Sutton is across the street. It looks like a mountain of lights from up here. We can see into the rooms looking over the parapet. But I only see men who are on the telephone or reading. Someone is watching television.

Everybody seems to have a television now, but we still haven't gotten one, or a phone, either. The welfare doesn't allow them, my mother says, but I don't know why we couldn't hide them and add them to our famous list of secrets.

"I wish I had binocs," Johnny says.

"What's binocs?" I ask, wondering why he knows so many things I don't.

"Like they look through in the navy pictures, you know, to see if any Jap kamikazes are coming."

Johnny is lying across the roof edge, and I am thinking that he is getting his clothes dirty because I know no one ever cleans up here.

"C'mon," he says, "lean up here, and you can see better."

Suddenly, I hear the squeak of a roof door opening, and I am hoping that we don't get caught up here on the roof. No one is allowed. If I get caught, I don't know how I will ever explain anything to my mother. What would I say? That I was up on the roof to play cards? To talk with Johnny? She will know for sure that I came up here to do something I am not supposed to.

"Shhsh," I whisper as Johnny slides down from the roof edge. "Let's take cover."

We run to the other side of the roof and wait in the dark to see who is coming. We are crouched low by a wall that looks over an alleyway. I can see, two roofs over, that a guy is there with his dog. Johnny sees him, too, and puts his mouth by my ear.

"If that dog comes over here," he says, "I am going to throw him off the roof."

"Shhsh," I say, "he won't come if he doesn't hear you."

We are kneeling down now for more than ten minutes, until finally the guy takes the dog back into his building.

"Whew," Johnny says, "that was close."

I stand to take the stiffness out of my legs. It is like I've been kneeling for an age at a High Mass. We are next to a wall that looks over to a back alleyway. I look down, and I feel instantly frozen.

"Shhsh," I say.

"What?" Johnny says.

"Shhsh," I say again. Looking down between the clothes hanging from the clotheslines, I can see Sue Flanagan. If Johnny talks now, I think I'll kill him.

"Let me see," he says.

"Shhsh."

I am leaning over the alleyway wall, and there on the top floor, just below me, is Sue Flanagan in her bedroom. There are curtains over her window, but I can see right through them. There is not much space in her room, but she is moving around like crazy, and each time she moves, her skirt waves one way and then the next, and I can see the curves of her legs. She throws something on her bed, and then she leans over the bed to get it back, and her skirt goes up to her thighs. Her skin is so white. I don't know if I have ever seen skin as white as hers. And then she leaves the room, and I am straining to see into her kitchen window, but the shade is down, and I can't see anything.

"Where'd she go?" Johnny asks.

"Shhsh."

I am hoping that she will come back again, and I am staring into her room, past the curtains and into her empty bed. God. Does she sleep in the bed for everyone on the roof to see? God.

Sue comes back into the room, and I am so happy to see her again. It is thrilling. She is still moving quickly, as if she has ten things to do and time for just three of them. She throws something on her bed again, and she begins to unbutton her blouse. I can feel myself trembling, the way I felt before I ran in to call the cops on Quigley. This is maybe the most exciting thing I have ever done in my life, to be here watching Sue Flanagan.

But there is also something strange happening.

Something is bothering me, something I don't like. I suddenly begin to think that I am doing something only because I have the edge of being in this darkness. It doesn't sit right with me, and I wonder why I am doing this. I am thinking that I am embarrassed, and I can hardly talk. I feel a little like I have been listening to someone else's confession at church.

I want to tell Johnny that maybe we shouldn't be here.

Sue has her blouse open, and I can see her brassiere clearly as she turns around quickly. I can remember being so close to that brassiere, and dancing around the stoop with her, rocking back and forth, feeling wanted, and I am thinking that I want to close my eyes. I know she is going to take her blouse off, and I am having trouble swallowing. But she unbuttons her skirt instead, and the skirt drops to the floor. My mouth is dry and sticky. I feel myself moving in my underwear, feeling the famous boner all the guys love so much, but yet I

know something is wrong. I feel that I want to punch out at somebody, maybe like Mr. Dempsey there in the back of his delicatessen.
Why am I so young, I am thinking, and why can't I just be in that
room with Sue, talking to her as she prances around in her underpants
and a blouse that is opening and closing like a flapping flag? I can
hardly breathe as I watch her lean over to pick up her skirt, the silk of
her underpants so close to me I can almost feel it. She folds the skirt
and puts it into her drawer by the bed. I can't watch anymore. I feel
like I should be punching out at myself because I know that I am
wrong being in this darkness like this. And I know, too, that she is
going to take her underpants and her brassiere off, because I know now
that it is her nightgown that she put on the bed. I can't look anymore,
because every time I see her I want her to hug me, and to call me Dapper Dan, and to laugh, and I know if I watch her take all her clothes
off that I am going to feel funny the next time I see her, odd and different. And I know that she would hate me if she knew that I was here.
I am breathing so heavily. I have to do something.

I can hardly talk, and I can see that Johnny is big-eyed and smiling. I know I have to say something to him.

But what?

I can't just tell him that I think this is wrong. He thinks that this
is just another one of those great things that come with living in the
city, things that don't happen in Brooklyn.

And so I kneel down again, and I am low enough so that I can't
see over the wall. It is a strange relief now, like I am out of it. And I
take a moment to think what to say.

"We better go before we get caught," I say, putting as much alarm
in my whisper as I can.

"Are you crazy?" Johnny says. He isn't whispering now, but talking loud, like he was surprised and shocked that I would say something
so out of touch.

"Are you crazy?" he says again. This time he yells, and I know he
is not asking a question.

"Shhsh," I say. "I'm getting outta here."

Someone opens a window. I can hear the metal chains of the window moving as it opens. Someone yells up the alley.

"Who's there? What's going on?"

God, I think, God, get me outta here before anyone finds out.

I am running now, and Johnny is running behind me. We get to the roof door of my building, and it creaks louder than any door has ever creaked as I open it. The No One Allowed on Roof sign slams behind me.

"Shhsh."

We are in the hall, tiptoeing down the stairs. I am praying that no one opens their door until we get to the fourth floor, apartment 26.

"Man, did you ever see tits like that?" Johnny says. I know now that he is asking a question like he wants an answer.

"Shhsh," I say to him. "Shhsh."

We are going down my long hallway. I don't want to answer Johnny. I don't want to talk about it, and I know that if I just go to bed, I won't have to talk to Johnny until next time he comes to New York to sing Irish songs, and I can just lie in my bed and think about the beauty in the eyes of the Rose of Tralee, and try with all my might to not think about the whitest skin I have ever seen in my life.

Chapter Twenty-five

I am in Bobby Carney's house down on 51st Street, around the corner from Kips. He is taking me over to the residence of St. Patrick's Cathedral, where I have an appointment to take the special Latin exam for Cathedral altar boys.

"Why are you doing that?" Billy asked as I was leaving the house.

"It's a good deal," I answered, "because the Cathedral is like being in the championships for altar boys. Not everyone can get in."

"Big deal," Billy said, "it's ten blocks away, long blocks. And it will snow every time you have the six o'clock Mass."

"Ahh," I said to Billy, "you're just in a bad mood all the time because the Knicks lost the play-offs."

Basketball is most of Billy's life. He's an altar boy at St. John's, but he doesn't like the Cathedral. I don't know why. He says he would rather spend his altar boy time at our church doing the weddings and funerals for the tip money, rather than going to the Cathedral for the fanfare of it.

I don't know why some people like to do one thing, and other people like to do something else. Maybe it depends on who your friends are, who you're hanging around with. When Jurgensen became an altar boy, I wanted to join up with him, and when Walsh became a choirboy, I wanted to do that, too. And when Carney said I could go to the Cathedral if I wanted, that was good enough for me.

Now there is no one home at Carney's, and so we are sitting on a couch in a dark living room. The couch and a chair are covered with a thick plastic. If Carney's mother was home, she wouldn't let us in the living room but would make us sit at the kitchen table.

"Did you bring the Latin book?" Carney asks.

"I forgot it," I answer. "It's on my brother's bed. You know he's got the lower bunk and it's dark there and I didn't see it, and he was breaking my horns when I was leaving, anyway. So I forgot it."

"Shit," he says, "how are we gonna go over the Latin?"

"Don't you know it by heart?" I ask. I know that Carney is good at the Latin. We have been altar boys at St. John's for a few years now, and ordinarily I would know the Latin pretty good, too, but this was for the Cathedral. Your Latin has to be exact at the Cathedral or they'll give you the bum's rush, twenty-three skidoo, get lost, kid.

"Yeah," he answers, "I know most of it. You can start after *Ad Deum qui laetificat.*"

"*Quia tu es, Deus,*" I say, "*fortitudo mea, quare me repulisti, et quare tristis . . .*"

"Okay," Carney says, "okay."

He goes on through the Latin, and I am amazed that he knows it as good as any priest. I am trying to answer as quickly as he says it.

I am doing fine as Carney gets to "*Domine, exaudi orationem meam.*"

"*Et clamor meus,*" I answer, "*ad te veniat.*"

"*Dominus vobiscum,*" he says.

"*Et cum spiritu tuo,*" I say, being careful to form my words exactly.

Carney shakes his head. "*Et cum spiri tutu oh,*" he says.

"That's not how you say it," I say. I know that he said it wrong, and a little mess-up like this could keep me out of the Cathedral altar boys.

"Bullshit," he says. "It is so."

"It's not," I say. "It's *et cum spiritu tuo,* and not *spiri tutu oh.*"

"Bullshit," he says again, this time very sarcastically. "I'm telling you, I've been saying this for years. It's *spiri TU-TU oh.*"

"Look, Carney," I say, getting a little hot under the collar, "I don't want to say you're wrong, but you're wrong. I mean, I can see the words the way they are written on the page in my Latin book."

"Do you know what the Latin means?" he asks, and I can see he wants to lord it over me.

"No," I say, "I don't know what any of it means, but it doesn't matter, 'cause they don't ask you what any of it means."

"Well," he says, "it tells you in the book what it means, and it was you who forgot the book. I didn't."

"Doesn't matter," I say. "I know what it says. It says *et cum spiritu tuo.*" And, for emphasis, I yell, "*Tu-oh,* you see, not *tu-tu-oh.*"

"Well," Carney says as he gets up from the couch, "if that's the way you feel about it, you can just go over there for the test by yourself, and see if I care."

"All right," I say, getting up also, "who needs you, anyway?"

"Don't get smart with me," he says, "or I'll punch you in the mouth. You wouldn't be having this test if it wasn't for me."

"You punch me in the mouth," I say, "and you'll be picking up your eyes off the floor."

"Yeah?"

"Yeah."

I am feeling a little angry that Carney and I are arguing about this, but I know I can't let him push me around. And, anyway, I think I know the Latin enough to pass the test. So I begin to head for the door when I am suddenly shocked as Carney punches me square in the back.

I am falling forward now and thinking, Holy God, do I have to fight Carney over the Latin right here in his living room on East 51st Street?

I know I can take him, for I have wrestled with him a hundred times at Kips Bay, and I think of the pain in my back where he punched me. I could give him a black eye right here in his living room, but this isn't the same as when Shalleski pushed me around. Carney is a good kid, and he's just being stupid and selfish, and I guess he wants to show me that he's not afraid of me. I don't know why guys get like this. Why does he so need to be right even though he's wrong as Wrong Way Corrigan?

I just look at Bobby, hard and angry, and he puts his fists up. He wants to duke it out in his living room where we'll break all the lamps and ashtrays. It's crazy, especially since I know I can take him in a minute.

But I don't want to beat Bobby Carney up. He did get me the test at St. Patrick's Cathedral, even though I didn't ask him to. He just came and asked me if I wanted to get in the Cathedral altar boys. It was a nice thing for him to do.

I am always remembering the story about turning the other cheek. Carney is wrong to hit me like this, as wrong as he is about the Latin, but I don't have to do anything about it. I know it is *spiritu tuo*. It is enough to know I am right, without getting into a fight about it.

Et cum spiritu, big space, *tuo,* and he's got a lot to learn.

And, I think as I skip down his stairs two by two, he's lucky I gave him the other cheek.

Chapter Twenty-six

I passed the Cathedral Latin test. It was like a breeze. It is now morning dark, two months later.

It doesn't seem like there is anyone in the Cathedral, except me and this priest who doesn't speak any English. He is looking at a framed diagram of the altars in the Cathedral, each one numbered. It is hanging on the sacristy wall next to the cabinet where they keep the wine and the incense. There must be about twenty altars upstairs, and he is trying to figure out what to do.

It is good I know the Latin, for this priest would go thirsty if he tried in his own language to get any wine from me. Maybe he is a guinea priest, or spick, or Portugee. Billy was right. All I seem to get here in the Cathedral are the six o'clock Masses, and most of the time with the priests who don't know the English.

I don't like it so much at the Cathedral, but I guess it's fair. The new guy on the block always gets the dirty work in any job. That's the way it is on the basketball team, too. The new guy never starts the game, never gets in the middle of the action at the beginning.

I was yawning and thinking about this when I was walking here this morning, getting up in the dark like I was a farmer going to milk the cows, and then meeting some foreign priest in the sacristy who tries to tell me what to do with hand signals, like in the deaf school. And I am so tired I can hardly speak, let alone read hand signals.

The priest doesn't seem much older than Billy. He waves me over to him. The sacristy is made of stone, and has a high ceiling that goes up in the middle like a fancy tent. He gets a pencil and paper and draws an altar of a table and a cross and then puts a question mark next to it. It's like charades with a pencil, and I know right away what he is asking.

But how should I know what altar we should go to? Pick a number, one to twenty.

Since I don't want to appear that I don't know what I am doing, I write *#1* next to his question mark. The priest smiles. It is the way the Italians and the Spanish in New York smile when they don't know the language but want to believe that everything is all right. We begin to walk up the long, steep and narrow corridor of the sacristy stairs, and I know that this priest is going to take me right to where we shouldn't be. We then continue right on to the main altar, me trailing behind him when I should be in front, smiling as well, holding the cruets in one hand and my cassock in the other, trying to keep from tripping over myself.

I have been on the main altar of the Cathedral only once before when they called me in to fill in for a sick acolyte at a High Mass. It was a fluke, for altar boys don't get to serve at High Mass until they've been around for a couple of years. In the Cathedral they make the High Mass on Sunday mornings their biggest deal, like being in a movie. I never had so many layers of vestments on. They have a woman who dresses you. First, in a kind of an alb, a long white surplice, and then a cincture to tie around it like a belt, and then over this they make you wear a very fancy surplice with more lace than I have ever seen, and, finally, they put a red velvet cape around my shoulders, the material flowing like a waterfall down to my wrists. Then I was really surprised when the sacristy lady pulled a small gold ring out of a box and put it on my middle finger. I felt like I was a cardinal like Cardinal Spellman and asked one of the guys next to me if he would kiss the ring so I could tell Billy that it was all so great and they were kissing my ring and everything.

I was hoping I would see Cardinal Spellman, for I have never seen him except for his picture in the *Daily News*. But the cardinal was off with the Pope or something, and we had to settle for a bishop who said the Mass with about fifty priests around him. I thought I was an actor in a play, but then some guy started to sing the "Panis Angelicus," a hymn that means the bread of the angels, and I felt that the hymn was so cool, the singer was so great, that I had to think about being in church and talking with God. Not in a cathedral, but just in a simple church where just you and God can get together. And I kept looking at the angels painted on the ceiling, up over the three red hats of the dead cardinals, because I thought that they might get off the ceiling and fly around.

I get a feeling of belonging when I am in church, that there are no problems in my life that don't have answers. Not long ago a Capuchin monk came to St. John's to give a retreat. Father Luke was such a cool guy, and dressed cool, too, in a long brown robe tied around the waist by a white cincture. There was a red heart over his breast, a symbol of the Sacred Heart of Jesus. And on his feet he wore thick leather sandals that the monks make for themselves.

"You made those shoes?" I asked him.

"I made them," he said, pointing toward the ceiling, "with a little help from the Big Guy."

He kept twirling the ends of his cincture in different directions as he told us that a retreat was not like running away from anything, like an army retreats when their goose is being cooked. "This retreat," he said, "is taking a time-out from the everyday stuff of your life, and taking in a deep breath, but while you're doing this you're remembering that God is in the deep breath."

I sat on that hard wooden pew of our church, breathing hard, and thinking that being in church made me happier than in any other place. Breathing God like that made me feel that maybe I was born to care about people the way Father Luke cared about us. No one ever asks me what I want to be, because they are always spending their time telling me that I should learn about my abilities. But, maybe, I thought, I want to be like Father Luke.

I went every day for three hours to listen to Father Luke, and at

          Dennis Smith

the end of it he brought everyone into the school auditorium and gave us punch and cookies.

I asked him what I had to do to go to a seminary where I could make my own sandals, and he said that he would talk to my teacher about it, and he would write me a letter. And then he shook my hand, like we had made a deal.

I haven't heard from him yet, but I remember that I skipped home that day, singing like Bing Crosby.

There are no lights on the main altar, and the priest seems very confused. But we are already there, across the black and white marble floor, walking up the final five marble stairs to the platform beneath the gold canopy, and it seems he isn't going to give the spot up just because there aren't any lights. So we grope along in the dark. I know there is a huge marble pulpit to my right, but I can't see it. And the big wooden cardinal's throne is to my left, but I can't see that either. I am wondering how I'm going to pour the water and wine into his chalice if I can't see a foot in front of me. Then, suddenly, the dawn begins to spread out through the Cathedral, and all the big stone columns begin to change color, and there are shafts of yellow light and blue shade all around. It is very beautiful here on the main altar, like in a picture at the Metropolitan Museum, with some of the saints on the walls and the angels on the ceiling being half in shadow and half in glittering gold.

But I wonder how long it will take before the smiling priest realizes something is wrong, because there are no lights on anywhere, except for two of the small side altars, which is where we are supposed to be.

The priest, though, is as happy as a prince sitting on his father's chair, and the Mass goes along without a hitch. I remind myself, as I always do, that being in church is supposed to be a swell time and that I should be thinking good and wholesome thoughts.

But today, for some reason, I can only think of Sue Flanagan, and seeing her moving around her room, her skirt waving, her blouse open showing the soft cotton of her brassiere, and I know I shouldn't be thinking of things like this in church.

But maybe this is exactly the place to think about it, to get all these thoughts straight and unconfused.

It's getting lighter, but I can still hardly see what the priest is doing between the shafts of light pouring into the darkness.

When we get to the Consecration, I can see him leaning over, and beginning to change the Host into the body of Jesus, but he moves out of the light shaft, and I can hardly see him as he lifts the Host into the air. But at least I see some action, and so I ring the bell, and then ring it again when it seems he is lifting the chalice with the little bit of wine I poured into it. I guess I got it right, because he doesn't turn around to give me a dirty look the way priests do when you make a mistake.

I love this part of the Mass because it is the part only for good Catholics. I guess no one else believes that the priest is changing the bread into the body of Jesus, that's what Billy says.

But, I am thinking, maybe they can believe that it's okay for other people to believe it. I am not sure which part of the body of Jesus it gets changed into, and sometimes I wonder if it isn't a little like having chicken for dinner where you get a leg or a wing. But I know it happens, and Father Ford taught us that you can have faith in a lot of things, like if you have faith that it is really Arthur Godfrey playing the ukulele on the radio when you hear the ukulele, or that Joe DiMaggio will bring a base runner home if he gets at bat, but that you can never be a good Catholic unless you have faith to believe that the Host is turned into the body of Jesus when the priest lifts it up to God.

I like this, this having faith, because it makes us different from everybody who doesn't have it.

When the Mass is over, we return to the sacristy, and a man there in a powder-blue suit begins to speak to the priest in what is like French, and he is shaking his finger at him. The priest has his hands out, and his shoulders are hunched up like he is innocent and can't figure out why he is being accused of some crime. The man is the sacristan, I guess, because no priest would wear a powder-blue suit.

The priest is explaining his story, going on, shaking his finger back at the sacristan, looking at me from time to time.

The sacristan looks at me, too.

"What is your name, son?" the sacristan asks me.

I tell him, and I squirm a little as I watch him write my name down on a pocket pad.

"You should know better," the sacristan says. "The main altar is never used for the six o'clock, and the side altars are always for the visiting priests. You should know better."

The sacristan leaves, and I immediately start to worry if he is going to tell Cardinal Spellman on me.

And what Cardinal Spellman will do about it.

God, I hope the sacristan isn't a stool pigeon. How am I to know it's a sin to do the six o'clock on the main altar?

The priest finishes up in the sacristy, putting his chalice into a big black box, and I hang my cassock in the big wooden closet. He is now talking to himself, whispering, really, and I wish I could know what he is saying. He doesn't seem as happy as he was.

I am ready to go home. I am still tired. My eyes are beginning to close even as I walk up the sacristy stairs.

And I have to go now and deliver the papers on 57th Street, and I suppose I'll worry all day about what Cardinal Spellman is going to do to me.

It's too bad they don't pay us for the six o'clocks the way they do for delivering the papers.

Chapter Twenty-seven

$\mathcal{I}$ am standing in the courtyard yelling up between the corridor of the high walls. "Hey, Mom," I am yelling, trying hard to avoid looking at the spot where I remember crazy Mario Giambetta sprawled out like a pancake. The courtyard is dirty, garbage piled up in the corners, a couple of old tomato cans and some old newspapers blowing around in the breeze. They keep the buildings on 56th Street pretty clean most of the time, but the supers don't do such a good job in the backyards.

"Hey, Mom!"

Looking up, I try to see between the lines of sheets, pillowcases, and underwear that are in lines from window to window, and from window to the line pole shooting up like a ship's mast in the middle of the alleyway.

"Hey, Mom!"

Where is she? I wonder. I want to see *The Greatest Show on Earth* with all the guys from 56th Street. And the girls. Marilyn Rolleri is going, and there is no one in the seventh grade that has grown to be as pretty as Marilyn Rolleri.

Finally, between the army of flying sheets, I see the fourth-floor window open, and my mother is sticking her head out, though not too far because she is afraid of the height.

"Yes," she says, "stop yelling."

"Mom," I say in a slightly lowered yell, "can I have a quarter to go see *The Greatest Show on Earth* with all the guys?"

I wouldn't tell her about Marilyn Rolleri.

"No," she says, "not today."

The window closes and she disappears.

I feel very sad suddenly, because I can see in my mind all the guys walking down to the Loew's Lexington, cracking jokes under the Third Avenue El, trying to sneak up past the lobby goldfish pool to the balcony where you have to be more than sixteen, or going off to the side of the loge and grabbing a smoke on the sneak.

And I can see one of the guys putting his arm around Marilyn Rolleri's chair, and then bringing his arm down until he feels her arm, and then maybe over more until he has a good feel of her chest until she slaps him. But maybe she won't slap him, and if she doesn't slap him, then I very much want to be the boy she doesn't slap.

"Hey, Mom!"

The window opens again, and I see my mother, but she doesn't say anything.

"Mom," I say, "please?"

"No."

"Mom, come on, Mom, please. I really want to go. All of my friends are going." I am hoping here that she doesn't mention jumping off the Brooklyn Bridge.

"No."

"Please," I argue. "Why can't I go when everyone else is going?"

"Come up here," she says, and then she closes the window again.

"Hey, Mom!"

I see her head once more.

"C'mon, Mom," I say. "I don't want to walk all the way up the stairs. I just want you to wrap a quarter in a piece of newspaper and throw it down to me."

"No," she says, "and you come up here right this minute. Don't answer me again."

I can see the window shutting, but this time it is slamming down. I know she is mad about something. I don't want to climb the stairs, but I know now that she is mad, and she'll only be madder if I don't go up. I know, too, that she is going to say no again, and I am wondering as I count the gum stains on the stairs what I will do then. It is Sunday. Kips Bay Boys Club is closed, and there is nowhere to go, and nobody to hang around with. At least at Kips there are a hundred things to do, but a Sunday in New York is like being in a ballpark when the game is called for rain.

In my living room I am sitting on the hard spring that is popping up almost through the cushion of the couch. Mom comes in from the kitchen and sits in the small chair across from me. There is just room for the couch and the small chair and the radio. I wish as I always wish when I look around my living room that we had a television set like everyone else, so I could watch Milton Berle on my own television set, and not on somebody else's, like on Dante Vescovi's television set that was sent to them by his uncle who is a bishop in Italy, where you can't say a peep because Dante's father will throw you out on your ear if you say a peep when they are watching television.

"I wish you wouldn't do that," my mother says.

"Do what, Mom?"

I am in for it, because she always begins complaining when she says "I wish."

"Yell up in the yard like that," she says, wringing a dish towel in her hands, "asking me for money, so that all the neighbors on 56th Street will know that I am a woman that does not have a quarter to give her own son when he wants to go to the movies. You have to learn better manners than that."

Here we go again with the better manners, I am thinking. My mother is always saying that I should get better manners, and my brother Billy, too. It's like an excuse to not talk about something. Don't talk about that or you'll hurt someone's feelings, and all that. But it's my feelings, too.

I don't know how much good manners you have to have, anyway. We are always saying thank you like a broken record, and we always have the clean shirts, and if there's meat, we don't pick it up with our fingers, except if there are pork chops. I like to hold the pork chop in my hand like a hatchet, and she lets me get away with it.

My mother is looking at me now in a kind of hard way. Not in an angry way, but, still, I can tell she is unhappy.

"It is not right," she says, "that I don't have the quarter to give you to go with your friends, but I don't. Can't you see that I would give it to you if I had it in my bag, or even saved up somewhere? But there are no quarters, Dennis, not even any of your money from the newspapers, or Billy's, and you shouldn't make me say that out the window to the whole world. Can't you understand that?"

Well, I do understand her. But I also want to go see *The Greatest Show on Earth* and try to get my arm around Marilyn Rolleri's chair. I can't say it, though. Even if she did understand, I couldn't say that to her. It's just a quarter. Some of my friends get a quarter whenever they ask for it. Some of them don't even have to ask, like Dante. His mother is always giving him quarters, an unending supply of quarters, like she just got them from the bishop's collection basket.

In the street again, I tell Bobby Walsh that I can't go with them to the Loew's Lexington. I don't say anything except that I don't have the quarter.

"Let's go steal some bottles from Rossi's," Bobby says.

"What happens if we get caught?" I ask, knowing that my mother won't be able to get the milk there anymore if someone saw us.

"Are you yellow or what?" Bobby says. "Rossi keeps the bottles in the cellar, and we just have to open the outside grating and climb down there. Then we can give the bottles right back to him for the deposit, thirteen for the quarter. C'mon."

Bobby has his own quarter, and he's being a good friend trying to help me get the money up, but I know I don't want to do this. If we got caught, Rossi would never again give me a roast pork hero, and my mother wouldn't be able to have a bill there anymore, and I don't know what. She would disown me like I was an orphan.

"Naw," I say, shrugging my shoulders, "forget it. You go, Bobby. Catch up with the gang and those girls, but don't try to cop a feel of Marilyn Rolleri's anything."

"What's an anything?" he says.

"You know," I answer, "anything what's soft and round."

"Hey, c'mon," Bobby says, "come with us, anyway. You can do your own copping, 'cause I'll sneak up to the balcony and open the emergency exit there. I know how to do it, and you can get in through the back door."

I am alone now, and a little scared. I wish there was someone with me. But everyone had a quarter, and I didn't. That's the breaks, and why I'm here in the backyard of the Loew's Lexington, trying to get up the fire escape stairs to the balcony door.

It's a wide fire escape, and it has outside bars that go completely from bottom to top, so there is no way I can get into the stairway. But, looking up, about four flights up, I can see that there is an opening at the top of a door that connects the landing and the stairs. If I could just get to that door, I could squeeze through the opening. Maybe. It looks like more than a foot high and two feet wide. I know I can fit.

It is like a mathematical problem, and I can see my seventh grade class now, and I can hear Sister Regina's squeaky voice as she is teaching. Just Greta Schmidt and Ronnie Santina say they like mathematics, but the rest of us have these blank and ignorant faces, and our heads going up and down as if we understand it all.

"Always study the problem a few minutes first," Sister says. "First you see it straight, then sideways, then upside down, whatever helps you get to the middle, because that is where you want to be, right smack in the middle of the problem. When you are there, you can always figure a way out."

Maybe she's right, I'm thinking, for I want to be in the middle of the stairs, and the only way I can get there is to climb up the outside of the fire escape until I get to that fourth-floor opening. Only, I wish that somebody else was here to help me, because I know that if I fall, it might be days before someone comes back here to find me.

God. This wave of questioning suddenly comes over me. What is it about us, about Billy and my mother and the way we live, that I can't even get a quarter together? Maybe I should have thought more about Rossi's bottles.

Goddammit, I want to be in that balcony. So whatever I have to do to be there I want to do it.

I am thinking now as I climb carefully up the outside of the stairs about nothing more than how far it is to the concrete of the backyard below. My foot is wedged between the iron steps and the thin metal bars of the fence. Just for a moment, I think about Harry Shalleski, but I know I shouldn't think about him. Not now. One by one I climb up the outside of the steps, carefully, the breeze sweeping stronger across my face the higher I get. My hair is blowing all around. I am being careful to grab firmly onto the fencing before I move my feet. I do this for three flights, slowly, like I am on a very high monkey bar, until I am up on the fourth floor on the outside of this fire escape, and the opening I want is just up a little higher. But, suddenly, my foot slips out of the wedge because there is not enough room where this one step is, and I fall down, and I'm falling fast, but my hand is still firmly around the fencing rod, and it slips down as I fall into the midair, and now I am swinging in the midair, my hand caught at the bottom of the fencing because I have slid all the way down, Holy God, and I can feel a sharp pain in my hand and in my shoulder because my body is swinging with nothing to grab onto.

Oh, God, this is just what I was afraid of, something like this, and without somebody here to help me. And now I think of Harry Shalleski again, falling from the RKO fire escape, and Mikie Harris sliding down the rope, and Harry dead and splattered below. God.

Why couldn't I just buy my ticket like everybody else, and walk in past the big marble goldfish fountain, past the candy stand, and into the dark of the movie house, feeling my way around until my eyes adjusted and I could see the lovely form of Marilyn Rolleri? Here I am swinging by one hand above the end of my life. Like that guy in "The Pit and the Pendulum," a story Sister Regina made us read, I have to do anything I can from falling into the black hole.

I know I have to use all my strength now to pull myself up, and so I try to rest for a minute, but the shoulder is hurting too much to rest. So I swing as hard as I can, to get a foot up and catch it between the fencing rods, and so I begin to say a prayer, and shift my weight with as much force as I can. Oh, yes, I have it, I have my foot between the upright rods, and now what? I have to inch my hands up, little by little, and I do, sliding my hands upward, each inch giving me a little more room to get a better balance, until, finally, I am again standing upright, my foot firmly wedged again between the stair and the fence. God.

My heart is beating so loudly I can hear it through the breeze, but

I climb up to the opening and slide my body through, like a snake, headfirst, and I climb down the fencing on the other side with my hands down below me. When I get down on the landing, I am sprawled out flat, breathing hard, trying to get over the shock of almost being flat like a pancake like crazy Mario Giambetta, down on the backyard concrete when he took a flier out the window, or like Harry Shalleski, probably wrapped in silk that looks like cellophane in his small coffin.

I am now at the door of the balcony. There is only one door, and so I know I haven't made a mistake, but I can see that it isn't open. I can't believe that Walsh hasn't gotten up to the balcony, and I never thought about what I would do if the door wasn't open. But I have to get into the middle of this problem, too, because I know I can't go headfirst back out through that hole because there is nothing below but air for four stories.

Oh, Sister Regina, what now?

I know I am going to have to bang on this door, as hard as I can, until somebody comes and gets me out of this mess, this fire escape jail. But I'll be caught then for sure, and I better think about what I am going to tell my mother. Maybe I can tell her I was playing hide-and-seek down here on 51st Street, but then I'll be lying and the whole rest of my life will be ruined and I'll have no friends, because nobody likes a liar.

God. I'll have to tell her I was sneaking into the movies because she didn't have the quarter to give me. But I'll hurt her feelings for sure. And then I won't have the good manners.

I've been on the fire escape a while now, and I'd better start banging on the door and get it over with. No one will like banging on the door during *The Greatest Show on Earth*, and they will come get me soon.

I hope Marilyn Rolleri doesn't see me when they kick me out.

My fists are now tightened, and I am about to bang on the door, when, without a squeak, the door opens, and Walsh sticks his head out. He is like an angel coming out of the clouds, and he is holding a little paper cup of water.

"Quick," he says. "C'mon."

"I almost got killed," I say, moving into the darkness. I am so happy to be out of the fire escape prison.

"Don't complain about being killed," Walsh says. "The usher almost didn't believe me when I told him my mother needed a glass of water before she had a heart attack, but I told him my father was a doctor and I should know when my mother needs a glass of water, and if she doesn't get it, her heart attack will be on his conscience. It was a close call."

"Where is everybody?"

"All around. Some downstairs, some in the balcony here."

"Where is Marilyn Rolleri?"

"Her? She couldn't come, 'cause her grandmother came to visit by surprise."

"She's not here?"

"A no-show for sure."

After all of this there is no Marilyn, and suddenly I have lost all interest in the *The Greatest Show on Earth*. I feel like going home, but I know I can't. I can't just leave Bobby Walsh after everything he's done to get me in the movies.

And, anyway, maybe I should just sit down, even if there's no one to put my arm around. Maybe I could get my breath back. Maybe I should rub my shoulder a little. God, my hand hurts.

Chapter Twenty-eight

My Aunt Kitty lives down on the ground floor of our building, and she always has her door open. She is my father's sister, the one that always has a bottle of beer in her hand, and even though she was born in Ireland, she never comes up to sing Irish songs on Sundays like my mother's family does.

Aunt Kitty has a high whining voice, and I can hear it as I jump the last five steps of the stairs. So I walk down the hall to her apartment and find her sitting at her kitchen table with my Uncle Tracy, who has come down from Mount Vernon. Tracy is married to my father's sister Josie.

Kitty and Tracy are sitting there in the kitchen, and there are two quarts of Ballantine beer on the table. I begin to think about the empties. I wonder if Aunt Kitty will give me the empties if I ask her, but I know that I won't ask, because my mother would be pretty mad if I asked Aunt Kitty for anything.

"How's the little rug rat?" my uncle says to me.

This is what my Uncle Tracy calls everyone under fifteen, so that he doesn't have to remember anyone's name. He's got eight kids, my Mount Vernon cousins, and he calls them Doodlebug, the Wheel, Sore Thumb, Kat Kat, Hole in the Head, Granite Head, Betty Boop, and Tarzan. They have real names like Tommy, Joey, Janet, Elizabeth, and so on, but I think he has forgotten the originals. I know that he doesn't know my name, but he knows that his wife is my father's sister.

"Great, Uncle Tracy," I answer. "What are you doing?"

He's got a puddle of beer in front of him, and he is soaking a dollar bill in it. On the other side of the table he is soaking a twenty.

"I'm going to show Aunt Kitty," he says, "how to make eighteen dollars seventy cents, and two beers, out of absolutely nothin', that's what."

I sit across from him, next to my aunt. She is talking at the top of her lungs, and so I pretend to lean on my elbow and hold a hand over my ear to soften the cackle of her voice. I am interested in what Uncle Tracy is doing.

It is only ten-thirty in the morning, and they are both red-eyed. I wonder if they've been here since last night, or maybe two days ago. My Aunt Kitty never wears a brassiere, and her small breasts are pushing against her housedress. I can see the roundness of her nipples clearly through the material, and I wonder if it counts as a sin to be looking at her nipples even if they are behind the material.

"See, Kitty," Uncle Tracy says, "just take the corner of the bill like this and keep picking at it, slowly. You don't even have to look. See? The corner will begin to separate, because a bill is nothing but two pieces of printed paper stuck together. See how it is splitting apart at the corner here? Now you can just tug at it, very easy, like it's your missing husband's privates. And now you can break it, like you prob'ly wanna to your missing husband's privates. And look, see, it is splitting apart."

The twenty-dollar bill is now in halves, and he lays them out carefully in the puddle of beer, pressing every wrinkle out of them. And now he does the same with the one-dollar bill, which comes apart much more easily because it has been soaking in the beer for so long. It is so interesting to watch him. He is like a surgeon doing an operation, and when he has the four parts of the two bills laid out before him, he puts the back part of the dollar on the front part of the twenty, and then he puts the front part of the dollar on the back part of the twenty so that it appears he has two twenties when the twenty sides are laid faceup.

"You see," he says as he presses them smooth, "you have to do this in a bar that has just a little light, 'cause the bartenders never turn the bill over. And so you lay the twenty down, dollar side down, twenty side up, and he picks it up and you pay the fifteen cents for one beer, and he shoves it in the cash register and gives you nineteen eighty-five change. And then you go into the next bar and you do the same thing. So, for your twenty-one-dollar investment, you have given yourself thirty-nine dollars and seventy cents, and two beers to boot."

Uncle Tracy always does things that are like magic. He works at the Brooklyn Navy Yard, and since he has so many kids, he never has enough money for a couple of drinks after work. So he has all these tricks that he bets on at the bar, and he can get a free half a load on. Most of his tricks have to do with toothpicks, the tools of his trade, he calls them. Uncle Tracy can make an eight-toothpick square into an eight-toothpick rectangle by moving just two toothpicks.

"Uncle Tracy can do anything," Aunt Kitty says, wiping up the beer on the table.

Uncle Tracy is the only relative I know who has a car, except for Uncle Phil, who had one before he died a couple of years ago. And he has a great car, too, a '38 Buick, a huge boat with a floor shift. I was in it once, and I am thinking now that Uncle Tracy doesn't seeem to be doing anything with Aunt Kitty, and so maybe he'll take me out and teach me how to drive.

Uncle Phil would probably teach me if he didn't die. He was always helping out, and he used to drive my mother up to the hospital to visit my father. He also used to give us the best Christmas presents, things my mother could never afford, like shoulder pads for football and real-leather basketballs.

"Hey, Uncle Tracy," I say, "can you teach me how to drive?"

"Are you kiddin'?" he says. "The cops will throw away the cell key 'less I get three hours' sleep to get sober. Don'tcha know anybody else?"

"I know lots," I say, "but they don't have cars."

"Why don't they have cars? I could put a car together with milk boxes and an old washing machine."

Aunt Kitty laughs at this and pours another beer for Uncle Tracy.

"They did before the signs and the insurance," I say.

"The signs?"

"Yeah," I say, "they put signs up saying you can't park some days."

"So why don't they move 'em?" Uncle Tracy asks.

"They can't," I explain, " 'cause they're at work, and anyway they can't afford the insurance."

"That's too bad," Uncle Tracy says, like he really cares about it.

"Yeah," I continue, "so that's why the cars out on the street belong to people like you who don't live in the neighborhood, or who don't have jobs and have no insurance."

"That's too bad, too," he says, "about the insurance. I don't have the insurance, either, but I got the job, and I'm lucky to find an extra dollar now and then to get gas to drive the goddamn thing."

"So," I say, looking up at him and smiling, "I can't find a car to learn how to drive."

"Hey, rug rat," Uncle Tracy says, "here."

And Uncle Tracy throws the keys to his car into my hands. I am twelve years old, and my uncle has given me his car keys.

"Find someone to teach ya," he says. "The car's in front, but don't use too much gas, will ya?"

Aunt Kitty is now bent over as she laughs.

"Uncle Tracy is a riot," she says in a very loud voice, and I hope my mother isn't passing in the hall. My mother would give back these keys faster than a camera could take a picture.

On the stoop, I see Davy Weld coming up the block. I think he is sixteen, and maybe he has one of those junior licenses I heard about. I know he's got a piece of a sister named Tuesday, and they live down on 53rd Street. She's a model, and I heard she's an actress on television. We still don't have a television, but Uncle Andy said he was going to find a cheap one for us at the railroad where he works.

"Hey, Davy," I call out to him. "You have a license?"

"Yeah, sure," he says. "I have a license from California."

"You want to teach me how to drive?" I ask.

"Sure," he says, grinning. "You got a Cadillac? I only drive Cadillacs."

"No," I say, "I got a '38 Buick, floor shift with an on-the-floor starter."

"No bullshit?" Davy says, his eyes now open pretty wide.

"I wouldn't bullshit," I say.

Fifteen minutes later we are driving down the East River Drive.

The speed limit is thirty. But Davy is going seventy, and I am beginning to worry that the cops might be around.

I am yelling over the wind that is pushing through the car.

"Do you have any cigarettes?" I ask him. I don't smoke yet, but I am thinking that this might get him to slow the car up so that he can teach me how to drive, and so we won't have to go to jail if there are any cops around.

Davy pulls a cigarette out from his shirt pocket and hands it to me. There is no cigarette lighter in the car, and Davy has to pull over on 14th Street to strike a match.

"Maybe later," I say, putting the cigarette in my pocket, "but, for now, could you teach me something?"

Davy lights one and then drives into a deserted street by a large Con Edison plant down by 14th Street. He tells me to get behind the wheel.

"You can drive home," Davy says.

I can drive home, I am thinking, and I haven't even had my first driving lesson yet.

"Anyway," he says, "I don't want to take the risk anymore."

"What risk?" I ask.

"Getting caught," he says, "without a license."

I think about this as I go around the car to get behind the wheel. Uncle Tracy would be happier if Davy had a license, even a phony one.

"I thought," I say to him, "you had a license from California?"

"Naw," he says. "I have a sister lives out there, but I'm not sixteen yet."

I should have known that no one likes to say they don't have something, so it doesn't surprise me too much to learn that Davy doesn't have a license. I just better not let Uncle Tracy know.

Davy offers me another cigarette.

"It looks cool if you are smoking behind the wheel," he says. "It will make you look older."

But, I am thinking, I'm still only twelve, and I can't even see over the steering wheel. So how cool can I look?

I am not so sure I want to try to smoke yet. Maybe if I just hold the cigarette in my hand, it will make me look older.

I think of Humphrey Bogart as I take the cigarette. I want to learn how to blow smoke out of my nose the way Humphrey Bogart does in all his pictures. He is always such a big shot. If I ever smoke, I want to blow the smoke out of my nose and talk at the same time with the smoke coming out of my mouth, too, just like Bogart.

I am behind the wheel now, the cigarette between my fingers, and feeling like I have been graduated to some new level of life. I am learning to drive and I am getting older.

I have only been in a car a few times before, and even though it is Uncle Tracy's car, I feel that this one is mine, that it is in the family. I put the cigarette between my lips, and both hands on the steering wheel. This is as close to king of the mountain that I've ever been. I turn the wheel back and forth, and I remember a movie I just saw and think I am like James Cagney speeding away from the cops. Maybe I'd rather be Jimmy Cagney than Humphrey Bogart, because what mother would name her son Humphrey, anyway?

Davy lights a match for me. He is already smoking heavily on his cigarette, and flicking it like crazy before the ash has a chance to grow thicker than a strand of hair. He lights the match with one hand, which I think is a pretty hotsy-totsy thing to do. But I think of my mother and what she would do if she ever found out I was smoking. She has a way of finding out everything. She will smell smoke in my clothes or in my nostrils. She will sniff at my nostrils, and she will say you've been smoking. And then she will take me to Father O'Rourke, who will throw me out of the altar boys and make me take an oath of some kind, a don't-upset-your-mother pledge or something. Or worse, he'll give me to Father Hamilton to face my punishment, and I'll have to say three months' worth of prayers.

I hand the cigarette back to Davy.

"Not today," I say. "I don't want to smoke and drive at the same time."

"Okay," Davy says. "So step on the clutch and put the gearshift way up into first."

I look down, and I can see that there is about three inches between the clutch and the end of my foot, even with my toes stretched out. I am already on the edge of the seat, and the only way to press the clutch down is to go over on the right cheek of my ass and stretch my whole body out.

It is impossible to drive this way, and so I get out of the car.

I know, though, that this is an opportunity for me, and I don't want to miss it. I really want to know how to drive, and I have to learn as much as I can. Davy gets back in the driver's seat.

"So teach me how to drive, anyway," I say. "Just show me."

Davy goes through the motions, and I ask him to do a couple of things twice, like how he presses down on the gas and lifts the clutch up easily, and how he presses the clutch in just before he brakes the car to a complete stop.

I think I know it all by the time Davy parks the car back on First Avenue and 56th Street, and I can't wait until I get another three inches on my leg. I know how to drive now, anyway, and I can tell everyone, Bobby Walsh and Jurgensen and those guys, that I can drive better than them.

Uncle Tracy really is a riot, I am thinking as I begin down the hall to my Aunt Kitty's to return the keys.

Aunt Kitty has the door open, and I can hear her jabbering a mile away. They are sitting in her living room, which on the first floor is smaller than ours because of the big lobby space in the front of the building, and I hear what they are saying as I go in the door and into the kitchen.

"It's rotten what they do to him," Aunt Kitty says. "They are always beating him up and taking his smokes, and he never has a drink."

Who is she talking about? I am wondering as I lay the keys down on the table. I stand by the kitchen door and wait.

"He tried to run away once," Aunt Kitty goes on, "during the time they were giving him the shock treatment, and they beat him up good. They said he fell in the shower. What a mess he was."

"Holy shit," Uncle Tracy says. "Where is this place?"

"Someplace called Greenland State Hospital," Aunt Kittty answers.

I know that Greenland State is the insane asylum. The nuthouse. I've heard guys in the street sometimes say that other guys in the street should be sent away to Greenland State, like Charlie Ameche, who beat his father up so bad they had to keep the old man in the hospital for months before the broken bones in his face healed, and I am still wondering who Aunt Kitty is talking about, and how come she never told me anything like this.

"He'll never get any better," she says, "and I always feel sorry for poor Mary and the burden she has with those two sons."

What burden? Is this my mother she is talking about? It can't be Mom, because Mom is always saying how lucky she is to have such two healthy sons around the house.

"And the welfare," Aunt Kitty says. "She's gotta have the welfare. What a mess. At least I have the pension, and I don't have to go on the welfare. But she's lucky, anyway, that she got that apartment upstairs."

My mind is now racing. Is there somebody upstairs who is on the welfare and has two kids and is named Mary, and who isn't my mother?

I am running up the stairs now, two by two, and I feel the tears running as quickly down the sides of my face. I'm twelve years old and I shouldn't be crying, but I want to yell at her, to tell her how mad I am that she has told me all these years about my father having the bad legs, and that the hospital won't let me and Billy in because we are too young, that something fell off the truck at Railway Express and landed right on top of him and on top of his legs, and all these years I have pictured him being squished underneath some great package and his face tormented by the pain, and I always thought he was getting well, and he would come home and meet me after school and take me home, and someday take me to the ball game at Yankee Stadium.

But it is all a lie.

Why didn't she tell me?

The O'Dwyer for Mayor sticker is still on the window on the fourth floor, and I stop there to catch my breath, stretching my eyes as wide as they will go, thinking of the words I will say to her.

I know, every time I think of something, that I won't say that. I can't. I can't yell at my mother. I can't make her sad. I am already a burden, Aunt Kitty said. And Billy, too. She has to carry us everywhere, like big things that wear her down. I can't make her sad.

And it is my fault. How could I believe that he was in a hospital with bad legs? All these years, no one said anything, not Billy, either. Maybe Billy wanted to believe it, too, maybe Billy just said to himself that his father is in the hospital with bad legs, or bad something, but not because he was flipped, not because he was walking around with wide eyes and a blank, scary stare, or pacing back and forth like a palace guard, or beating himself against a wall, or lying in a corner of a padded cell with a straitjacket on.

But who knows what Billy is thinking, or my mother, or anyone else? We don't talk about these things, we keep them packed away in a dark closet like a pair of old gloves that will never fit again.

I am thinking of all I have learned today, as I now lie with my eyes closed on the top bunk. Billy is below me, and I want to tell him everything, that I saw Uncle Tracy make forty dollars out of twenty-one dollars, and that Davy Weld taught me how to drive the car, and that Daddy was in Greenland State. Just like that, pop, pop, pop. But I don't know if Billy knows. And if he does know, why hasn't he told me all this time?

Jesus, I am twelve years old. I should have known.

My mother should have told me.

Why doesn't she trust me?

Chapter Twenty-nine

It is one of those mornings when my mother is making us do things we don't want to do, and I want to go out and play baseball under the bridge on 59th Street. It is Saturday, and the living room is bright with sunshine. We are on the west wall of the courtyard, and so when the sun goes over the East River, it brightens our living room for half the morning. After that, the apartment goes dark.

The welfare inspector is coming today. He always comes on Saturday, I guess so that he can talk to Billy and me, and Mom makes us put on our best shirts. Mine is the white shirt I wore at Confirmation. My hair is combed, and Mom has made me shine my shoes with the liquid polish she bought at Woolworth's.

Mom has piled the magazines and books neatly on the table next to the couch, and on top of the pile is the Family Bible she bought recently for one dollar a month for thirty-six months. It is a beautiful book, filled with color pictures of saints and angels, and God, and on the first page is all our names written in big printed letters. It is the first new book that has ever been in our house, and every time I read in it I remember that I still have a ton of those book-bricks in my building to read.

The radio is blaring the Top Ten, Martin Block and his Make Believe Ballroom. Billy is in a plaid shirt, a little heavy for this weather, and is sitting on the windowsill of the living room, washing the windows. His shoes are shined with the liquid polish, and are gleaming. He puts vinegar in the spaghetti pot and fills it with cold water. That is the best for the windows, Mom says. He wipes the rag from one end of the window to the other and then dries it with old newspaper. His hand is black with the ink, but the windows sparkle. He is singing as he wipes, "That Old Black Magic," and he sounds like a crooner.

I have put an old army blanket over the television that Uncle Andy just gave us, for the welfare doesn't allow television sets. It is great to have a television set, and not to have to go to Dante Vescovi's house to watch Sid Caesar and Imogene Coca.

My mother takes a look around the living room and says that the phonograph has to be covered, too, for the welfare also doesn't like phonographs as much as they don't like television sets. I look for another army blanket on the top of the tin closet my mother has bought for her room. But I don't see one, and so I take the bedspread off her bed and lay it across the phonograph. The bedspread is light green and the army blanket is dark brown, and it looks like there are two pedestals in the living room waiting for us to put stuff on top of them like in Bloomingdale's. I am thinking that we could put picture frames on them, or maybe the spaghetti bowl, which is painted with flowers.

My mother comes into the living room and takes a look. She shakes her head.

"It will never do," she says.

"What's the matter?" I ask.

"Just the colors," she says, "green and brown. That will never do. Look for something yellow or blue, a sheet maybe, something so that the colors go together."

She rubs my head like I am a little boy. I hate it when she does this, but I never turn away or say anything.

"They can come all they want," she says, "just because we're on home relief, but I don't want them to say that we don't have any taste."

Mom sits on the couch and looks around the room. It looks okay to her, I can tell, for she is smiling.

"It won't be long," she says, "before we are off this welfare, and I'll be glad when that day comes. You guys are big enough to be on your own now—pretty soon, anyway."

I know she is talking about me, because Billy is fourteen, and he told my mother recently that the famous Romeo of *Romeo and Juliet* was already in love and dead at his age.

"And," she continues, "I am going to try to get a job at the telephone company. At the telephone company, they won't care if we have a television or not."

"And then," Billy asks, "maybe we could get a telephone?"

"Maybe," she says.

An old colored man comes to the door, carrying a large notebook that has paper hanging out from all sides. He has a small mustache, and it looks like he cares about it a lot, for it is very straight and trimmed. He smiles, and my mother asks him in.

He sits at the kitchen table. It is a new table made of something called Formica, and it has chromium legs. Mom loves this table, I guess because it is new. She loves anything that shines and sparkles. There are four chairs with stuffed plastic seats and chromium legs, and Mom has washed all the fingerprints off the chromium.

We don't get many new things in the house. All the furniture, the chairs, the lamps, the dishes, came from people who gave it to us. Especially Uncle Andy, who gives us all his old things when he gets new ones.

We can see the colored man studying the pedestals like they were works of art. I don't think he would ask to go into the living room if he is not invited. Mom would tell him that it is impolite to invite yourself wherever you please.

The colored man asks me and Billy to sit down, and we do.

"What did you have for your supper last night?" he asks.

"Magpie and Muff," Billy says, fooling around. Mom shoves his shoulder.

"Tripe," I say.

Now she shoves my shoulder.

"We did not have tripe," she says. "Why do you say tripe?"

"I hate tripe, Mom," I say.

"We haven't had any tripe in a year," she says.

"I just wanted to remind you," I say.

The colored man doesn't think this is funny, and to get our attention he slaps his hand down easily on the new table.

"Well," he asks, "what did you have?"

"Hamburgers," my mother says.

"And mashed potatoes," Billy says.

"I'm not so good on hamburgers, either," I say.

"Did you bring us any turkey?" Billy asks. I guess Billy is think-ing of the turkeys that the James Farley Democratic Club gives out at Christmas.

No answer. Instead, the man asks, "How many days of school did you miss in the last month?"

"I guess you don't know Sister Sylvester," I say. "You don't miss school in St. John's. They come to your house to yell at you."

He looks at Billy.

"Same thing at Cardinal Hayes High School. I never miss."

"Okay," the man says, "that's all I have to ask."

I think all his job consists of is making sure people are who they say they are, and that if you say you have two kids, that you really have two kids. My mother calls them "checker-uppers" when they come.

"So I'm going out, Mom," I say.

"Where are you going?"

"Just out," I say.

"I'm going to Kips," Billy says.

The colored man is still sitting there, writing in his notebook.

I change my clothes and grab my baseball glove from the top of the tub. It is the old one that was given to me by Uncle Phil a few years before he died.

"I guess," I say, "I'll play ball under the bridge with the PAL team."

I kiss my mother goodbye, and I would say goodbye to the col-ored man if he would only look up from his writing. But he doesn't.

On the stoop, I linger for a moment. Billy is standing next to me.

"Who are you playing with?" Billy asks.

"I don't know," I say, "the Police Athletic League team up on 59th Street, I guess."

I am biding my time, for I don't want to walk with my brother. I am always a straight shooter with Billy, but I don't want him to know that I started smoking just after I learned how to drive, and I have a package of cigarettes hidden under the stairs in the hall. He is always straight with me, too, except for not telling me about my father. But, still, I don't want him to be mad at me for smoking.

"I think," I say, "I'll just wait here for a few minutes and see if anybody comes around."

"See ya."

"Yeah," I say.

I watch Billy until he turns the corner at First Avenue, and then I take the smokes from under the stairs. They are burning a hole in my pocket, but I don't light one up until I get far down toward Sutton Place. Finally, I take one out and hold the book of matches with one hand. The way Davy Weld did it. I've been practicing this for a few weeks now, and I want to get it right. I fold one match over and close the cover, and still with just one hand, I bend the match again until it hits the striker, and then I zip my finger across, and the match lights.

I am proud of this new trick, and I wish someone would have seen me do it. But the street is empty until I turn the corner on York Avenue and walk toward the baseball field at 59th Street. There I see Jimmy Burton, sitting against the rough concrete of the sitting steps that go around the ballpark. The park is empty except for a couple of boys playing catch near home plate. They are waiting for the head of the PAL team to come with the bats and the bases.

"Hey," I call out to him, "where's your glove?"

"I don't need a glove," he says. "I have a car."

Burton is fourteen, a big guy with curly hair, and he looks old enough so that he can buy smokes in a store without anyone asking his age.

"Where did you get a car?" I ask, thinking that my Uncle Tracy may be in town again.

"Right here in my shirt pocket," he answers.

He is wearing a red and black plaid shirt and pulls a chewing-gum wrapper from the pocket. The wrinkles have been smoothed out so that it is a shiny sheet of silver, like silk. I know exactly what he is talking about.

"So where's this car?" I ask.

"Down by the smokestack," he says, talking about the big Con Edison smokestack on 59th Street by the river. "I was hitting the windows and the best '49 Ford opened up."

I picture him pressing every side and vent window of every car until he finds one open.

"Did you get it started?" I ask.

"I didn't try yet," he says. "You wanna come?"

"No," I say. "What if you get caught?"

"Don't be such a chicken ass," he says. "You don't even know how to drive. You don't get caught if you just drive around and obey all the rules like stopping at the lights."

"I do know how to drive," I say. "I can drive as good as anyone."

I don't like it when people tell me that I can't do something when I know I can.

"C'mon," Burton says, getting up and pulling me by the sleeve. "C'mon."

Burton is one of those guys in the neighborhood that are liked by everybody, mostly because he is a little crazy, but also because he is loyal. Even if you are wrong, like, say, you cursed in front of somebody's girlfriend, Burton will always back you up if you need him, for he is good with his dukes, or he will give you a quarter for the movies if you don't have one. He took me to the movies a few times, and I guess this is why I don't want to disappoint him now.

And so I walk down toward the river with him, knowing that I am getting into something that could end up with me holding the shitty end of the stick. Joyriding in a stolen car is not something any of the guys I know have ever done. Walsh and Scarry and those guys wouldn't have the balls to put it together that you could act the part in a '49 Ford, you could put your arm out the window, and the girls on the corner could give you a look that could work when you passed them by.

This '49 Ford is a beauty, gleaming dark blue paint, woven black and white plastic seats, a big black steering wheel. It has a smell of mint in the car, coming from one of those odor things that is hanging from one of the radio knobs. Burton shoves the silver paper up underneath the dashboard behind the ignition key mount. There is a spark, and he flinches backward, dropping the paper.

Maybe this is a sign, I think. Maybe he won't get it started, and we can get out of this car before somebody comes. But he picks it up and tries again, this time starting the car.

"Go, baby, go," Burton says, and he rams the car in first gear and pops the clutch. The wheels squeal, and the car lunges forward, just missing a parked car in front. Burton forgets to put the clutch in again as he brakes at the red light, and the car stalls.

"Shit," he says, shoving the paper underneath again. But the car won't start. He tries and tries, but the contact with the silver just does not happen.

"The paper must be all scratched up," he says. "I don't have any more gum. Do you have any gum?"

Suddenly, a car comes up behind us and beeps his horn.

"Christ," I say. This could be an off-duty cop, or someone who knows this car and the car's owner. I can feel my eyes tighten at the corners.

We are sitting at a red light on 59th Street and York Avenue, and I know I don't have any gum. The car is stolen, and all I can think of is that my mother never lets me chew gum because it is bad for the teeth, and my teeth are bad enough ever since the dental students pulled out the ones with the cavities. And now there is this car behind us beeping his horn like he is an ambulance driver delivering a stretcher.

Burton is looking all around, and I can tell he is wondering what to do.

I am suddenly scared, and my mouth begins to tremble. If this guy would only stop beeping his horn. Everybody up and down Sutton Place must be turning around to look. I can hardly speak, for if we got caught in a stolen car, it would be Lincoln Hall or some other reform school for sure, and all the boys I know who went to Lincoln Hall were practicing to be murderers. I don't know if I could ever live in a place like that.

"Christ, Jimmy," I say, "I don't want to cop out on you, but let's get the hell outta here, huh?"

"Right," Burton says, "just get out and run like hell."

And so we leave the car right there at the red light, sticking out like an elephant in the middle aisle of the supermarket, with the beeping-horn guy now stuck and cursing with every beep. All I can think of as we run back to the baseball field is that this guy must think he is in some circus act with these two kids jumping out of the car in front of him and disappearing around the corner.

Burton does not say anything as we enter the park. I try to say something, but I still can't control my speech, I am so scared. There are a few more boys on the field now, and they are about to choose up sides. At least I'll get a game, and that will take my mind off of how close I am to going to Lincoln Hall for Delinquents. I can hardly catch my breath. Bobby Walsh is there and sees me. He comes over and puts his arm around my shoulder.

I am still thinking of what would happen if we were caught. Holy shit. I don't know what would happen. Except for the trouble, and Lincoln Hall. But what would my mother say? God. She would never believe it, that I got in a stolen car. And if she did, she would be so disappointed and sad. And she'd beat me with a hanger or a baseball bat or something.

"Hey," Walsh says, "s'matter you?" I guess he sees me shaking.

Burton comes over and punches me in the arm.

"Nothin's s'matter him," Burton says, laughing. "He's gonna loand me his baseball glove is all."

I look at Burton. I am feeling strangely strengthened, like I did something that was different than anyone else can do, that I have won a sort of trophy in my own mind. I want to smile, to laugh it off like Burton, but, still, I know that I have done something stupid and that I have gotten away with it.

This time.

Chapter Thirty

Finally, I am thirteen, and old enough to go to the teenage canteen at Kips Bay Boys Club, but my mother is acting like I am still twelve or something.

"I'm in the eighth grade now," I am saying, "and I don't know why I can't stay out until midnight, 'cause everyone else stays out."

I am sitting at the kitchen table, trying to draw a bird in a back page of my schoolbook. I like to draw birds, because they are easy. You just have to start with a circle, and you will always get to something that looks like a bird.

My mother is at the sink cleaning those little pork chops that she boils with the sauerkraut and potatoes.

"C'mon, Mom," I say, protesting. "C'mon. Just until eleven-thirty, then."

"You have a lot of nerve," my mother says finally, "to expect to go gallivanting around, to ask for any favors with the report card you brought home. When you start getting marks like your brother Billy, I will think about giving you any special privileges, but for now you'll be home here at ten o'clock if you know what's good for you. Otherwise you can stay home and brood about it."

This, I am thinking, is exactly the trouble with trying to make sense with my mother. She's always saying if I know what's good for me, as if I don't know what's good for me, but when I tell her what's good for me, she never pays attention. It is only her definition of "good" that we get to talk about in the house.

Billy is up in the Bronx at school, Cardinal Hayes, and he is probably still at basketball practice. Even on a Friday. He made the varsity team there, and he is only in his second year. He is such a good player. Billy is good at everything, and when he graduated from St. John's, most of the parents got pretty mad at him because he won so many of the medals, and their kids didn't get very many. He is good at remembering things, like how many errors Ty Cobb made in his career, or who was the king of England or the king of France when America was discovered by the Vikings, or even before when the Irish came.

Just recently, Billy won the Boy of the Year at Kips Bay, and they gave him a scholarship to a place called Exeter up in New Hampshire, a boarding school. Mr. McNiven at Kips Bay said it was a good school, but Mom went up to Cardinal Hayes to talk to the principal there, Monsignor Fleming, and he told her that Exeter was a Protestant place, and it would not be good for Billy's soul to go there. So he is not going. He's got a scholarship at Cardinal Hayes, anyway, because of the fact that we are on welfare and Billy plays basketball.

I wonder about Billy's soul, and if being at this place Exeter would make a Protestant out of him. And then, I wonder, what is a Protestant, and why is it so bad to be one? I have never been inside of a Protestant church, and I don't think I have ever met a Protestant person except for the Jehovah's Witnesses who knock on the door every once in a while to give out magazines. I only know that being a Catholic is better. We have to do things, like love God, do good, avoid evil, and provide for the propagation of the faith. I always try to provide for the propagation of the faith, which I think is that you have to be ready to be a martyr, like those guys who had to fight the lions in the movies. But Protestants don't have to do anything special. They don't even have to go to church on Sunday if they have something else to do. If we don't go to church on Sunday, we go right to hell when we die.

We never miss Mass in our house, and even if we did miss once in a while, I don't think Billy would be available to be a Protestant, no matter how many teachers at Exeter tried to get him to be one. Anyway, Billy's too tough, and he's such a good athlete it would take four or five guys to hold him down if they wanted to make a Protestant out of him.

I wish my mother would treat me like a teenager.

"I don't want to stay home," I say, trying to draw feathers that look like something other than sticks on the side of the bird. It comes out better if I use the side of my pencil instead of the point.

"Then be home at ten," she says, now scrubbing out a big pot, the one where there is only one handle, "and do your homework the way your brother always does his homework before he goes to sleep."

She is always telling me that I should get better grades, and I guess she doesn't have any choice except to use Billy as an example. Sister Alphonsus always does that, and Archie down at Kips does it, too. Everyone thinks Billy is doing great in everything, and it's easy for them to say I'm not doing so great.

"Maybe," my mother says, "if you paid closer attention to your homework, you will begin to apply yourself better to your schooling. You have to build on the stuff God gave you, and I'm not just talking about those blue eyes of yours, either. It's too bad we can't put our fingers in our ears to feel our brains, because that might remind us that we had one."

She smiles, but I don't think it is funny. I wish I could tell her how much I think school is a waste of time. That I would rather be out working somewhere, and having a quarter in my pocket to go to the movies or get a hamburger at Riker's if I want one. But she would just argue with me, and tell me that I don't know what's good for me, that I will never get near to meeting my abilities without getting high marks at school.

Besides, everyone at school is always yelling at you, making you feel like you did something wrong by getting up in the morning. My mother doesn't realize that there is so much yelling at St. John's. The nuns yell at you for running in the playground during recess, the principal yells at you if you're late to lineup, the priests yell at you for pouring too much wine in the chalice, or not enough wine. And everyone yells about getting better marks.

My mother is very much against yelling. She never lets us yell in the house. "A gentleman never raises his voice" is what she says if we yell.

Sister Alphonsus doesn't hit anyone, but she doesn't let the smallest thing pass without yelling at you, either. And almost everyone stays after school every day for something or other. Like yesterday I had to stay because I got out of the line at lunchtime to tie my shoe.

"You stay after school, young man," Sister Alphonsus said as she pushed me back into the line. I feel like I am in some prison movie when I am in school, where everyone is against you, and you know your only job there is to find a way to escape.

I am sitting on the floor now in the auditorium-size game room of Kips Bay. On the walls are big paintings of dancing teenagers, ten of them, that were done for Kips Bay by students in an art school somewhere. The paintings give the room a feeling of a dance hall or a nightclub, anything but the dull gray–painted game room of Kips. The room is pretty dark, and there are spotlights shining down on the dance floor in the middle of the room.

Marilyn Rolleri is on the other side of the dance floor, sitting on a chair in the middle of a crowd of girls. I am in my powder-blue sports jacket, and I am talking with Walsh and Scarry, drinking the small bottles of Coke they gave us for free. Archie is at the door, checking the club cards, making sure that everyone who wants to get in is at least thirteen.

Some slow music starts, and there is a rush of boys going across the dance floor for the girls.

"I'm going to ask Rolleri to dance," I say, getting up.

"Good luck," Walsh says, rubbing his hand up and down the outside of the Coke bottle.

"Those Italian girls," Scarry laughs, "like the sausage."

"Yeah, yeah," I say as I walk away and toward Marilyn.

She looks at Gilda Galli as she gets up to dance with me, saying, "Mind my place."

I walk to the middle of the dance floor and turn to see if she followed me. She is there, standing with her hands at her sides, flat against a tight black skirt, which wraps her down to her ankles. It is so tight I can see the outlines of her thighs.

I don't know what to say to her, and just grab her around the waist and pull her close to me. The nuns say that you should leave room for the Holy Ghost when you dance, but I don't think there is enough room between us for one of Uncle Tracy's toothpicks.

Her hair is falling behind her, halfway down her back, in long black curls. I can smell it, and it is like canned peaches. We are dancing, but we are hardly moving at all. She smells so good, and I put my face against hers. My lips slide softly over her cheek.

I could ask her any number of things, like, "How are things in school?" or "How are your ballet lessons?" or "How do you get along with your parents?" But I wonder how many opportunities like this I am going to get. Just get it over with, I say to myself.

I slide my lips up to her ear, and I whisper, "Could I take you home tonight?"

She knows I like her, like I have been liking her since the fourth grade. But she doesn't seem impressed. It is almost like I said, "The moon always comes up when the sun goes down." Knowing I want to take her home is nothing new.

"I have to go," she says, "with Barbara Cavazzine and Gilda Galli to Emiliano's for a pizza after the dance."

The three of them, I think, are like the Italian mopsy triplets. I picture myself, just for a moment, saying, "I can't go. I have to be home before ten, or my mother will kill me."

I could never say that to Marilyn. She would think I am a stupid schmo, a kid.

My mother is a whack job when it comes to time and schedule, and if I'm late, each minute becomes a crime of some kind. "Being on time," she says, "is as important as wearing clothes. If you're late all the time, people will see you as nothing more than a little naked oddball."

Oh, Marilyn.

I pull my head back a little to look at her, as I have been looking at her since the fourth grade. I like her more each year, and I am beginning to think about what I am feeling as I hold her so close to me as we dance.

Johnnie Ray begins to sing "The Little White Cloud That

Cried," and I feel myself up against her thigh, the inside of her thigh. It feels like she is pushing into me. Oh, God. Johnnie Ray sounds like he's in tears. There are a hundred kids around us, some doing the fox-trot, some doing the fish, but I have Marilyn stiffly around the waist, and we are grinding. She's doing the grind with me in the middle of the floor, behind a curtain of others. I feel like I won the grand prize in some happiness contest, and I'm hoping that Archie doesn't see us. You're not supposed to do the fish, and you're especially not supposed to do the grind.

"As I went walking down by the river," Johnnie Ray is singing, and I am thinking that I would like to take Marilyn down by the river, to sit with her on a 51st Street park bench, to put my hand all over her tight skirt, to watch the Pepsi-Cola sign blink on and off across the river, to kiss her big, red Italian lips, and to move my hand into her blouse, softly, quietly, to feel the cotton of her brassiere.

I'm not sure if she is pressing into me deliberately. I only know we are grinding slowly, hardly moving anything but our hips on the dance floor. Am I grinding into her, or is she grinding into me? Nothing matters as long as her thighs are against mine, and I can feel her breath on my neck.

"Why don't you come to Emiliano's for a pizza with us?" she asks in a whisper.

"I can't," I say, " 'cause I have something to do."

"What do you have to do?"

Her breath is going all over my neck and the side of my face, and her legs are like hot wax against me.

"Just something to do," I say, "that's all."

"Something to do?"

"Yeah, something to do."

"What are you," she says, "a bookie or something, going off with something to do that you can't say what it is?"

"Some other time," I say, "maybe I could go with you."

She doesn't answer, and I am too excited by all the grinding that I don't think much about how sad it is that I can't go with them for a pizza pie. All I can think about is how hard I am pressing into her, and how I would like to take her to see the Pepsi-Cola sign.

* * *

Now, though, I am realizing that I can't go with all my friends, and I am getting very pissed off. I don't care if it is better to be pissed off than pissed on. Walsh, Scarry, Jurgensen, all of them are going for the pizza, and I have to go home. Just because my report card is not so good.

And I feel very sharp in my powder-blue jacket, too, and the white shirt with the big collar. My hair is combed in the front into a drop curl. I combed it after I left the house, in the dark of my hallway, because my mother doesn't like my hair in a drop curl, and says that it makes me look like an Italian. She thinks the Italians all end up in jail because of the way they comb their hair, and so she wouldn't let me out of the house with my hair combed like that. But I like it, the hair coming down in one big curl in the middle of my forehead, and in the back, combed into a duck's tail. It makes me feel tough and with it.

Marilyn Rolleri seems to like it, too, for every time I ask her to dance she dances with me.

But something is missing. I feel like everything is okay, that I look sharp, feel sharp, be sharp, like the razor blades, and Marilyn Rolleri and the other girls have been noticing me, but, still, I feel like I am naked, that I am standing here with all my friends, and I am absolutely naked without a stitch on, and I am hoping that they don't see me like this.

My mother, if you think about it, has ruined my whole night, just because of my report card. And I don't care what anybody says, it isn't fair to get punished like this. I could get good grades like Billy if I wanted, don't they know that?

It just doesn't matter to me, the famous report card, is all.

Martin Block, the disc jockey from the Make Believe Ballroom show on the radio, introduces the special guest he has brought tonight. Block's been here many times before with Dinah Shore, Tony Bennett, Johnny Mathis, Rosemary Clooney, and big stars like that. Tonight he has Les Paul and Mary Ford. They don't say anything, but they start to play "How High the Moon," and everybody begins to move and shake their bodies. Imagine, Les Paul and Mary Ford right here in our dance at Kips Bay Boys Club, just for us kids. Maybe Martin Block used to be a member here, or something like that, but he has brought Les Paul and Mary Ford right here into the club, and all of us feel like we were born on Sutton Place and we have front-row seats at Radio City Music Hall.

Mary Ford is wearing a big crinoline skirt, all black with bangles and beads, and Les Paul has a shoelace instead of a tie, and they are both playing guitars that are bigger than me, and the music is going through the room and through the bodies of all the kids, and everyone is smiling, and I forget for a minute that I can't go to Emiliano's with Marilyn after the dance.

When the dance is over, I can see by the big hall clock that I don't have time to hang around, and I'll have to run home if I am going to be there at ten.

On my way out I see Martin Block. I think about my mother's harping all the time about being polite, and I know I should say thank you to him. But there are a bunch of other kids around, and they will think I am such a brizzer if I go right in the middle of them to thank Martin Block.

It's too bad about Emiliano's. It doesn't matter that I don't have the money to buy some pizza. Someone would give me a bite of theirs, probably.

I'll have some money soon, more than my paper money. I am supposed to get a delivery job with the East River Florist. If I could buy my own pizza, I would split it with my friends.

But I could live without pizza if I had to. It would be okay to just sit there.

If only, I am thinking as I skip alone down the stairs of Kips Bay, I could see if Marilyn Rolleri would make room for me to sit next to her at Emiliano's.

I guess my mother thinks that somewhere between ten and eleven o'clock that, because of a bad report card, I am going to murder someone, or that someone is going to murder me. So I have to leave everyone and be home at ten, if I don't want to get murdered or if I don't want to do the murdering.

It's not right.

No one has to go home at ten o'clock. And everyone but me is going to get a chance to see if they can get Marilyn Rolleri down by the river to watch the Pepsi-Cola sign.

So now I am still alone on Second Avenue. Everyone else is behind me, walking slower, taking their time. I suddenly want to run, and I sprint forward. It's not that I am late. I am running like mad because I want the wind against my face, and if I didn't have to be home at ten, I think I could run all the way to the Bronx.

Chapter Thirty-one

$\mathcal{I}$ am lying here under the bunk bed, thinking. It's dark. All I can see above me is the metal of a bedspring and squares of swollen mattress protruding down.

Yesterday was a two-time-terrible day. A Friday. A fragrant and feeble friggin' Friday, and it all makes me want to puke to think about it.

Diane Gillespie threw up in the girls' clothes closet, and Sister Alphonsus sent me down to the basement to find Mr. Greendust, the school custodian. I don't think anyone knows his name, because all you ever hear is the name "custodian." "Where's the custodian?" and "Go get the custodian," which is what Sister Alphonsus said to me. We call him Mr. Greendust because that is what he spreads around the floor when someone gets sick.

On the way up from the basement I met Marilyn Rolleri in the stairway. I guess she was late for school or something. I thought she was a gift from heaven when I saw her there, kneeling down to pick up a pencil case she had dropped. Her blue gabardine uniform skirt was tight around her round Italian thighs, and her great Italian breasts were pushing out against the white of her school blouse. I knelt down next to her and put my fingers around the pencil case just as she was picking it up. Her large brown Italian eyes were in a dance of some kind, looking me up and down.

Oh, Marilyn, I was thinking, what am I going to do? You are here in the quiet of the staircase, you with a smile of perfect teeth and a backside molded by an artist.

We were both standing then, she had her book case by her feet, our fingers were wrapped around her pencil case, and her smile was coming closer to me. No, I was moving closer to her. I don't know what got into me. I closed my eyes a little and leaned in so close to her I could smell her breath. I thought her breath smelled like what love should smell like, soft and airy and warm. I let go of the pencil case, and it dropped again to the floor. I put my arms around her, and we leaned back onto the wired glass of the staircase wall, and we kissed. I wanted to open my mouth, but she pressed her two beautiful Italian lips together and pushed them hard against my own lips, and they felt like soft and moist pancakes as the breath from her nose covered my face.

Oh, Marilyn, I thought, this is better than watching the Pepsi-Cola sign. I did not try to open my mouth, but just breathed in her life's breath and let the wetness of her lips enter my mind so that it will never be forgotten.

Not a single word was said between us. She gave me that one long kiss, and then she picked up her pencil case and her book case, and she trotted up the stairs so fast that I couldn't catch her. She was already sitting when I opened the door to Sister Alphonsus' eighth-grade class.

I waited for her in the school yard when we broke for lunch. She was walking out of the yard with Barbara Cavazzine, and I asked if I could talk to her.

They both stopped, and Marilyn came toward me. She whispered.

"I know," she said, "that you want to ask me to go out with you, but I am going to go steady with Raymond Connors."

"Right."

That was all I could get out. "Right."

But it wasn't right, not after being like that with her in the staircase, not after having her lips pressed against mine for, what, a minute at least. One glorious, historic minute. It was like she had given me a hundred dollars and then takes it away after I bought presents for all my friends. And now it feels like I have the tab for the presents but no money, like I have this love in my heart for her but there is no her.

I wanted to shout, but I remembered what my mother said about being polite all the time. If you are polite in the good times, you will also be polite in the bad times, when it matters the most. And so I didn't shout, but just turned and tried to get in the punchball game going on in the corner of the school yard.

Raymond Connors, who had enough red hair and enough teeth for triplets. I like Raymond Connors, but he doesn't even know how to do the lindy. Why would Marilyn go steady with him when she could, well, get anyone she wanted?

All afternoon at school I could hardly pay attention to Sister Alphonsus. We were going over the English part of the State Regents examination. Mostly, they were grammar questions, and I was getting all the right answers. At least, when I did them, for I was doing one and skipping one, and every time I skipped one I thought about Marilyn sitting up there in the front of the class.

Sister Alphonsus kept looking at my answer sheet and shaking her head, and at the end of the day she asked me to stay. It is always a bad sign when the teacher asks you to stay after school, and I sat alone in my seat drumming my fingers until she came back from the dismissal.

"You're hopeless, Dennis," she said as she stood before me, "and I don't think we will be able to let you graduate unless things are changed around here."

I thought of a wisecrack. If you want a change, I wanted to say, put curtains on the windows. But Sister wasn't in the mood to laugh, and it is always a good rule to say nothing until you find out what is going on.

"I want to see your mother," she said.

"What for?" I asked. I was already agitated, and I suddenly got very nervous. I just knew that my mother would be upset. She so hates it when things are not going right.

"Your report card was not good," she said, "and you are falling behind in everything."

"I do my homework," I said.

"You have not done a complete homework since the term started, Dennis," she said, "and do not argue with me. Bring your mother in, fifteen minutes before the start of school on Monday morning, no ifs, ands, or buts about it, please. Good afternoon."

Good afternoon, I was thinking, bullshit. I was exploding inside. I am so tired of all of it, everyone telling me what I should be doing, nobody doing anything to help me, Father Luke the Capuchin writing me a letter and saying that I should pray for my future vocation for the next few years, Sister Alphonsus saying things have to change, Marilyn Rolleri making out with Raymond Connors, my father walking around in circles in some upstate hospital, I don't even know where because they keep moving him from place to place, Archie telling me I could be great, but he never says what I could be great at, and my mother crying, sighing, yelling, and pleading with me almost every day to read more, to write more, to spend more time with my homework. It is just too much bullshit to put up with every day.

"Good afternoon, Sister," I said quietly, holding my head down, being polite.

But something inside me was running, running away from Sister Alphonsus as fast as I could, running into some dark forest where you can't see two inches in front of you. I felt myself walking slowly away from her, but my feet were going fifty miles an hour, and the next thing I knew I had changed my clothes, and I was in my mother's room, and I was searching through the drawers of her dresser looking for the welfare money that she kept hidden away. She always keeps the money in her drawer until she pays the rent or pays the bill at Rossi's. I looked everywhere, in every drawer, in every closet. Even on top and below. I needed some money, but I didn't know why. I only knew that I had to keep running, that I couldn't stay and talk to my mother, and tell her that Sister Alphonsus wants to tell her that I am not going to graduate, because I only did some of the grammar questions when I wasn't thinking about Marilyn kissing Raymond Connors with teeth enough for three people.

I needed a cigarette. I have never smoked a cigarette in my house, but I needed a cigarette, and so I grabbed the carton of Old Golds that my mother had in her bottom drawer, and shook out a pack. I know that she knows how many packs are left, the way mothers just know these things, so I can't take the whole pack. But I know I can get a cigarette out without her knowing, the way Uncle Tracy would do it, and I carefully opened the bottom end of the cellophane, making sure not to rip it in any way, and then I opened the paper at the bottom of the pack just as carefully. The opened bottom looked like a honeycomb of tobacco, twenty cigarettes all tight together. I pulled out one cigarette from the exact center, knowing that she will open one side of the pack or the other, and she will never see the empty hole in the center of the pack. I ran to the kitchen for the glue bottle, and I glued the paper and then the cellophane back together again, and put the pack back into the carton.

In the living room, I lit the cigarette and leaned far back into the pillow of the couch. I knew that my mother was cleaning some apartment down on Sutton Place, and so I just relaxed. And I sat there feeling for a minute that I owned the building, that I owned my life.

But only for a minute.

What was I going to do? I was thinking. What? I couldn't tell my mother that I was going to get kicked out of school. I just couldn't.

Run away, I thought. I had to run away.

Anywhere.

Maybe be a cowboy out west. If I was only older, maybe as old as Billy, I could get a job on a ship and sail the seas like Sinbad. I began to feel so alone there on the couch, smoking that cigarette, but I was thinking about my life. I realized that I didn't really care about Marilyn Rolleri or Sister Alphonsus or the Regents exam. I just cared about what I was going to do next.

It is not easy to run away when you are only in the eighth grade, because people spot you right away in the train station. But I had to do it, rather than face my mother and watch her become furious with me.

And, worse, I didn't want to see her cry again just because of me.

If I could run away, everything would turn out okay. Something good might happen somewhere, and I wouldn't have to explain about why I am not doing what they all expect me to do. I only want to be left alone, and to get a job, and to stay out until eleven, and to earn money so that I can get a pizza at Emiliano's.

I knew something lucky would happen, and the first person I met on Second Avenue was Henry Castle. I know him from the baseball games under the Queensboro Bridge, a little guy with big ears, and I have hung around with him a few times. He goes to public school, because his father is a Mohammedan, or a Buddhist, or something where you would think they were Chinese. But they are Irish and Mexican from the West Side, that's what Henry told me.

I told him there was a reason God gave him such big ears, so that he could listen better to me, and I told him everything that happened and why I had to run away.

Henry promised that he would stick by me all the way. I think he liked the excitement of somebody running away. Or maybe he wanted to be better friends with me so that he could hang around with me and Scarry and Walsh. It didn't matter to me why he would stick by me. It was just lucky.

But it was a little unlucky that Henry didn't have any money left from his allowance. So a bus or a train was out of the question. At least I didn't have to think of where I could take a bus or a train. I don't even know what stop to get off at when I visit my cousins in Brooklyn.

We went to the 54th Street Gym, because Henry wanted to work out to get in shape for the Golden Gloves. We hit the bag a little and ran a zillion times the running track that goes around the ceiling of the gym, and then we were hungry.

I sat on a radiator in the hallway while Henry went in to have dinner at his house. He put a fish stick in a paper napkin and brought it out to me, and I was glad Mrs. Castle didn't make spaghetti. My mother usually makes spaghetti on Friday instead of fish, and I was thinking that spaghetti would be hard to cart around in a napkin.

We then went down 53rd Street and watched the older guys play craps, and I grubbed an English muffin off Fatso Cassidy, who was winning. I did this by volunteering to go to Riker's to get him six English muffins, and then I ate one on the way back to the crap game. He never missed it.

Barbara Gabelli came around with a girl from 49th Street I didn't know. Her name is Lillian, and her skin is so dark I thought she had to come from some mountain village in Italy that was close to the sun. Her eyes are jet-black, and her hair is blacker and goes way down below her waist. She is very beautiful in that way you see in the old, dark pictures in the Metropolitan Museum.

We talked for a while, and then the four of us walked downtown. Henry walked us past 49th Street and past the construction barriers where they are building a tunnel underneath First Avenue for the United Nations building.

"Let's see what's in the U.N. tunnel," Henry said, and we followed him deep into the hole. I could tell that Henry was going to try to make time with Barbara, and so I sat with Lillian on the steps of an emergency stairs that went up to the street level.

Lillian was shy and quiet, and so I did all the talking. I told her about Marilyn going out with Raymond, and she told me she could never have a boyfriend, anyway, because her father was strict and he would kill her if she had a boyfriend before she graduated high school, which was four years away.

I told her that her father would never find out if she would let me be her boyfriend for just a half hour, and then I kissed her. I closed my eyes and put my lips on hers, and she opened her mouth suddenly and I felt her steaming tongue slopping away in my mouth like she has been kissing guys for ten years already, and then she got up.

My whole body was shaking.

This was nothing like kissing Marilyn Rolleri.

"I can't see you again," Lillian said, "because I can't have a boyfriend."

And then she yelled out Barbara's name and her voice echoed through the tunnel until it was covered by Barbara's voice as Barbara and Henry ran toward us, thinking someone was coming to catch us in the tunnel construction.

Henry and I left them on the corner of 49th Street, and I shook Lillian's hand. I watched her walk down the street, her skirt clinging to her legs down to her ankles. I was thinking I will always remember my first real kiss there in the United Nations tunnel, and I was wishing that Lillian was Irish, or at least that she wasn't Italian, so that she wouldn't have a father who was so strict, and I could give Lillian another French kiss here in New York on the grounds of the United Nations.

All Henry could talk about as we went uptown was Barbara Gabelli's stack, and I didn't pay much attention to him. I just kept trying to keep Lillian's taste in my mouth.

I think Henry felt that I would just go home at eleven o'clock, but I stuck to him like roof tar. There was no way he could get rid of me. After all, who said he would stick by me? I couldn't be alone at a time like this, and he knew it. So we went back to his house and crept quietly up the creaking tenement stairs.

Henry lives on the third floor of a building next to the Old Brew House Restaurant on 54th Street. It's an old building, probably as old as the Civil War, over near Third Avenue, and I was again in the hall as he searched the apartment for somewhere to hide me. Henry has a younger sister and two older sisters. I know their house. There are two bedrooms off the kitchen, and so I took my shoes off and tiptoed into the bedroom, where there were two sets of bunk beds, with maybe six inches between them.

Henry's younger sister, Madelaine, was sleeping on the couch in the living room. She is a year younger than we are, and good-looking, too. It would have been a lot easier to just sleep with her, but Henry made me get on the floor and pull myself under the bed like a grease monkey under a car. His sisters were already sleeping. I asked Henry for a pillow, and he threw me a blanket to put under my head.

I lay there, in the dark and under a bed, and wondered what my life was coming to. I put Lillian out of my mind. I did not know what to think, because everything was all confused. I only knew that I was running away, and if I didn't, everyone would be sad and angry. No one was going to forgive me, anyway. I was wrong in everybody's eyes, and I just said to myself that I wasn't going to think about it anymore.

So I said my night prayers and made all the blessing requests like nothing had ever happened. I blessed my mother and asked that my father gets okay again and that Uncle Tommy forgets about the airplane crash and is happy.

And now I am here. Still under the bed. I am just opening my eyes. It is a new day, and I am hoping it will be better than yesterday. Forget about Lillian's taste, I say to myself. I raise up a little and bump my head on the bedspring. Shit. It is like being in a tiny sewer or cave. There is nowhere to move.

Now I am hearing voices, and I remember where I am. What are those voices? Is my mother here? Where is my mother? Probably sitting in the police station. Oh, shit, she is going to give me blue murder, and now that I've been out all night I can never go home.

I listen for a minute or so. I don't hear my mother's voice. The whole Castle family seems to be sitting around the kitchen table. I will just lie quietly here under the bed, waiting for Henry to figure out how I am going to get out without anyone seeing me.

Henry comes in, and he lies on the floor next to me.

He whispers.

"My father," he says, "will pull my eyes out of my head if he finds out you're here. It's like harboring a criminal."

"You want me to jump out the window?" I ask.

"That would work," Henry says in a whispering laugh. "But that gives me an idea."

"Yeah, so?" I ask.

"I got it," he says, his eyes sparkling like he invented something. "We'll have seven seconds, maybe less, so you gotta run like hell. You got it?"

"I got it," I answer. "I think."

"Run like hell," he says, "when you hear me making a commotion, but quietly."

"Got it," I say. The Irish-Mexican mind is a mystery to me.

I don't have a clue about what is going on.

I have my shoes in my hands now, lying under the bed, and waiting for something to happen. I hear Henry opening the front window of the apartment.

And then Henry begins to scream.

"Holy God," he is yelling to his family at the top of his lungs, "look at this!"

I can hear all six of them now running to the front window, and everyone is crying, "What, what, what?"

I am now bolting like a racehorse to the front door, and I can hear Henry in the background, saying, "It's not even raining today."

*   *   *

It was just about seven seconds, and I am now out in the hall, and I run down to 54th Street and onto Second Avenue and then to 56th Street.

I stop running in front of Billy's Bar and Grill, and I am thinking hard about what I can do now. I still have nowhere to go. I can't go home. Kips Bay doesn't open for another hour or so. I will have to hang around somewhere, but where? My neighborhood is so big, maybe the biggest neighborhood in the country, and it is changing. There is a lot of construction, and the high buildings that are going up will make the neighborhood even bigger. My mother says that when they tear down the Third Avenue El, the whole neighborhood will get ritzy, and our apartment will finally be worth the thirty-two dollars a month we pay in rent.

The bright light of the sun is gleaming off the copper roof of St. John the Evangelist, and the sunbeam is like a halo over the church. Maybe I should stop in for a while. I could just sit in church until Kips Bay opens. To think about God, to ask Him to get Sister Alphonsus to change her mind. But it is too late for that. I could just go up to the altar and wait for the Virgin statue to smile at me like when I was a kid, and ask her to watch over me specially, to help me get better marks, to make me as smart as Billy, to make my mother happy.

I could add onto my night prayers for my father, to make him better so that he could come home again. But does anyone ever get better in one of those asylums? What is it really like there for him? Does he ever think about us? About me? But I've been praying to make his legs better for so many years, all wasted prayers when it had nothing to do with his legs, when I should have been praying that the Connors' family would inherit a house in Cleveland or somewhere like that, so that Raymond wouldn't be in the neighborhood and Marilyn Rolleri wouldn't be going steady.

At least, a prayer like that could be on the level.

I know deep in my heart that I should be sorry for running away like this, that my mother is probably sick with trying to find me, and that I should feel sorry, too, that everyone thinks I am not worth anything if I don't get all As in school. And if you're sorry for something, there is no better place to be than in church.

But I don't feel sorry at all.

I know that I should feel sorry, but I don't want to go into church and pretend that I am sorry for being a holy terror for my mother, just so I could ask for things in my prayers. I'm not sorry.

I have to begin to do things in my own life that I want to do, not the things that people think would help me to recognize my abilities, and not spend my time going around being sorry for everything.

And if you're not sorry, then I don't think you should go to church and ask for all kinds of things.

So Uncle Tommy and my father and Sister Alphonsus and the Cleveland house for the Connors family will have to wait.

It is not yet noon, and Bobby Walsh and I are playing pool in the intermediate game room at Kips Bay. The room is reserved for boys between thirteen and sixteen years old.

In Kips, the little kids are called midgets and have black membership cards. The cards are made of a kind of hard graphite. You can't get in the club without your membership card, which has your name imprinted on it, and which costs twenty-five cents a year. And you can only get a card if a parent comes in to sign you up. When you are ten, you get a junior card, which is red. I have the gray card for intermediates, ever since I turned thirteen, and Billy has a white card made of cardboard which is what the sixteen-to-eighteen-year-old seniors get.

Bill Egan is the instructor for the room. He's an older man, retired from the post office, and a great Ping-Pong player. He's swinging the paddle now on the other side of the room, near the three big windows that look out onto 52nd Street.

The room is bright, and filled with two big pool tables, a small pool table, and the Ping-Pong table.

Walsh is taking a shot on a big table in the corner of the room when I look up and see my brother Billy. He has rage in his eyes, and I have never seen him like this.

"There you are," he says, "you freakin' punk."

He is coming after me. I am in the corner, behind the pool table, and he is on the other side of the table. He is coming fast, as if he can't wait to get to me. So I sprint the other way. He stops and reverses himself. There is nobody as fast as Billy. I go back to the corner, and I wait here. He fakes to one side, and I fake to the other, and we both stop. It is like a standoff.

"You tried," he says, snarling at me, "to steal Mommy's money."

"I did not," I say, knowing that I was saying an outright lie.

"You're nothing but a punk," he says, "you know that."

He fakes again. My heart is pounding. I know that he is going to beat me good when he catches me.

"Lookit," I say, "just leave me alone. It is none of your business, anyway, what I do."

"Just a goddamn punk," he says, "stealing from your mother."

"I didn't steal anything," I say. This, anyway, wasn't a lie.

Walsh drops his pool cue on the table and slips past Billy in a flash. Bill Egan has stopped playing Ping-Pong and is looking our way. Billy picks up Walsh's cue stick. He takes the small end in his hand, and I know now that I can't get past, but I have to do something, I have to make my way to the door so that I can get to the street. And so I fake one way and then run the opposite way at full speed. Billy swings the pool stick, and it is a blur coming at me. I raise my arm, and the stick hits me just above my elbow.

It is like there has been an explosion, and I feel myself falling to the floor.

It feels like the stick is stuck in my arm, that the bone has broken and wrapped around it. The pain is shooting through every part of me, through my shoulders and into my head and down into my legs. The room gets dark for a moment, and I can't see anything.

Bill Egan is now on his knee and has my face cupped in his hands.

"Dennis," he is saying, "Dennis. Look at me. Say your name."

"Dennis," I say resentfully, like some cop has asked me a question.

"What's my name?" he asks.

"Bill," I say.

"Good," he says, leaving my face go, "let's see now."

Billy is standing just behind Egan as he lifts my arm and squeezes it where it is now swollen. He is bending it, and squeezing it, and pulling on it. It hurts like the skin has been burned away, but

I don't say anything. I don't want to give my brother the satisfaction that he has nearly killed me.

"It's okay," Egan says. "No break, anyway."

"It's okay?" I can hear Billy asking.

Billy's voice seems nervous.

"Just hit a nerve is all," Egan answers. "It will leave a bruise big as a house, though."

Bill Egan turns to my brother. "What the hell is going on?" he asks. "You think your brother is a baseball or something?"

Right, I'm thinking, or an old rug to beat the dust outta.

"I just wanted to stop him," Billy says. "It's a family matter, you know?"

That's all you have to say in the neighborhood if you don't want anyone asking questions. Just mention the word *family*, and the mouths shut like clams.

We are outside the club now, and I am sitting on a car fender on 52nd Street.

"I have to take you home," my brother says.

"Yeah?" I say. "Well, I don't want to go."

"Mommy is worried," he says. "She was up all night."

"I don't want to go through it all with her," I say. "Sister Alphonsus wants to see her, and they are going to kick me out of school."

"They are not going to kick you out of school," he says.

"Sister said it, that I won't graduate."

"You just have to go home," Billy says, "and talk to Mommy about this. Just tell her, and she'll go see Sister Alphonsus and get it all straight."

"I don't want to go home, Billy," I say. "She is going to hate me for causing all this trouble."

Billy is quiet for a while. The cars going down Second Avenue are beeping their horns, and a bunch of kids are lined up now to get into Kips Bay. Finally, he grabs me by the neck, but gently, and pulls me off the car.

"Let's walk a little," he says as we begin to walk toward Second Avenue, " 'cause I want to tell you what I read at school yesterday. It's a poem by this poet Robert Frost, and in it he is talking about what we are talking about now, and he says that home is the place that, when you go there, they always have to let you in. Get it?"

"So?" I say, because I really don't get it.

"So," Billy says, "you have to feel that there is something between you and Mommy that will let you tell her all about Sister Alphonsus, and let her at the same time believe in you so that she'll go to Sister Alphonsus and work it out."

It all sounds easy, but I know it is more complicated than just saying "work it out."

"What about running away?" I ask.

"Work it out with Mommy," Billy says, "and take your punishment."

That's the thing I don't like, the punishment part, and I am wondering why Billy is saying "Mommy" all the time? I wish I could just get out of all this kid part of my life.

"What kind of punishment?" I ask.

"You can handle it," he says.

"And why are you saying 'Mommy' like a kid?"

"I don't know," he says. "She's feeling so bad, it just seems right. Mom, Mommy, what difference does it make? You know who I mean, right?"

Billy puts his arm around my shoulder as we walk the concrete. We walk a couple of blocks like this, without saying anything more.

Then, as we're passing 55th Street, I look into his eyes. I never saw his eyes so blue. I smile at him, saying, "So they hafta let you in when you go home, huh?"

"Yeah," he says, "they have to."

Chapter Thirty-two

I am in the library now at Kips Bay Boys Club, a long and narrow room with polished wooden walls. It is like being in an apartment on Sutton Place, because it has a rich smell, and the furniture is all made of wood, and is shining.

Betty Fallon is the librarian, and I have been sitting with her almost every night for the last few months, trying to read more, like I promised my mother I would do. She has been giving me a different book every week, like *The Last of the Mohicans* and *The Prairie,* books that tell the story of how wild America was when it started to be a country with people from Ireland and France and England. I don't take the books home, but read them in the library, sitting there at the end of a long, spindly table. We talk a lot about the books whenever I'm there, and I tell Betty how I pretend I am in the books, too, that I am behind a tree or hiding in a shed when everything happens, and I have to try to save my own skin. And Betty laughs. She is always laughing and putting her hand on my arm. I feel I can really talk to her. She gave me a book called *The Corsican Brothers,* and the book made me feel sad because of how close these brothers were. One could know what the other was doing even if one was in Italy and the other in England. I wish I had someone who I was so close to that I could feel it if they were hit in the head, even if they were in another country.

I guess I feel close to Billy, no matter what happened with the pool stick. But he is so much older than me, two years, that it would be hard for us to be close like the Corsican brothers. Maybe, if I had a girlfriend, I could be close to her.

"You know, Betty," I say, "I don't have anybody to be close to like in *The Corsican Brothers*."

"You have your friends," Betty says. She is sitting behind her desk at the front of the room, up on a step, like an altar.

"I do have a lot of friends, like Walsh and Scarry, and those guys."

"Well, you can be close to them, can't you?"

"No, not with guys. You can't tell guys things that are bothering you 'cause they'll call you a faggot."

Betty smiles in a kind of surprise.

"Oh, Dennis," she says, "don't use words like 'fag.' It's like using bad words against Negroes or Puerto Ricans or the Italians."

"Yeah," I say. "My mother always says 'guineas,' and the other words."

"She probably grew up with those words," Betty says, nodding. "Some people just grow up combing their hair one way, and it never occurs to them to comb it another way. That's true with the way we speak as well. I don't think your mother means to be mean, ever. Do you?"

"I don't know," I answer. "She doesn't like the Italians much. But the only girls I like are the Italian ones."

"Anyway," Betty says, "now, what about you? What kind of things are bothering you?"

"Lots of things, I guess." I say this looking away for a moment. "I am always thinking about things in my life."

"Like what?"

Betty smiles at me, and I smile back at her.

I begin to think about the talk my mother had with Sister Alphonsus, and how I had to promise that I would work harder to do all my homework and to study for the tests. I never told them about the library down at Kips. Maybe if I told them, my mother would have let me come to Kips instead of keeping me in the house every night for a week because I ran away.

I close my eyes for a minute because I feel my heart beginning to beat like a tom-tom. I am thinking now how happy it makes me to talk to Betty. Not just having-a-good-time kind of happy, but I have a good feeling that she is my friend.

But no matter how things are going, if they are good or bad, I still am not crazy about school. And there's something else lately. I've been thinking a lot about my father, that I don't know what is going on with him, and what kind of a place he's in, and if people are still being mean to him, tying him up or beating him. The thoughts about him just come up without expecting them. I could be washing my toes in the kitchen bathtub and I could suddenly wonder if my father washed his toes, too, or if someone was washing them for him. Or I could be in the movies and suddenly forget the movie and wonder if he ever goes to a movie, or if they have television there in that upstate hospital. Does he ever listen to Bing Crosby or to Dennis Day?

Shit, it bothers me all the time.

"Betty," I say, opening my eyes, "can I tell you something that you can't tell anyone ever?"

"Sure you can," she answers.

"I mean it is like confession, where you can't say anything even if I murdered someone."

"Did you murder someone?" she asks, pretending to be surprised. "Maybe Father O'Rourke for his long sermons?"

I am laughing now. Betty makes things so easy.

"No," I say, and I begin to choke on my words. "I . . . I . . . I want to tell you about my father."

Betty leans over and cups her face in her hands.

"My father," I say, "is in a place where they beat him up and give him shock treatments—you know, they put wires into his brain and all that." I am trying to be as casual as I can be, like I am talking about the color of my brother's basketball uniform.

"Your father is in a mental institution?" she asks.

I am staring at Betty. It is so hard to speak, and I think she knows this. She doesn't say anything, but waits until I can put the words I want to say together in my mind.

"My mother always said," I continue, "that my father was in the hospital because he fell from a truck when he worked for the Railway

Express, and he can't walk, but I heard my Aunt Kitty talking about him being in this mental place."

"You mean a hospital?"

"A state asylum."

"Oh, Dennis," Betty says, reaching out to hold my hand, "that's too bad he is sick like that, but you know it is just another sickness, like having the mumps."

I know Betty is just trying to put flowers around the coffin, which is something my mother says when she thinks people are trying to be nice.

"Yes," I say, pulling my hand back a little, "I guess I know all that, but my mother doesn't know that I heard Aunt Kitty, and she keeps talking about him being in the hospital because of his legs and all, and I can't go because kids aren't allowed in, and she thinks I don't know about it being a different kind of hospital."

I feel like crying now, but I know I won't. So I look around for something to count to take my mind off my mother and the way she lied to me.

I see all the books lining the shelves from one end of the room to the other, and I stare at them and begin counting the spines.

"What are you doing?" Betty asks. I guess she sees how I am trying to count the books.

"I am counting the books because . . ."

"Because?"

"Oh," I say, now feeling a little embarrassed. "I . . . I don't know, I just count things if I think I might start to bawl."

"Oh, Dennis," she says, putting her hand on my arm. "Why do you want to cry?"

I move away again, but just a little.

"Because my mother didn't tell me the truth about my father being in the hospital because of something mental."

"But can't you see, Dennis," Betty says, sitting back in her chair, "that your mother doesn't want to hurt your feelings, that she wants to protect you?"

I see that Betty's eyes, big and blue like the Virgin's coat, have gotten bigger and shinier. She is such a pretty woman, and she is smiling. She has the kind of smile that tells you she could be anybody's friend, if a friend was needed. I know that she doesn't want me to feel bad about my mother, or about my father, either.

"Yes," I say, "but . . . but . . . why should she lie to me? Why couldn't she just trust me?"

"Did she tell Billy any different?" Betty asks.

"I don't know," I say, shrugging my shoulders. "I think I'm mad at Billy, anyway, because he hit me with a pool stick."

"Your brother didn't hit you with a pool stick." Betty looks like she really is surprised this time.

I roll up my sleeve and show Betty the bruise that is still on my arm, the one that I don't think will ever go away. I don't say anything, but I wonder why she would think that I said something that wasn't true.

"Well," Betty says, "brothers fight sometimes. Look at the Morgan brothers. They fight a lot, but they are always together, aren't they?"

"I suppose," I answer. "But I don't know if she told Billy, and I don't want to ask him."

Betty gets up from her chair now and puts her arms around me. I try to move away a little, but she holds me firm, and as I feel her pressing me into her I just relax there until she holds me out by the shoulders.

"Maybe," she says, "you should ask. You have these questions in your mind, and they will have nowhere to go unless you let them out of your mouth, and there is no one better than your mother to ask about them."

She gives me another little hug and takes a book from her desk. It is called *Tom Sawyer*. She hands it to me, and I look at it. It is pretty ragged, but the cover has a picture of a boy without shoes, and he's painting a fence.

"You'll like it," she says, "I promise. And you don't have to read it here. Take it home for a week."

I run out of the library and jump down the black marble stairs in twos. It is a surprise to me that Kips Bay has all these men, in the pool, the gym, the woodworking shop, the clay and the jewelry shops, and the game room, and, besides all that, they have a woman like Betty who can help you out if you are in a jam with homework or have trouble with a drunken father or something.

I wouldn't mind so much if I had a drunken father, though. At least he'd be home.

I am thinking again about what a big neighborhood this is as I turn the corner on 52nd Street and walk up Second Avenue. The East Fifties, from here to the Queensboro Bridge, from Sutton Place over to Third Avenue. I know guys, and girls, too, on every street, almost in every building. Over a hundred people, I suppose. I wonder where they go when they need to talk to someone about something that is bothering them. Maybe they can go to a police station if they don't belong to Kips. Maybe to a church, if they don't mind confession.

I throw *Tom Sawyer* on the kitchen table. I am going to also tell my mother about all the books I've been reading at Kips. The kitchen light is out, and I can see her legs in the living room. She is sitting on the couch, reading a magazine. She is always reading something whenever she sits down. She hardly ever watches the television. This one is the second television Uncle Andy has given us, but the first one worked a little better. The new one is probably older and has too many lines rolling from the top to the bottom.

My mother has been pretty mad at me since I ran away, and I wonder how she'll act with me now. Mothers, I think, usually forget about it when their kids hurt their feelings, but when it comes to running away, I don't know.

I sit next to her. She kisses me but doesn't say anything. She is staring at me, and I wonder if she smells the cigarette smoke of the one cigarette I had before I went to Kips. A long time passes as she continues to stare at me, as if I was a painting at the Metropolitan or a statue.

"How are you?" she says finally.

I lean in next to her, and I inhale the smell of Clorox coming from her white blouse. Anything white in my house smells of bleach, because my mother is such a stickler about getting things clean. Her hands, too, usually smell of Clorox, because when she is not reading she is always with her hands in the sink, washing shirts and things for people. It is a hard smell, but it is such a clean smell that it is relaxing.

And I do need to relax as I figure out a way to ask her about my father being in the hospital.

"Okay," I answer.

"I've been reading this interesting story about the Pope," she says. "Let me read it to you."

Good. If she wants to read to me, that means running away is something she is forgetting about.

My mother loves to read to us. When we were kids, my mother used to read the Letters to the Editor and the Inquiring Photographer columns to us every day, and get excited about the things she was reading.

"Yes," she would say, "I agree, and we should all write to President Truman about that," or "That is such a load of baloney that they could get rich by selling it in Brooklyn."

"How come, Mommy?" I once asked her.

"People love baloney in Brooklyn," she said.

And so she is reading now about how the Pope was the first Pope ever to come to America, when he was a monsignor or something, and her voice is light and singsong. She has a real New York accent, and when she wants to say *bottle,* she says *ba-ull.* The nuns are always harping about the New York accent, like saying *toid* for *third,* and that the bosses at the insurance companies will never give us jobs if we have New York accents. But I love to hear my mother read, and especially when she says *ba-ull.*

Now, though, I am trying to figure out a way to get her to stop reading. I am not certain how I can bring the subject of the hospital up, but I know I want to say something before Billy gets home. He is allowed to stay out an hour later than I can if he is finished with his homework.

I guess I will just interrupt her, although she will probably say that I am being impolite. The only thing my mother thinks is worse than wearing a dirty shirt is being impolite. "Thank you" are my mother's favorite words, and "yes, please," and "may I this" and "may I that," and excuse me, pardon me, and get on your feet if a lady enters the room or else you'll be like all the ragamuffins who live over on Third Avenue and turn into a statue glued to your chair, and don't forget to take your hat off indoors, because gentlemen never wear a hat with a roof over their heads.

Finally, I work up the courage to risk being impolite. It is not easy because I don't really want to talk to her about this. I don't want her to have to admit that she has been lying. "You will never have any friends if you lie," that's what she always says.

"Mom," I begin with a hesitation, "could I make you a cup of tea?"

She puts the magazine down beside her and takes her glasses off.

"You should say excuse me," she says. I knew she would say that.

"I'm sorry," I say. "Excuse me, your most worshipful lady."

She laughs now and pats my leg.

"No thanks, Dennis," she says. "I could never sleep if I had tea now."

I shift some on the couch and then say, "Could I ask you something?"

"Sure," she answers.

"Did you ever have a conversation with Daddy about me? I mean, doesn't he want to see me? Does he ever ask about me?"

"Of course he does, honey," she says. "But they don't let kids in the hospital there. I told you a hundred times."

I was hoping she wouldn't say that again, even now when I'm thirteen, and I can't just let her say it again and leave it alone. It's been too many years of saying this, and me believing it, too.

"I know, Mom," I say, shaking my head, "but you never told me he was in a mental place."

I can feel all the muscles in her body get tight, and she picks the magazine up again and begins to flip through it. She doesn't look at me, but keeps flipping the pages. Two minutes must pass. It is so silent, no noise at all except these pages in the magazine being flipped.

Finally, she stops.

"Who told you that?" she demands.

"I heard it," I say.

"Where did you hear it?"

"I heard Aunt Kitty talking to Uncle Tracy, that's all. And I told Betty about it down at the Kips library, and she said I should just talk to you about it."

My mother turns on the couch and faces me.

"You told Betty," she says, "about your father being in an insane asylum?"

"I told her you told me he was in the hospital because he hurt his legs."

I can almost feel how upset she is, because the couch seems to be shaking.

"Dennis," she says, her voice getting louder now, "you must never tell anyone these things, about your father, or about us being on welfare, or about not having any money. Or anything in our lives. This is our secret. It's our lives. People are always trying to butt in."

She stops now and points her finger at me.

"Nobody," she says, "should know our business. Do you understand, Dennis?"

She makes this ugly face when she is mad at me, like she is disgusted with something, like there is some dead fish around or something that smells wicked. I am so sorry that she is angry with me, and I am sorry now that I said anything to Betty. How would Betty know that my mother would get so mad at me and that everything in our family is such a big secret? And that people are trying to know our business?

I am feeling ashamed now, and I don't know why. There is no reason for me to be ashamed, but still that is what I feel. I don't say anything more, but I get up from the couch and go into the kitchen and turn the light on. I grab *Tom Sawyer* from the table and go into my room and throw the book on the upper bunk. I can read, maybe, and calm down.

Why are we so different, goddammit? Different from everyone I know. Why do we have to have all these secrets that separate everyone, including us here in apartment 26? Why should I have to feel so apart from my mother?

I am in my pajamas and reading as my brother comes home. He doesn't say anything and quickly gets into the bottom bunk.

I am wondering if I should ask him what he knows about Daddy and about the mental asylum. He has never mentioned it to me. But what if he doesn't know? What if he never heard anyone talking about poor Daddy getting beat up in the shower at some mental asylum?

What will he think if he doesn't know? Will I make him sick with worrying about it?

"Turn the light out, will you?" Billy says.

I can't read, anyway, and so I turn the light out. But I know I'm not going to get any sleep, not when I have all these questions. Like Betty said, they will have nowhere to go unless I let them out of my mouth.

"Billy," I say, "what do you know about our father?"

There. I've said it, asked it. I can't do anything about it now.

"He's in a mental institution," Billy says, and I can hear him pulling the sheet up over his head.

"How come you never told me?" I ask.

"There's never any reason to talk about it, Dennis," he says. "And a long time ago, Uncle Andy told me that I shouldn't talk to anyone about it, so I didn't."

"Uncle Andy told you that?"

"Yeah," Billy says. "He told me about the hospital and all, and then said not to talk about it."

"Shit," I say.

"Why," Billy says, "what's the matter?"

"How old were you?"

"I don't know, eight, maybe nine."

"Shit, you knew all this time and never said anything?"

"We never talk about it, Dennis."

I am climbing down from the top bunk now.

"Shit," I say, over and over, as I walk through the kitchen and the living room and into my mother's bedroom.

I pull the light cord, and my mother jumps up.

"What's the matter?" she asks.

"Could you get up?" I ask.

"What's the matter?" she asks again, sitting up in the bed.

"I just want to know one thing, Mom," I say, standing there in my pajamas. "Why didn't you tell me about it a long time ago? Why didn't you think I was old enough to know about my own father?"

I can see her shoulders going into a slump. She suddenly looks so tired, and she begins to whisper. "Oh, Dennis, Dennis, Dennis."

"Well?" I ask, folding my arms.

"I just never thought," she said, "that you wouldn't feel bad if you knew. I didn't want you to feel bad, Dennis."

"That's not it, Mom," I say. "I don't care about feeling bad or not. I just want to know why you don't trust me?"

My mother looks away for a second, and she says, "I do trust you, I trust both of you. What do you want to know, what do you want me to tell you?"

"Is he okay, is he hurt, is he getting beat up?" I ask these questions like they are bouncing off the sides of a pinball machine.

My mother smiles at these questions. "Yes," she says, "he is not in that awful Greenland hospital anymore but up in Poughkeepsie State and the people there are very nice to him. Believe me, I have seen them being nice many times."

"All right, good, Mom," I say, turning. "I'm sorry to wake you up."

"You didn't wake me up, Dennis," she says.

"Good, Mom," I say, "because I wouldn't want to disturb you."

I go to our room and climb back to the top bunk. I pull the sheet up and adjust my eyes to the dark. Billy doesn't say anything at all, and I leave him to his own thoughts.

God, I am thinking.

Shit.

God.

Anyway, I'm thinking, at least I'm not alone in all of this anymore.

Chapter Thirty-three

*B*illy is a junior counselor at Kips Bay Summer Camp this year, and so I'm home alone. It is a hot night, and I have a wet rag around my neck, and I'm trying to sleep on the floor. Anything to cool off. My mother is asleep, and probably dreaming about how mad at me she is, because she found a couple of the tiniest pieces of tobacco in my shirt pocket.

She treats me like I'm in the third grade. And she never would have found it if she didn't have to iron my polo shirts all the time. I'm the only guy on the street who has ironed polo shirts.

Goddammit, I hate that I can't get out of this being a kid.

She made such a big thing about it, smelling my breath, smelling my shirt, smelling everything around me, searching for the dreaded tobacco stench. I wanted to say that she could be smelling her own cigarettes if she smelled anything at all. But it's better to keep cool and collected.

"Tom Harris," I said to her, making up a fast story, "put his wallet in my shirt pocket yesterday when he got up at bat, when we were playing stickball in the street, so it wouldn't fall out of his pocket, in case he had to run fast if he hit a homer down over two sewers, and so I guess he had some tobacco in his wallet or something."

It's not a complete lie. We were playing stickball, and Tom did put his wallet in my shirt pocket, next to my cigarettes.

"Go to bed," she said, "just go to bed. I don't want to talk about it."

"I can't go to bed, Mom."

"Just go to bed."

"Mom, it's only seven o'clock, and it doesn't even get dark until nine."

"Okay, then," she said, her arm gliding like an ice-skater over the ironing board, "just read a book first and wait until it gets dark. Then go to bed. You are making a spectacle of yourself, thirteen years old and smoking like you were a truck driver or a stevedore."

Sometimes I don't understand the way my mother develops her thoughts. She is always saying that I am making a spectacle of myself, like I am in the center ring at the circus, and I wonder how I am such a spectacle. And she says it's because I am being like a truck driver or a stevedore, who are not such spectacles. Nothing goes together. It would be like seeing monkey wrenches instead of knives and forks on the linen napkins at Joe's Original Restaurant. And so I just picked up *All Quiet on the Western Front,* the book Betty gave me a few days ago, and I read about dirty foxholes and dying soldiers until my eyes hurt.

I wish I was back at camp. At Kips Bay Camp up in Valhalla, New York, everything is bright and green and clear, and there is no mother to be on you about this and that. And even if there was a mother, there would be no time to listen to her complaints because you are always off somewhere hunting frogs or snakes, or playing flag football, or making lanyards for key chains and bracelets and necklaces.

I've been going to Kips Bay Camp for two weeks every summer since I was six years old. I think they give it to my mother for free, because I could never stay for a long three-week trip. If I had a three-week trip, I would still be there.

The first time I went to camp I went because I won first place in a "why I want to go to camp" essay contest. I was in the first grade, and I wrote a composition which was about a page long. I remember I wrote that I wanted to get away from the cars, because you can't play stickball in the street with all the cars coming through 56th Street, and that I had never been out of New York City except when I was four and went to Canada on a train when my Uncle Ronald died there, and my Aunt May paid for my mother to take Billy and me to the funeral so's all the relatives could see us.

The winning composition was more a letter than a composition, and I guess they sent it to everyone in the neighborhood. A director guy must have read it, and so he sent me a camp package, which, besides having cookies and candy that I had to share, also had a baseball glove and a baseball hat. My Uncle Phil had bought Billy a baseball glove for Christmas, but I just got a sweater.

But this package came as a complete surprise, and I yelled when I opened it. That baseball glove was the best present I ever got, and I used it all the time for years until Uncle Phil bought me a professional one.

But it came with some bad luck, because the man who sent it, this director, decided to stop in the camp one day to pay me a visit. He had another big box of candy and cookies, and he went looking for me.

Archie was the head counselor that year, and he and Archie searched for an hour, but they couldn't find me, for that was the day my counselor made me make my bed three times before I got the hospital corners right, and I was so mad at him that I decided to run away. I took a flashlight, even though it was before lunch, and went into the woods. I still remember how frightened I was, because I got lost in five minutes, and it seemed like I was in the woods all day before they found me.

Archie was ready to send me home. He showed me the box that the man had left for me, filled with all kinds of stuff, cookies and candies and games, but said that I didn't deserve it. So he left it out in the dining hall at dinner for the counselors to give as rewards to their best campers.

It did not bother me that Archie gave away the goodie box. That's the way things are at camp. You're supposed to be having a great time, and if you're not, it's probably your fault. And if it's your fault, you don't get the prize, and that's the way it goes. Archie would never do anything bad to someone, but he will never let you get away with anything bad, either. That's the lesson at camp.

*   *   *

Now the sweat's coming out of my neck like Niagara Falls. All I can do is toss and turn on the hard floor, and so I decide to sleep out on the fire escape. It could be cooler there, and it's cleaner, anyway, than the roof.

The fire escape window is in my mother's room. I don't want to bother her, and so I grab a blanket and go out the front door and then down the long, narrow hall to the hall window. The hall back here is never mopped, and I'm walking in my bare feet through an inch of dust. I have to wrestle with the window a little before it opens, which makes me sweat more, but I can feel the live air as I climb out to the fire escape, and I am thinking that at least I'm out of the dead air of the apartment.

I am in my short cotton underpants, barefoot and bare-chested, and I throw the old army blanket across the rusty iron strips of the fire escape. I lie down. There is not much room between the building, the rails, and the fire stairs, and I'm curled up like a puppy in a corner. Still sweating like mad, I say a prayer to Saint Jude, the patron of hopeless causes, to send a breeze my way. I'm maybe as uncomfortable as I have ever felt in my life. I'm not sure of what is bothering me. The spaces between the iron slats of the fire escape, or thinking that I could be up at Kips Camp if we could afford another two-week trip, or maybe just that my mother still hasn't mentioned anything about our father since we had that talk in her bedroom.

I don't know why she avoids it. She could tell me what happened to him, how he got that way, why they won't let me in to see him. There is still this big absence, this big empty hole, in the middle of our lives.

And, then, there is Barbara Cavazzine, who I now like more than Marilyn Rolleri. I asked her to go to the movies with me or to meet me there some Saturday.

She said no.

She didn't say "No thanks," or "My mother won't let me," or "I like you but I like some other guy more." She just said "No," and that was that. I guess I will have to ask her again.

But I saw someone else I also liked, but I don't think she comes from this neighborhood. All I know is her name is Virginia. Maybe I can get to meet her.

Why is it so hard to get a girlfriend on 56th Street?

I don't know how long I have been sleeping, but I awake suddenly because I feel the whole fire escape shaking. I smell smoke as I open my eyes, and try to adjust to the night's dark. There is a giant in front of me, like a character in "Puss in Boots," with big boots folded over below the knees, and he is picking me up as a group of other firemen are running up the stairs behind him.

"Hey, kid," the fireman says.

"Let me down," I say to him, thinking, I'm not a kid, for Chris-sakes.

A cloud of smoke sweeps down over us, and I begin to choke uncontrollably. I look up and see the flames coming from the apartment window above us, Mr. Sorenson's apartment. My eyes are hurting like someone put mud in them.

"Sure thing, kid," the fireman says, putting me down. "Let's get you off this fire escape, anyway. You'd be in a lot of trouble when they break the windows upstairs."

He has me by the hand as we go to the hallway window.

"The firemen," he says, "have to break the windows, you know."

He grabs a huge ax which he had put down, climbs in first, and helps me into the hallway. The fire is above, but I can still smell the smoke here in the hall.

"Hey, kid," the fireman says as we walk into the hallway, him in his huge boots and me in my bare feet, "what do you think of that DiMaggio? Is he a hero, or what?"

Mr. Sorenson's apartment, and maybe even Mr. Sorenson himself, is burning up, and he's asking me about Joltin' Joe DiMaggio.

"Nobody better," I say.

I love this fireman. This fireman is like Father Luke, and I wonder what you have to do to be a fireman.

There is a lot of noise in the hallway as the firemen are dragging up the hose. I see that my mother is sticking her head out of the apartment door.

"Just stay in your house," the fireman says to her, "and you'll be okay."

He messes my hair and runs back to the fire escape, and in a second he is gone out the window. My mother has no idea that I was out on the fire escape, and it must seem to her that I came out of thin air. She puts her arm around me and squeezes hard as the door shuts.

"It's Mr. Sorenson's apartment upstairs," I say. "There's a lot of smoke."

"Ohh," my mother says.

I look at her hazel eyes, and they show that she is afraid. Her eyes are like street signs to me, because you always know where she is when you look at them, and now I can see the fear in them.

"It's okay, Mom," I say to her. "The fireman said so. He said that we'll be okay and that DiMaggio is a hero."

I am back on the floor in the living room, the wet rag again around my neck, and in the new quiet of the dark I am thinking about that fireman. It must be something to be a fireman. He was so cool, a real cool cat.

I wonder if he has children, maybe a boy or a couple of boys, that he takes to Yankee Stadium to see DiMaggio.

Chapter Thirty-four

$\mathcal{I}$t is now fall. I am fourteen years old, and in public school.

There was a big ruckus about going to a public school. Everybody knows that kids go to Catholic high schools when they graduate St. John's, and it's like getting caught at first on a bunt to go to public school, like you're destined to be out. Even Sister Alphonsus, who was going to fail me in everything, told me that I would be better off going to a minor-league Catholic school like St. Agnes than to go to public school.

And my mother, too. She went on and on about how good Billy is doing up in the Bronx at Cardinal Hayes High School. Billy would do good at Nortre Dame if he was there, but my mother doesn't realize the difference between us, which is a simple difference. Billy *likes* school.

I begged her.

Another Catholic school would kill me, even if I could get in one of the not-so-good ones, which I thought pretty doubtful because of the bad grades. I just want to be out of it, away from the nuns and the priests. It's like being a duck-stepping Nazi storm trooper to be in Catholic school. Everything is all precision and discipline, and you can never talk without being first asked a question. And you are reading all the time, breakfast, lunch, and supper, in these big books they give you with stories about history or people who invent things or about soldiers going off to war to fight the Japs and the krauts.

All my friends who go to public school tell me that no teacher ever makes you do things like read, or gives you a bad time, and you can either do your homework or not, no difference to them, no sweat off their back. That was for me, to get away from the standing-up-straight-in-line stuff.

Public school is like heaven, where nobody bothers you.

And so now I'm in a school where I never go.

The School of Aviation Trades is on East 63rd Street. I get up in the morning, and I go to Jimmy's candy store on 62nd Street where "Sh-boom, Sh-boom" is always playing on the jukebox, and the guys who hang around wear leather jackets and have key rings hanging from their belts.

At least I don't have to wear a white shirt and blue tie anymore. I have this black windbreaker with my name printed on the front pocket. I know my mother would never be able to afford to buy me a leather jacket, but those leather jackets are so cool. Some of the guys put gloves through the shoulder flaps, like Marlon Brando in *The Wild One,* and nothing looks cooler than that.

I did go to class a few times, but the homeroom teacher kept changing, and each teacher who came in thought he was just there for the day, and no one ever took attendance. There is no point in going to school if no one takes the attendance, because you'll never be missed, and no one will think that you are in Jimmy's candy store where you can use the fifteen cents your mother gives you each day to buy singles, Lucky Strikes or Camels. And you only had to stick around the candy store until noon. The school is on a half-day schedule, because there are so many students who want to fix airplanes, and there's not enough space for everyone to go at the same time.

I never thought much about fixing airplanes, but SAT was a public school, which I wanted, and I could walk there from 56th Street, which by itself is a good enough reason to go there.

My mother thought I was doing great things in my new school, because each day I would tell her about these swell guys I knew, and how smart they were, and I would mix in a few names of books to make everything sound A-OK.

My mother would ask about the teachers, and when did the school have parent-teacher day like they did at St. John's, and I told her that they did things differently at public school, that they sent reports in the mail at the end of the term.

I was thinking that I could always tell her that the reports got lost in the mail.

Today, most of the guys went over to play pool, but I don't have the money for even a game of eight ball, so I am sitting in the rear of the candy store, on the back legs of an old wooden chair, leaning against a wall, watching Antone and a guy named Bullboy whose real name I don't know as they are dancing to the new Frankie Lymon and the Teenagers tune, "Why Do Fools Fall in Love?" They are not dancing with each other, but they have imaginary partners and they are twirling them out and in and it looks pretty funny.

Antone comes over to me when the music stops. He's a couple of years older than I am, and I think he lives in Queens or Brooklyn, maybe the Bronx.

"Hey, Smitty," he says, "give me a butt, huh?"

I have only two cigarettes left, and it isn't even noon yet. If I give him one, I'll be stuck for the rest of the day until I get back to 56th Street where I can grub some.

"C'mon, will ya," he says, holding his hand out.

His black leather jacket is open, and all the zipper chains are swinging back and forth. He has on a white shirt, and the collar is open and standing high in the back. He told us he has his shirts starched and pressed so that the collars stand up like this, like billboards. His hair is in a million curls and falls down into a point just above his nose, and with the collar sticking out like wings it looks like his head could fly away. He'd fly fast, too, I'm thinking, because the sides of his hair are greased down with Vaseline petroleum jelly, and smooth like the sides of an airplane.

He doesn't like it that I'm taking so long.

"C'mon," he says again, "give me a fuckin' bitchin' bastard cigarette. What are you, some guy who hugs the pillow and takes it in the brown spot, or what?"

The guys I grew up with don't talk like these guys do. Up here at SAT there is a never-ending contest to see how many curses you can get into a sentence. I look over and see that Bullboy is laughing. I am hoping that he doesn't ask me for a cigarette, too, as I reach into the pack and take out one cigarette.

Antone doesn't say thank you, but this doesn't bother me too much. He'll never meet my mother, anyway.

Some other guys come in, and Antone and Bullboy leave, and then some more guys come in. The candy store is just a place to smoke, and to waste time, and I am tired of just sitting back on this chair. No one has put any money in the jukebox, either, and so I think about going around to the school yard to see if anyone is playing against-the-wall stickball. I look around to see where I left the three-ring binder I carry around, and I see that some guy is sitting on it, on the floor next to the jukebox.

"Hey," I say to him, "you're sitting on my book."

The guy looks me up and down and gets off the book.

"Here," he says, shoving it across the floor, "take your fuckin' book."

It's easier most of the time to keep your mouth shut when somebody curses at you up here, because most of the time they don't mean anything by it.

I am walking down 63rd Street, toward the school building, and I suddenly hear my name called out.

"Dennis," I hear.

I am stunned to hear my mother's voice. I know I'll be in big trouble because I should be in class.

"Hey, Mom," I say. She is wearing her red coat that ties around the waist, and she has her head wrapped in a red kerchief. She looks good in these clothes, like she coordinates it before she leaves the house.

I am trying to be nonchalant. It is always good to be nonchalant because it is cool not to be raveled by things.

"Give us a kiss," she says. She is carrying a big paper bag, and she swings it as she puts her arms around me.

I know I am not in such trouble now, because she would never want a kiss if I was in trouble. And so I kiss her on the cheek, hoping none of the guys are around to see me.

I know I have to think fast, before she asks me any questions.

"I just came from shop class," I say. "Now I'm going around to history and social studies."

I know I am lying.

"Where is shop class?"

Her eyes now are like pinpoints, like she is a detective studying some clue.

"Around on 64th Street." The school is divided between both streets.

She thinks for a minute and shrugs her shoulders.

"I have a surprise for you," she says.

She is smiling as she changes from a detective back to my mother. I can tell she is happy for some reason. My mother is not happy so much, and I always feel good if I see her smiling.

"What's that, Mom?"

"Just take a look at this," she says, opening the bag.

She pulls out a green wool jacket and holds it up, here in the middle of the street. Across the back, in big white letters, it has the name of the school: AVIATION. It is brand-new, and I wonder how much money she had to pay for it.

My mother just began working for the New York Telephone Company. After all those years on welfare, I am finally old enough to leave home alone after school so she could go out to work. I know she doesn't make much money, especially as an operator in training.

Oh, man, I think. I feel so bad that she went and did this, spending all this money on this jacket.

Maybe I could have gotten a cheap leather jacket with all the zippers, and here she has gotten me this jacket from the school where I never go.

She is looking at me now, waiting for some response.

Now is the time I could tell her about the black leather jackets, but I don't know if she would like those. There are certain clothes she hates, like pegged pants with pistol pockets, and maybe she would think leather jackets are bad for me.

But she is gleaming at me. She is so proud that she has given me this jacket.

I should smile, I think, and I do as I take my windbreaker off. Even if I don't like it. I can see in her eyes that she has a little happiness, and I wish I could add to it by loving the damn jacket. But I can't. The only thing I can do is to not cut down that little bit of happiness that came to her by giving the jacket to me.

And so I put it on. It fits just right, and I put the collar up, so that I feel a little like a brizzer, a king of the hill, a guy who's cool and with it.

"It looks great," she says. "It is just the thing, now that you are in high school and everything is going so good for you."

She stands back a little and folds her hands one into the other the way she does when she is studying something. Her smile goes from one end of her face to the other.

I am feeling worse now, because the first thing I think about is I wonder if the guys around the jukebox will think the jacket is for faggots.

But my mother has taken the windbreaker, and I have no choice but to wear this one.

"Thank you, Mom," I say, giving her a kiss on the cheek. "I have to go or I'll be late."

I am walking down Second Avenue when I again hear someone call my name. This time I don't recognize the voice. I look around, but I don't see anyone.

"Over here, Dumbo," the voice cries.

I turn and see a guy I know from 56th Street, an Italian named DooDoo, his head hanging out from a window of the Second Avenue bus. The bus is stopped for a light, and I walk over to it. I can see the bus is packed with people. I look up at him.

DooDoo is a kid who works on a garbage truck that his father owns, and is maybe a year older than me. His little sister could never say Dominic, so he got tagged with DooDoo, because his father could never stop laughing when the sister called him that.

It is a stupid name, but it is the only one that anyone knows to call him, and reminds me of guys who have names like Lipshitz or Fokker or Handman. And then there's the Dicks of the world. I don't know a single Dick who doesn't wish they named him something else.

"Who you calling Dumbo?" I say. "At least my name doesn't mean crap in a diaper."

"Oh, yeah?" he says, laughing, and squinting his eyes so that he looks Chinese.

"Yeah," I say.

DooDoo then fast pulls up a lunger from deep within his throat, and he spits it out at me. I jump away as quick as I can, but part of it lands on my face. More goes on the jacket that I haven't been wearing more than an hour.

I can feel the blood rushing to my cheeks. I must be beet-red, and I look around to see if anyone has seen what DooDoo has done.

DooDoo is laughing, and I feel my face stinging from all the redness. The muscles around my eyes are tightening. I don't know what to do, being out here on the avenue, all alone, looking up, the whole busload of people looking down at me.

"Dumbo," he yells again as the bus pulls away.

I can't just stand here, and I begin to run with the bus. I am pointing my finger at him as I run. I have to let these people on the bus know that I'm not going to just stand there and do nothing.

"I'll get you later," I yell in return. "You punk."

I realize as I am running that I am not just yelling. I am screaming. And everyone on the street is looking at me.

"Yeah, yeah," I can hear DooDoo say as the bus gains speed down the avenue.

I am sitting on a car fender now, across the street from DooDoo's house. Walsh and Scarry are with me. Scarry has in his hands a *New York Times,* folded in three parts like a letter, and he is rolling it up. Rolled and tied together with strings, it is the closest thing to a free football that exists. A *New York Times* football sails through the air like a glider when you throw the bomber pass.

"Let's play touch," Scarry says as he knots the third and last string.

"Let's wait a little while longer," I say, " 'cause DooDoo's gotta come out sometime."

"Why don't you just forget about it?" Walsh says.

"You can't let somebody spit on you, Bobby," I answer.

"He could kick the crap outta you," Scarry says, "maybe."

"So," I say, "as long as he knows he can't spit on me, I don't care."

"C'mon," Walsh says, "let's play football."

I can feel my stomach turning, waiting here for DooDoo. I don't want to fight anyone, but you have to take a chance on getting hurt once or you'll get hurt all the time. I learned that with Shalleski.

Finally, I see DooDoo come out of his building, which is next to the Hotel Sutton on the other side of the street from my house. There is only one step on his stoop, and he is just stepping off it when he sees me charging toward him. He knows what to expect, and he puts his hands up fast. But it is too late, and I punch him five times in a row, right, left, right, left, right, and DooDoo is falling to the sidewalk.

He gets up slowly and turns his back to me.

I could hit him again, but you can't Jap someone like that, hit someone whose back is to you. It would get around the neighborhood that you were a Jap puncher, and people would think you're a creep and a coward.

DooDoo turns, points his finger at me, and says, "I'll fight you Saturday, down by the river. I'll get you."

DooDoo then turns and walks back onto his one-step stoop and into his building.

It is Saturday morning, and a crowd of us are down by the river, in the 56th Street park. Walsh is holding my Aviation jacket. Doo-Doo is taking things out of his pockets and putting them on a park bench. Other guys, like Jurgensen and the Harris brothers and Jimmy Burton, are standing around us. They heard there was a fight, and they came around to see.

I got DooDoo good the other day, but I took him by surprise then.

Now he is waiting for me to come toward him, his fists out to either side of him, clenched tightly.

He moves in and throws a punch. The last thing I think of before it hits me is that I have to be fast and quick like my brother Billy. But I am not being fast enough, and it crashes into the side of my face. And before I can recover from this punch, I get a second one, just above my eye on the other side of my face. Shit, I am thinking. It is hurting, stinging like a hard slap.

I know I have to move fast, and so I lunge forward at him, grab him around the neck, and pull him to the ground. He gets out of the headlock easy, and now he is on top of me, and he is fast, fast like Billy, punching like he was hammering nails. He gets me in the eye again, and in the mouth, and I feel the skin smarting, burning.

I grab him around the neck again, and this time I squeeze like a vise, and there is no way he can get out of it. He is punching and flailing, but he isn't hitting anything but my back. I am holding on like I'm on a branch over a cliff, and now he is pushing his hand just under my arm so that he can breathe a little. He keeps trying to punch with the other hand.

But nothing is happening in the fight. He can't do anything, and I don't want to do anything except keep holding onto him. My face is hurting a lot now, and I know that if he gets a chance to belt me a few more times, I'll get hurt good.

"It looks like it's even," I hear Scarry say.

"Yeah," Frankie Harris says, "it's even."

"You guys wanna break it up?" Marty Harris, Frankie's twin, says.

"Yeah," Walsh says, "break it up."

"You want to break it up, DooDoo?" I ask.

"If I get free," DooDoo says, "I'll kick the shit outta you."

"You're not doin' anything," Scarry says.

"If it's even," DooDoo says, "I'll break it up."

And so I let go of DooDoo's neck, and he gets up.

I put my hand out.

"Friends," I say.

It would be hard, I know, for DooDoo to refuse to shake. No one would like him if he didn't shake.

DooDoo shakes, and goes off up the block with a couple of guys. Walsh is putting my Aviation jacket around my shoulders. I don't feel bad that it was even. At least I didn't lose. I stood there, face-to-face, and he knows I stood there because I couldn't just let him spit on me like that.

It is worth a black eye and a bloody lip to let him know that.

Chapter Thirty-five

$\mathcal{I}$ am on my way to Kips Bay Boys Club. It is early afternoon, and it has just stopped raining. I walk past the Hotel Sutton, just across from my building. Charlie Ameche, a squat, fat guy, is the doorman there, and he calls me over.

"Here, kid," he says, handing me a dollar, "go get me some coffee, four sugars, no milk."

He doesn't ask me to do this. He just orders. But I don't mind, and I go to Harry's Luncheonette next to DooDoo's house for the coffee. It's hard to get Harry's attention because he's talking to his wife about a bunch of Puerto Ricans who broke into the Congress this morning and mowed down five congressmen.

"Just leave me alone," Harry's wife says, "and let me do the scrambled eggs on toast, huh?"

I don't know any Puerto Ricans at all, I am thinking as Harry gets the coffee for me. Not even at SAT. Almost everybody in New York is Irish or Italian. There are a few exceptions, like the man in the Chinese laundry, or the Jews that run the delicatessen on 55th Street, but not many. Maybe Henry Castle on 54th Street could count as a Mexican, but I always think of him as Irish.

When I give Ameche the coffee and the change, he gives me a tip.

"Here, kid," he says, flipping a quarter to me, "go buy yourself a blow job."

I am laughing as I walk to Second Avenue. I would put the quarter in the poor box if I could just get Virginia Sabella to kiss me, and here is Ameche talking about a blow job.

Every neighborhood has a guy like Ameche, someone everyone knows to be a little off, a whack job they call him. The story is that he got to be crazy because when he was a kid his father beat him over the head with an anchor that was hanging in their living room on Second Avenue.

Ameche and Louie Daly were going fishing out in Sheepshead Bay in Brooklyn, and they had to leave at five-thirty in the morning to catch the boat. But Ameche had no alarm clock, and so they hung a rope down from the roof, a rope that Ameche was going to tie around his leg when he got into his bed down on the fourth floor. Louie was going to tug on the rope in the morning to wake him up.

"Just keep pulling on that goddamn rope, Louie," Ameche ordered him, "until I tell you it's okay, 'cause it's hard to wake me up."

"Right," Louie said, "right."

And then Ameche tied the rope to his father's leg when his father was sleeping, and in the morning the father was dragged out of his bed, and then his father practically went out the window before Ameche yelled up to the roof to tell Louie to stop pulling.

"You-a wanta to go fishin'," the father kept yelling as he hit Ameche's head again and again with the anchor, "you-a needa da boat, and den you needa da anchor."

The street is crowded with people because the sun has finally broken through the winter, and it's getting warmer out. I go toward Second, back past Harry's, past Ling's, the laundry down in the cellar, next to the auto repair shop, past the radio and TV repair shop, past Jasper's candy store where everybody plays the horses, past the empty lots and the corner vegetable stand. The old cobblestones on Second Avenue are shining with wetness, and everything in the neighborhood looks clean, like it has all been buffed with a rag.

I turn down Second because I'm meeting Walsh and Scarry and Jurgensen down at Kips, where they are playing basketball.

Pretty soon I won't have much time to just hang around and play ball. I've been going after this job at the East River Florist, and they just told me yesterday that I can work for them on Friday afternoons and all day Saturday. It's not a bad deal, either, thirty cents an hour.

I've been giving all my newspaper money to my mother, but I'm going to get to keep half of the florist money I earn, after I pay her back for a pair of Thom McAn shoes she bought me.

I see this guy I know, Frankie, on the corner of 54th Street.

I know him for a long time, since when we were kids and we all had bikes. We used to ride through Central Park, a gang of us from different streets. We all wore the same kind of hats, like that hat Marlon Brando wore in *The Wild One* when he walked around with his leather gloves through the straps across the shoulders.

Frankie is a quiet kid, but as tough as Rocky Marciano. Nobody mistakes his being quiet for a guy who can be pushed around. Now he is just standing here on the corner, and I am wondering what he is up to.

"Hey," I say to him.

"Hey, Dennis," he says, "where you going?"

"Kips."

"I never go there," he says.

"How come?"

"I dunno," he says. "Faggy stuff, waiting in line to play Ping-Pong. Got any smokes?"

"No," I say. "I'm gonna buy one-for-a-penny from Abbie. Want to walk me down to Moe's on 53rd Street, and I'll buy some potato chips?"

The quarter Ameche gave me makes me feel flush enough for a bag of potato chips.

"I can't," he says. "I'm waiting for a guy."

"What guy?" I ask.

"You ever smoke pot?" he asks.

"No," I answer. This is something we never thought about in our crowd on 56th Street.

"This guy," he says, "is supposed to come with some pot."

"You're gonna smoke pot?" I ask. I don't think I know anyone who smokes pot.

"Yeah," he says, "you wanna stick around I'll give you some tokes."

"What's a toke?" I never even heard this word up at SAT.

"A drag," he says. "You know, a puff."

"You ever smoke it before?" I ask.

"Yeah, sure," he says. "Everybody in my school smokes it."

Frankie goes to the Machine and Metal Trades High School up on 96th Street, and I am thinking if they are all smoking pot and working those big machines to shape the copper and sheet metal, they will all end up like Captain Hook looking for the alligator.

"I heard it makes you dizzy," I say.

"No, man," Frankie says, shaking his head. "High is not dizzy. High is like dreaming a great dream where all the colors are like on fire. And the sound is like you're in the middle of the phonograph. Stick around, Dennis, 'cause here he is now."

I do not recognize the guy who comes to us. Everyone says "Hey," and the boy gives Frankie a small brown paper bag. Frankie gives him two dollars.

"It's that easy?" I say. "Just stand on the corner and some kid brings you pot?"

"Naw," he says. "You hafta set it up. I set it up yesterday with this kid. He comes from Third Avenue, up around 59th Street, and he goes to my school."

"You like your school?"

"No," he says, "I never go. I just hang around there, you know? C'mon, we'll take a walk down by the river and smoke one of these."

Frankie lifts the opened bag up to my eyes, and I can see four hand-rolled cigarettes at the bottom.

"No," I say to him, "I gotta go play basketball. Maybe Saturday night when I get through with work."

"Yeah, sure," he answers, "maybe Saturday."

I don't think much about this, and I give him a small punch on the arm to say goodbye. He is such a friendly guy, but very different from my other friends. A mysterious guy, a loner. I could hang around with him, and I'd probably have a great time getting to know what makes him tick.

At Kips, I change into the club shorts and run out onto the basketball court in my undershirt. Scarry and Walsh and Jurgensen are there, doing layups, jump shots, sets from around the rim.

There is no place like Kips. The thing of it is that it's a building, and it is always there when you want to go there, like St. John's Church or the Metropolitan Museum. You can go as much as you want to these places, but some guys never go to any of them.

"About time," Scarry says to me. I guess they've been waiting to play two-on-two.

Scarry is semi-kneeling as he throws a set shot. It is a basket, but I knew it would be. Scarry is playing ball for LaSalle Academy, and he is the team's star. A basketball to Scarry is like a steering wheel to a bus driver, just something that makes everything else work.

Scarry is like my brother Billy, and he could even be better than Billy if he keeps working at it. He's broad-shouldered, and a tough player, elbows and hips all the way. If there is a way to get the ball on the rebound, he'll get it. Some college will pick him up someday, I am thinking, and if he was a little taller, he would go straight to the pros.

Walsh is big and skinny. Lanky. And his body moves like it was made of hinges. Walsh is more like me in playing this game, because he doesn't have that killer way to stop the other guy. He just wants to take shots from the outside and look like he has some style.

Jurgensen is heavier and stockier than all of us. He moves over the court like a farm tractor plowing a field of rocks, but he puts his heart into everything. Sometimes we call him Two-Wallet Joey, because he is always losing his wallet, and so he carries two, one in a back pocket and one in the front. He would be a good ballplayer if he was lighter and if he didn't drink so much beer. Anytime we go down to 51st Street park to drink beer, Joey always has his own package. Sometimes I'll drink two cans of Rheingold, and Scarry might drink one, but Joey gets two quarts, and puts his package between his knees and sips it in small gulps until he becomes legless. This is one of the reasons he is always losing his wallets.

It is a real pain carrying him to his hallway on 55th Street, and leaving him there to crawl his way up to his apartment. Joey's father has a good job, an engineer on a boat, or something like that, and so he goes away for days at a time, and that's when Joey puts his package on.

Joey was the smartest boy in our class at St. John's and got straight hundreds on all the tests. Things just come to him easily, and he made all the good high schools. He's in LaSalle with Scarry, but I know he likes the beer more than the books. His mother died when he was a kid, and maybe that's why.

I don't know what I would do if my mother died. Goddamn, it's something I wouldn't want to think about.

At least Joey has a good father who takes him to ball games, and if his father ever found out that Joey was drinking beer, I guess he would get beat, or maybe his father would send him away to a military school. I know his father wouldn't let him get away with swimming in a beer bottle if he knew about it.

Walsh and I play Scarry and Joey, and we have been at it for over an hour. We haven't won a game yet. Every time I pass the ball to Walsh, he shoots it. He never passes it back to me, even when I'm free and under the backboard. Walsh believes in himself and thinks that his one-man team is pretty good.

But Walsh never makes a basket. Sometimes I wave like I am trying to stop a locomotive, but he never passes the ball. I wouldn't pass it to him, except that Scarry is a hard and close ballplayer, and he gets so tight on me that I have to pass the ball out.

Scarry quits suddenly.

"I gotta go," he says. "I have homework."

"C'mon," I say, "we could do another half hour."

"I have homework, too," Jurgensen says. "If I don't get it done, they're gonna throw me outta school."

"It would take three Irish Christian Brothers," I say, "to lift you in order to throw you out."

"Naw," Jurgensen says. "I'm light, like a ballet dancer. You'd be surprised."

"Hey," Walsh says as they leave the court, "watch that talk about ballet dancers. I don't see you hanging around with the girls too much."

Jurgensen just raises his middle finger behind his back as the locker room door closes.

And so Walsh and I are left alone on the court to play horse, which is when one person has to duplicate the shot another person makes, if it is a bucket. I take three games straight because Walsh can't do the around-the-back layup that I have perfected.

I can tell Walsh is getting bored. He has a defeated look on his face.

"Let's quit," he says finally.

"How come?"

"I have to go home and do homework," he says, shrugging his shoulders.

"You're such a queer, Walsh," I say, "like Scarry and Jurgensen. Where is all that homework going to get you, anyway?"

Walsh laughs, saying, "It will get me through the night without my father beating my head against the wall with my algebra book."

Archie grabs me as I am pushing open the big doors to the stairs out to 52nd Street.

"Hey, son," he says, "give me a minute."

Archie has a different office ever since a guy named Russ came to work at the club, an office in the back by Mr. McNiven's office.

None of his trophies are in Archie's new office, but there are photographs of kids all over the walls. I see Scarry in a couple of them, and my brother Billy is in a few, too. There are a lot of the Friday night dances, and I see Barbara Cavazzine in a couple. I should ask her out again, I am thinking as Archie pulls his chair from around the desk and sits next to me.

"So," he says, "you're up at Aviation Trades, huh?"

Archie isn't one to beat around the bush, and I can tell what he is up to.

"Yeah," I answer, "right."

"And," he says, "you're going to school every day?"

"Right." I do go every day, anyway, so I'm not really lying. I just don't go to any of the classes.

"You are studying," he says, "and keeping up with everything there?"

"Right."

I feel I am being fried on a grill.

"Tell me about it," he says.

Archie wants to suck me into something here, but I don't know what. He must have heard something, maybe from Billy. Billy has been asking me a lot of questions about school lately, and I always try to put him off. I just mention the New York Knicks and he will automatically go off on a tangent about the McGuire brothers, and how either one of them can handle the ball better than anyone on the Minneapolis Lakers, who are the champs.

"There's nothing to tell," I say. "It's no different from any school, I guess."

I know I could just get up and walk out of Archie's office, like I did once before, but I don't want Archie on my back every time I see him. He's like the water fountain at Kips. He is here all the time, and never goes away.

"Do you like it there?" he asks.

"Sometimes I do, sometimes I don't."

"Do you have anything specific to say about it," he asks, "like is there a particular subject or teacher you like, or some sports?"

I don't want to outright lie to Archie, but I don't even know my teacher's name, except for Mr. Donahue in shop. And the only reason I remember him is that the guys called him Don't-a-You-Don-ahue the first day of class, because he told just about everyone to stop doing something.

"Don't bite your nails," he said to me as I was wondering what I was doing in a wing construction shop class.

"I like Mr. Donahue," I say.

"Mr. Donahue," Archie says, "good. Why do you like him?"

"I guess he's a good teacher. He pays attention, anyway."

"Are you paying attention to what you're doing?"

This is the setup now.

"What do you mean?" I ask.

"I mean," Archie says, leaning back in his chair, "you are telling me that everything is sweet and dandy, but that's not what I heard."

"Billy," I say. "I'm sure it was Billy who said something to you, right?"

"You know, son," Archie says, "we are not talking about another person here. There is just one name I am interested in. Dennis. I want you to know that people are interested in you, and I want to tell you what I think."

I begin to slouch in my chair, feeling that this is like a punishment just sitting here like this. People are interested in me? That's a big deal, right? It's just Billy bad-mouthing me to Archie, I bet.

"Sit up, son," Archie says, "will you? Be proud of yourself. You may be a smart, talented kid, but I think you are in danger of wasting your life away like an unwatered vine."

I don't say anything, though he waits to see if I do.

"Who," he says as he gets out of his chair, "who are the people we respect around here? Think about this, because you know the answer. It's the guys who jump up and say, 'Let's do it,' and 'Let's do it right and have a darn good time doing it.' Guys who stand up straight, and sit up straight, and who put their chins out for whatever is coming. Blow the trumpet, son, maybe holler a little bit, and get going. Lift your head up and think about pulling yourself together."

Archie now has his hands stretched out before him, and he pulls his hands together quickly, making a clapping sound. I jump a little in my chair. He walks to the window and pulls up the shade.

"Just look around the neighborhood," he says, "and think about who you want to be like, because I'll tell you this: If you don't start thinking about who you are and what you can do, you might be on the road to playing rummy with guys like Eddie Dunne up at Sing Sing."

Archie comes over to me and gives me a soft punch on the shoulder.

"We all like you, son," he says, "but you should know that wasting your life is as bad as taking food out of a starving person's mouth."

*   *   *

I'm on Second Avenue now. It's dark, and it's cold, and the trucks are backed up all the way to 55th Street and beeping their horns so that it sounds like the clown act at the circus.

What? I am thinking.

What?

How am I taking food out of a starving person's mouth?

Chapter Thirty-six

My mother is at work, at the phone company down the block near Third Avenue, and Billy is just finishing the cheese and noodles she left him in the pot. I am at the medicine cabinet mirror above the kitchen sink, putting a tie around my neck.

"Maybe you don't get it," Billy says.

"I get it good enough," I say. "I just don't want to deliver the papers anymore, now that I have the florist."

"You could do both jobs, Dennis," he says. "I'm doing the railroad, and I still do the papers."

I twist the tie until the double Windsor knot is just right, and I tighten it up as far as it can go. Billy has been throwing sacks of mail down at Grand Central, and he works all weird hours, never regular. Uncle Andy got him the job.

"Good for you," I say.

"Don't be a wise guy, Dennis," he says. "You were never much of a wise guy, and so why are you starting now?"

"I don't want to get up so early is all."

"What about the money?"

"I'll bring more money in with the florist."

"It's like throwing money away to quit the papers."

"I'm fourteen, Billy, and I can do what I want."

*   *   *

Joey Jurgensen has a cousin in the Bronx who is having a Saturday night party. And so we're going up there with him on the Lexington Avenue Express. It's what everyone wants to do, but I would rather just hang around the block doing nothing to see if Virginia Sabella comes around. I just met her the other night, and we went down to watch the Pepsi sign.

But a guy can't hang around with himself, and so I'm here with Joey on the subway. Scarry and Walsh are with us, and Tip-toe Tommy Moran who got his name because he is so quiet.

"Will there be broads there?" Scarry asks.

"More broads than in Julia Richmond High School," Jurgensen says.

"But will they be real broads," Walsh says, holding his hands just out from his chest, "you know?"

"Yeah, yeah," Jurgensen says, "broads with bazooms bigger than smoked hams."

I am smoking a Lucky Strike with Walsh, taking turns puffing, and I notice we are right below the No Spitting sign.

"How far can you spit?" I ask Walsh. I know how easy it is to press his buttons.

Walsh has a mouth bigger than the average toothy guy, and when he smiles he looks like the grille of a Buick Skylark. And he's smiling now.

"I could spit all the way to England," I say, "if I spit in the ocean."

"But," Walsh says, "we're in the subway."

"Yeah, sure," I say, "so I could spit to wherever the conductor is."

The train is just pulling into the 86th Street station, and we are getting out just for a second to see how far away the conductor is, but there are two cops running to the door as we step out. Walsh has the cigarette and flips it fast onto the tracks. But he can't hide the smoke, even after he has swallowed it, and the cops pull us all off the train.

I am immediately worried, because everything is dead serious with them. They ask for ID as the train roars out of the station. I don't say anything as I fumble through my wallet because I know not to say too much to the cops. Every word can be a shovelful in digging your own grave.

Scarry, though, is talking, and a little too much if you ask me.

"I didn't do anything, Officer," Scarry is saying. The blotches on his freckled face seem to be redder than usual.

I laugh to myself because I know he is right, that he did not do anything except getting on the train with us. But the cops are not going to care about who did what where. They just know they pulled five guys off the train, and now they have to do something with them.

"Shut up," a cop says to Scarry as he takes the ID out of my hand.

"But," Scarry says, "I don't want to get into trouble because my uncle is a chief inspector in the police department."

This gets the attention of the cops. My attention, too, because I did not know this.

"Who's your uncle, wise guy?" the cop says.

"Bill McQuade," Scarry says. It's a name the cops recognize.

"He's my mother's brother."

I am amazed now as the police officer gives me back my ID and walks away without saying another word. I am thinking that Scarry is like the Pope himself giving a dispensation.

Just now another train arrives and we get on it, all of us hoping the doors will shut quickly behind us.

We don't stay long at the party in the Bronx, just long enough for Jurgensen to find his uncle's booze stash.

"We're gonna be served in a goodly fashion by uncles tonight," Jurgensen says as he holds a bottle of Three Feathers to his lips.

In no time at all, half the bottle is empty and Jurgensen is staggering.

Scarry is pissed off there are no broads who will talk to him.

Walsh has his arm around a girl who looks ten years old, and Tiptoe is sitting in a corner, his arms folded, watching them silently.

It's not the kind of party we want, and so we head back to the subway.

Again on the train, Walsh is smoking, and I tell him to put it out until we get to 59th Street. The car is empty except for us, but you never know when a cop will come.

"Why do you wanna push your luck?" I ask.

"I just gotta prove to myself," he says, "that I don't have any luck, you know what I mean. So I'm gonna smoke until I fart smoke rings."

"Jeez, Walsh," I say, "just put the thing out, will ya?"

"Fuck you," Jurgensen says, waking up from a sleep. I don't know who he is talking to, and I don't think he does, either, but I direct his comment to Walsh.

"See, Walsh," I say, "even Jurgensen thinks you should get a new brain."

I look to Jurgensen. He is in a corner, and again sleeping like a Bowery bum.

Just now, four Negroes come through the car. They are about our age.

"Fucking monkeys," Tip-toe says, the first thing he's said all night.

None of them says anything, and they continue on through the slamming doors that separate the cars. But, in just a few seconds, as the train screeches into the 149th Street station, the four return. This time they are with four others. Some of them, I can see, are swinging bicycle chains.

I am thinking that I should apologize to them, tell them that Tip-toe is a spastic, and that he doesn't mean it, just as my mother doesn't mean it when she talks about guineas, but I know that they will not be convinced.

I guess we can fight them, but it looks like we are going to get beat pretty bad if we go against these chains. The train doors pull back, and I know we have to move fast.

"Who said it about monkeys?" the toughest-looking of the bunch says.

"Look," I say, "we don't want no trouble, man."

The guy then swings the chain, and it goes an inch from my head and down into my shoulder, biting into my skin like an electrical shock.

I get up and push him away and make for the door, and I see out of the corner of my eye that Scarry and Walsh have pushed those in front of them also, and are behind me. Tip-toe was the first one out the door.

We are on the platform now, running toward the turnstiles, and they are behind us, yelling like Comanches. And then, just as we get to the turnstiles, we are blessed with a visitation from the Holy Ghost

himself as two policemen, the very same two we had met earlier, come
out of the change booth. It is like the hundred-meter race in the
Olympics has come to a sudden end in the middle of the race, and I
stop before the two cops, and everyone behind me stops, too. I try to
recapture my breath. God, I have never been so happy, and I am thinking that maybe Walsh will begin now to have a streak of good luck.

"What's going on?" a cop asks.

"Not much, Officer," I say.

"Good to see you," Scarry says.

I don't see any bicycle chains now as I count the gang as the Negroes pass, each without a word. It doesn't matter that they're colored.
Size, shape, and number are the important things in a fight. There are
eight of them, and the smallest is bigger than any of us. Now here we
are with the cops, the four of us, and it's good to watch them pass.

God, just four of us.

Jurgensen is still on the train. He slept through Tip-toe's creation,
the bastard. I am the only one who took a welt, and I can still feel it
in my shoulder. Jurgensen will never know what he missed.

I think about Tip-toe. What is it inside of us, anyway, that we
have to talk about people because of their race? These guys were minding their own business when they went by in the subway. They didn't
mean us any harm. And Tip-toe was wrong to call them a name, any
name, that they would hate. I don't know why we are always looking
for trouble. Maybe we should change Tip-toe Tommy's name to
Treacherous Tom?

The two cops, I am thinking, know exactly what they have
walked into. They don't say anything, and neither do we, but we stick
very close to them as they wait for the next downtown train. They are
not more than ten feet away from us.

"Why don't you smoke now, Walsh?" I ask.

"Fuck you," Walsh says.

"Right," I say. "That's a courageous answer. Anybody notice that
Two-Wallet Joey is missing?"

"Where is that fat farm?" Scarry says.

I suddenly bend over in laughter.

"One thing for sure," I say, "if we don't know, Jurgensen doesn't know, either, and he'll know even less when the conductor wakes him up when they get to Coney Island."

Billy wakes up when I come into the room.

"Where were you?" he asks, picking up the alarm clock and checking the time. It's a little after midnight.

"We went to a party in the Bronx," I say, getting out of my clothes. "It was a dud."

"You going to do the papers in the morning?"

"Yeah, Billy, I'll do the goddamn papers, anyway."

"Good."

"It's no goddamn big deal."

"I'll get you up."

I can get five hours sleep, anyway, I'm thinking as I climb up to the top bunk.

I close my eyes, and before I know it the picture of Virginia Sabella forms in the darkness. Virginia, who I finally met, with those dark eyes and that dark Italian skin and those red, red lips, coming all the way down from where she lives on 68th Street, and walking up 56th Street with her cousin Maryanne Maniscalco, who brought her down to our block because she's friends with Catherine Gaeta, walking in those tiny steps because her pink skirt is so tight, her pink sweater swaying from side to side as her breasts move, the pink bandana around her neck flying in the breeze, her black Julia Richmond school jacket open and blowing behind her. I have every oval inch of her memorized, and especially the smell of her breath as we kissed down by the river. The first girl who has ever gone down to the 51st Street park with me, Virginia Sabella, her name like a cigar or a glass of wine, but to me her name will always stand for the first girl who looked into my eyes, and then kissed me, and then told me that she liked me, a lot.

Chapter Thirty-seven

Mr. Donahue is in my living room as I walk in the door. My mother's on the couch, crying, and Mr. Donahue has a sad look on his face. I know what he's doing in my apartment, and I hate him immediately for being here. For making my mother cry. Mr. Don't-a-You is from my shop class, and since I have only been to that class two or three times, he is the last person in the world I expected to find in my living room.

My mother looks up, and she stops crying.

"Sit down there," she says. She has a handkerchief to her eyes. I can see the anger in her eyes, or maybe it's sadness, I can't tell. Her voice is scratchy.

"What's going on?" I ask as I sit on a kitchen chair that's in the living room, the chair we brought in when the easy chair got a hole in the cushion and we threw it out.

I am in my green Aviation jacket, and I wiggle out of it.

"The worst thing about this," my mother says, "is that you lied to me. You lied to me every day for months about going to school."

I know I can't give an excuse, not with Mr. Donahue here, and so I know it is better to just say nothing. My mother is staring at me, and then she throws her arms out.

"Why do you do these things, Dennis?" she cries, her nose sniffling. "Billy never gives me a moment's problem, and you never give me a moment's rest. Why, why? When you are so smart? All the nuns at St. John's always told me how smart you are, and how you never meet your abilities, and how much everybody likes you. And you wanted to go to public school, and we let you go where you wanted, and now this?"

My mother is beginning to cry heavily again, sobbing, and then she screams.

"Why?"

I don't know what to say.

She is sitting there in her green housecoat, the one she wears when she is ironing, thin and pretty, the tears shining as they run down her cheeks, her nose sniffling red like she has a bad cold, and I wish I could hug her and tell her that there is nothing really wrong. Tell her that school is just not what I want to do. I want to be out in the world where there are no attendance teachers or so many years to go in a classroom. I just want my own life, and not have a life that has to be reported to every Tom, Dick, and Harry.

I just wish she wouldn't be so sad.

No one is saying anything. We all just look at each other and listen to my mother sobbing.

"We are going to have to give him a JAB card," Mr. Donahue says, finally breaking the ice.

"What does that mean?" I ask. I am trying to speak in a friendly voice, but I am madder than anything that my mother is crying. I guess these are those tenement tears she talks about, bad times that just come natural sometimes. Everyone knows that things could be better for all of us if we all lived on Sutton Place. The Walshes, the Scarrys, the Jurgensens, everybody. But everything would be the same for me no matter where we lived. If I could only get her to understand that— that I would still play hooky from school, because school is just not for me. It's a coop. You have no control over your life there. Look at my father, cooped up, he has no control over his life. We just get ordered around from minute to minute, do this, do that. I want to do something else, to work full-time at the florist on 53rd Street. At least I'll have my own money, and I can have a leather jacket if I want one.

"It means," Mr. Donahue says, "that you are fourteen years old and have to go to the Juvenile Aid Bureau regularly until you are sixteen."

"Where is that?" my mother asks between her sniffing.

"Up on 116th Street."

"They couldn't make it easier?" my mother asks. I know she is thinking that she has only so much time between working at the phone company and still doing apartments and all the ironing for Mr. Shurtliff next door.

"It is the way it is," Mr. Donahue says. "And he can quit school if he wants at sixteen, but until then the Juvenile Aid Bureau will be responsible for him going to school."

I know I can't wait until I am sixteen.

Chapter Thirty-eight

Frankie is waiting for me in Riker's on 53rd Street. I am getting paid thirty cents an hour at the florist, and I just got paid three dollars for three hours on Friday and seven hours on Saturday. I'll give my mother half, but I am still flush, and I order a hamburger on an English.

"You want something?" I ask him. You have to ask if you have the money.

"No," Frankie says. "I am going to keep my stomach empty. You shouldn't have too much in your stomach if we are going to toke on some smoke."

Frankie is laughing.

"I was on a boat once," I say. "Went fishing with Henry Casteneda and his father. Everyone got sick but me, 'cause I got an iron stomach."

After my hamburger, we walk down to 48th Street, where another Dennis, this one named Buckley, set up a club room in the cellar of his building. There is a lot of furniture around the room. It looks like it was taken from the street before the garbage trucks got there. A string light is hanging from the ceiling, and it is still swinging, and makes all the shadows in the room swing, too. Buckley is funny-looking, with a big wide mouth with a nose that almost comes over his lips.

And he's got a lot of pimples, like he has a disease. But his clothes are sharp, and his shoes look like they come from Flagg Brothers.

"Where did you get such cool vines?" I ask him. I am just trying to make conversation as I sit in a heavy brown sofa with a hundred cigarette burns in it.

Frankie has taken a bag from his jacket, and he opens it. He also opens a package of paper and pulls a piece out, folds it, and places it between his fingers. He then pours some of the pot out of the bag and onto the paper carefully, so that none of it drops to the floor.

It all reminds me of Gabby Hayes rolling a cigarette in the movies.

"The fags," Buckley says.

"What's that mean?" I ask.

"I would never let them near me," Frankie says.

"It's easy money," Buckley says. "It's all bullshit, anyway, 'cause I never let them go on top of me or anything."

I am getting nervous as I watch Frankie put the cigarette in his mouth and wet it fully so that it is closed all around the edges. It is all pretty sloppy with Frankie's spit all over it.

I am beginning to wonder what the hell I'm doing with these guys, when I could be around 56th Street waiting to see if Virginia comes around.

I don't like Buckley's talk. I have heard about guys who hang around Third Avenue by Clark's Bar, who walk up and down the street until some man offers them money to let them get kissed and worse in an alleyway. It is pretty sick, if you ask me, pretty sick and weird.

It makes me remember Mr. Dempsey, and I haven't remembered him in a long time. What kind of a man can do that to a kid? And what kind of a kid would do that willingly with a man?

Guys like Scarry and Walsh would never even know about this kind of stuff, making it with fags and smoking pot. I wish it was just Frankie and me here alone, so that I could swear him to secrecy like a blood brother or something. I don't want anyone to know that I am here with these guys doing this.

More secrets. Everything's a goddamn secret in my life.

I don't know this guy Buckley, and he gives me the creeps. I wish we could just get it all over with.

Frankie lights the cigarette and takes a deep puff, holding it in. He passes it to Buckley, who does the same, and then hands it to me. I take a little drag.

I am hoping that my brother especially never finds out about this because he would tell my mother for sure. He'd say, "You have to do something with Dennis, send him to reform school or something, because he never does homework, and he never even goes to school."

I could never do anything wrong to my brother, but I know he would tell on me for something as bad as this.

I am holding my breath, the smoke inside of me, and I don't feel anything.

I am expecting to feel something, but there is nothing. Good. I feel relieved that it doesn't affect me, and so I hand it over to Frankie.

"If I could get a job, I wouldn't let the fags near me," Buckley says, "but nobody wants to hire me."

I am thinking that I don't believe him. Everyone I know who wants a job can find one in my neighborhood. Even someone as funny-looking as him.

"I don't need a job," Frankie says, "because I just help my old man on the truck once in a while and he gives me the working wage, a buck ten an hour. Pretty good, huh?"

"A buck ten an hour," I repeat. "I could have made eleven instead of three for yesterday and all day today."

Maybe I could get to know Frankie better, and get to know his father, too. Maybe his father will let me help out on the truck.

Frankie takes another long drag and hands it off to Buckley. Some guys are so lucky, I am thinking, that they have fathers who give them a buck ten an hour.

I can't even keep my newspaper money.

Even now with my mother working and off the welfare, she still says that I have to give her the newspaper money, because it's not much, three dollars, sometimes four.

"Food and clothes," my mother says, "don't come out of the sky when you need them."

The cigarette is again between my thumb and forefinger. This time I take a deep puff, and I hold it in until I choke. I give it to Frankie, and then it hits me. I don't see colors that are on fire, but everything begins to spin, and the spinning is so out of control that I don't think I can sit up straight on the sofa. My stomach is trying to keep up with the spinning, and I can feel my breathing getting faster and faster, and I am suddenly scared and trembling, thinking that something awful is about to happen, that maybe the door will fly open and a thousand cops will rush in and beat us good until we are black-and-blue and bloody, and they will tell Billy, and Billy will tell my mother, and my stomach can't take the spinning anymore, and the hamburger on an English is now pushing up through my throat and pouring through my mouth, and Buckley is cursing like crazy, pulling me out of his clubhouse and into the dark, smelly cellar, where he shoves me into the blackness of a corner, where I am not hearing the sweet music of the inside of a phonograph, but I do hear Buckley laughing and a rat scurrying over some garbage as I hold my stomach and roll over into a knot and pray to God that the spinning will stop.

But it doesn't. It just spins and spins, and I am hoping it will be over soon.

Chapter Thirty-nine

Monsignor Ford looks over his desk at me. My mother and I are in the rectory of St. John's on 55th Street. There is a musty smell here, as if no one has opened a window in thirty years. The carpet is so thick, thicker than a blackboard eraser, but softer than a paintbrush.

We are all sitting on big leather chairs, the kind you see judges sitting on in the movies. There is a painting on the wall, with a brass sign under it that says it is Saint Thomas More, a man from olden days who looks so real I think he can talk. I am thinking that I could paint like that if someone would teach me. I get up and put my finger on the painting, to try to feel the paint under my fingers.

"Sit down, Dennis," Monsignor Ford says.

"Yes, sir," I say. Father Ford was just made a monsignor, and I know he is doing my mother a favor by taking the time to meet with us here.

He shifts a few papers across his desk, things my mother had given him.

"Do you think you want to try again?" he asks, folding his hands on the top of the desk.

He used to be my favorite priest, but then he took over the Catholic Charities, they made him a monsignor, and we don't see him

234

Dennis Smith

so much anymore. He has a little stripe of red at the bottom of his collar and on the wrists of his cassock, a stripe like a military man.

"Yes," I answer, "I guess so."

"Your record shows," he says, lifting a paper, "that you haven't been at school more than twelve days in two terms. Not much different from saying you've never been at school at all, for I doubt in those twelve memorable days they ever once had your attention."

"I don't know," I say. "I don't think they cared about me being there or not."

"Mr. Donahue cared," my mother says.

She smiles, and I know that she does not want to get into an argument with me, especially in front of Monsignor Ford.

I guess she was very surprised that the High School of Aviation Trades sent her a letter saying that I should find another high school to go to. That maybe Mr. Donahue would do something to make things right. I was surprised, too, that Mr. Donahue didn't make things easier on us, even if I attended classes for only twelve days during the whole year. Maybe he tried, and somebody forgot. Still, I'm surprised, because nobody gets kicked out of a public school, that's what I thought. But here we are with Monsignor Ford, trying to find a high school to go to.

Sitting here, I begin to think of Bobby Walsh, who sat in this chair just a month ago when his mother had him here to take the pledge, an oath where you promise before God that you will stay away from the booze. At fifteen years old, we guessed that Bobby is the youngest member of St. John's parish ever to take the pledge. All because sometimes New York can be the smallest town on the face of the earth.

It happened when Marty and Francis Harris loaned us their draft cards, but only for the night, a Friday night after the Kips Bay dance. The Harris twins were eighteen, and we thought we could just pass for the legal age. We looked pretty snappy, Bobby and I did, mature, we thought, and after the dance was over and most of the kids went to Emiliano's, we went to Happy's Bar and Grill on Second Avenue. We were acting the parts of the Harris twins, though we looked nothing like each other. But neither did the Harris twins. They looked like Mutt and Jeff, and if they could pass for twins, then so could we.

My mother was working the four-to-midnight shift at the telephone company, and so I could stay out until twelve, the latest.

We walked into Happy's Bar and found two seats at the bar and ordered two fifteen-cent beers.

"Get lost," Happy said to us.

"Whaddaya mean?" Bobby said, as if Happy insulted three generations of his family.

"You're not old enough to be in here," Happy said, wiping his rag across the bar.

"We got our draft cards," Bobby said, going into his wallet.

Happy gave us what could be thought of as a dirty look as he inspected the cards, but he drafted the beers and placed them before us.

I was sitting up real straight on the barstool, thinking that we've been allowed into some special club, maybe like the White House or the mayor's mansion.

After three beers we were feeling good and decided to go down the street to Abe Atell's bar on 55th Street. Abe was a middleweight champion of the world, and his place was always packed with the neighborhood athletes, guys who played basketball at the 54th Street Gym or softball in Central Park or baseball up under the bridge.

We shoved our way through the crowd and up to the bar. A tall man was standing with his back to us, his elbow leaning wide across the bar.

"Give us a little room here, buddy," Bobby says, confident, and in his best tough-guy voice.

The man turned around, and I was shocked.

I watched as Bobby just looked at the man vacantly, as if he didn't know where he was or who was with him. There was a long pause as Bobby stared out before him. I supposed, at first, that Bobby, being bleary-eyed from Happy's beer, didn't see who it was that was next to him.

But I saw right away. It was Bobby's father.

Finally, it all registered with Bobby, and I could see by the changing color of his face that he was more shocked than I was. He turned quickly, like a Harlem Globetrotter, pushed through the crowd, and ran down the street faster than a guy on roller skates. Mr. Walsh was right behind him, running like he was on the high school track team.

Mr. Walsh caught up to him a whole block away, down by Twomey's Funeral Parlor on First Avenue, and when I got there, Bobby's father was letting him have it from one end of the sidewalk to the other. *Bam, whack,* the clouts so loud I could feel them on the other side of the avenue.

The following morning, Bobby's mother marched him right down to the rectory where she could get someone to give him the pledge.

I began to smile, thinking about Bobby.

"What is funny about this?" Monsignor asks.

"Nothing," I say.

"That is correct," he says, "nothing. You have caused your mother nothing but grief, and now we are going to give you a final chance to get yourself together, to fly the straight and narrow."

"Yes, Monsignor," I answer in the kind of Catholic school way that got me through nine years of St. John the Evangelist's.

Monsignor is trying to help my mother, I know that. I figure I owe him some respect for that, anyway, and so I sit up in my chair, stern-faced and at attention.

"Can you play basketball?"

"Yes, Monsignor."

"That's something," he says, smiling. "They like basketball players up there at Hayes."

"Cardinal Hayes?" I ask, my eyes opening in recognition.

"Cardinal Hayes High School."

"That is where Billy is," my mother says.

"Good," Monsignor Ford says. "All the more reason for them to take a chance on Dennis."

I am suddenly excited.

It would be great to hang around with my brother. He's still two years older than me, but the age difference does not matter so much in high school, and maybe I can hang around with him and those guys from the Bronx who are his friends, guys like Buzzy O'Keefe and Tommy Henderson and Jimmy Dixon. I mean, everything can be different in high school with my brother. These guys are the stars, the jocksters, the guys who get the girls, the big shots. I could be a part of them.

Maybe.

I still have the East River Florist. Since I have been playing so much hooky, Mr. Schmidt has given me work three days a week, after I begged him to put me on as full-time as he could. He is paying me forty cents an hour now, three twenty a day, plus some tip money. Not many tips, though, because the maids always answer the doors on Sutton Place and the River House, and if the people leave any money for tips, you can bet the maids pocket it. I don't blame them, either, because if they are working as maids, they probably need more of everything in their lives.

Like my mother. She could use a new everything, especially a new ironing board. The ironing board she uses is covered with old sheets and stitched together at the bottom, and the sheets are always getting creased, and my mother is always saying Hail Marys to keep from cursing as she irons because she can't keep a flat bottom on the ironing board.

I don't think we have anything new in the house, except for the Bible and the Formica table in the kitchen with the four puffy chairs that she bought in a deal that took two years to pay off.

I have been saving my money, though, and I have thirty dollars tucked in an old sneaker under my bed. I saw a ring in Bloomingdale's, a little gold one with a blue stone. It is fourteen karats, and I just need ten dollars more to get it. My mother used to wear a wedding ring, a plain gold one, but I haven't seen it in a long time. I don't know if she lost it or sold it. A new ring would look nice on her hand, and as soon as I have the forty dollars I am going to get it for her.

I wonder if she would like a ring more than a new ironing board.

"The problem is," Monsignor Ford says, "you have to organize your time if you are going to go to a good school like Hayes. You can't work at that florist so much, you understand?"

I do understand. Things are changing for me, so I have to make some changes for myself.

After we leave Monsignor Ford, I walk with my mother to 56th Street. I can tell she is feeling better about things because she begins to whistle a Bing Crosby tune that I know. We are walking pretty fast, and she is whistling this tune, and I think of the words.

"You have to accentuate the positive," it goes, "eliminate the negative, latch onto the affirmative, and don't mess with Mr. In-Between."

Chapter Forty

I am walking up the hill to Kips Bay Camp, in Valhalla, New York. A big canvas bag is over my shoulder. The country air smells like a package of Chinese laundry, clean and soft. The dirt road under my feet makes me think that I am in another country, like Ireland, but Valhalla is just ten miles above the city. Still, it's greener than Central Park.

Forty shades of green, that's what Pop said about Ireland.

Pop is already dead a couple of months, but I think about him still, and especially when I see anything green—lawns, hills, forests, valleys, mountains, glens—they all remind me of Pop and his forty shades of green.

I am laughing now, because I remember that I don't think I have ever understood a complete sentence of Pop's in my whole life, except for one.

"In Eye-er-land," he used to say, "dere is ony da farty shades a green ta mak' a man smile."

I saw him the day before he died, a tube in his throat to give him some breath. All the pipes he smoked in his seventy-eight years burned his lungs out. I felt sorry for him, lying there, and I wondered if he knew who I was, or if he cared.

"Your grandfather," my mother told me at his wake, "didn't have much of a past, but whatever is there should be remembered, those fishing boats in County Cork, the warehouse in Manhattan, those endless roofs in Brooklyn waiting to be tarred and covered, all those Masses he went to, always in the same suspenders he wore for thirty years. Just keep all that in the back of your mind."

My mother's father hardly knew any of us, and spent all of his time smoking his pipe and reading the newspaper and drinking his beer. After he fell from that roof, running after that rolling log of tar paper, he never worked again.

He had no pension, no money, no stores laid up but his memories of Ireland. He was lucky to have my Aunt Kitty and my Uncle Andy there to put him up, and to put up with him. After Sunday Mass, a beer and a newspaper and a cushioned kitchen chair was all he wanted in his life, and his grandchildren were like shadows around him.

Billy got me the job of kitchen boy for the summer. He's a counselor, and he told me that next year, if I did okay at Hayes, I could become a counselor, too.

The kitchen boys' cabin is at the end of a long row of eight cabins and two double cabins. The cabins are just big enough for eight beds, four on each side, and have canvas shades instead of windows along the sides.

I throw my duffel on a bed, and I lie down to rest from the hike up the hill from the train station. I am still huffing and puffing, but I light a cigarette, anyway. The kitchen boys always smoke, and for as many years as I have been coming to this camp, since I was six, I don't remember a kitchen boy who didn't have a cigarette hanging from the side of his mouth.

A guy named Spango comes in with his suitcase tied together with a wash line. I know him from 55th Street. He has dark skin, a gold tooth, and he just moved into our neighborhood from some country in South America. He has brought with him a record player which plays the new 45 rpm records, and he has a collection of rock and roll.

It is great having Spango and having Frankie Lymon, the Platters, the Four Tops, all of them, always available on the 45s. I can tell there is never going to be a dull moment this summer.

Another guy named Charlie Spaskey comes into the cabin. I know him, too, from Kips Bay. He is from Brooklyn and has just won the Golden Gloves championship for fifteen-year-olds. The thing about Charlie Spaskey is that he is a very cool cat, a good-looking boy whose blond hair comes down over his eyes, and is known for getting any girl he wants. Marilyn Rolleri, Barbara Godotti, Barbara Gabelli, Catherine Gaeta, they were all in love with Charlie. Even Sue Flanagan would go for Charlie.

It is a hot day, but the cool breeze pouring through the window openings makes us feel that a new life is starting. Everything is different here, and so I offer my cigarettes around, and we have our first bullshit session, "Earth Angel" blaring in the background.

The time passes quickly at camp. Some days I have to work in the mess hall, cleaning tables, giving out food to the campers, or washing the floors, and on other days I have to work in the kitchen with Flora, who someone told me was Harry Belafonte's mother.

People are always making up stories at camp to have fun with the campers, and sometimes the truth mixes in with the stories, and I don't know what to believe.

Archie said that President Eisenhower's son is a camper here, but they have to keep it a government secret and so he's here using a moniker. Most of the campers believe him, and so, in a way, it makes their camp stay special. Archie also said that Ernest Hemingway won the Nobel Prize, and they were going to give it to him here at breakfast next week. Nobody believes that, but Flora could be Harry Belafonte's mother, for she is very black and she is always singing those calypso songs.

The work in the kitchen with Flora is hard, for all I do all day is Brillo out the pots and pans and wash the floors and the counters over and over. A schedule is posted in the kitchen boys' cabin telling us who has which job on which day. We sometimes trade the different jobs according to what days we want off. Archie is still the head counselor, and he tries to make things easy for us.

The easiest job is the porch duty, because all you do is stand on the mess hall porch and inspect the campers' hands to see if they have been washed as they march into the mess hall. Sometimes I pick out a little kid and make him go back to the wash house three times to wash his hands. When he comes back the third time, I have a muddy baseball which I throw to him suddenly. He has no choice but to catch it, and his hands are soaked with mud.

I would never send any of them back to wash their hands after the muddy baseball, but I tell them they better hide their hands from their counselor. The kids are great, and they take all the ribbing in stride. Archie did the same thing to me when I was seven, and I always remember it with a smile on my face.

Now the summer is half over. I have been practicing my set and jump shot every day, and reading as much as I can so that I will be ready to get off to a good start at Hayes. Billy gave me the complete works of Sherlock Holmes and the complete works of Shakespeare. I like Sherlock Holmes better, because he always knows what he is doing, but the characters in the Shakespeare book seem never to. My brother also gave me a paper edition of the *Confessions of Saint Augustine,* after he read it, and I keep carrying it around in my back pocket, half thinking that Archie will be impressed that I have such a book in my back pocket, and half thinking that I might find some time to read it.

Two days ago I was scheduled to work in the kitchen with Flo, and when I woke up I had a stomachache and heaved all over the place. It was a bug of some kind. It felt like Tom Thumb was in my stomach going through it with a lawn mower. I couldn't think about washing the kitchen floor four times, and Spango knew I was going to be late for work if I didn't get a move on. It was his day off, and I guess he felt sorry for me.

"You stay here, Dennis," Spango said, "and I'll work with Flo today."

He didn't say that he would change days off with me, or that I owed him something. He just said that he would do the job for me, and he went off to the kitchen as the sun was rising over Valhalla. I'll never forget him, that he did that for me.

He died last night.

The whole camp is in shock. He and Charlie Spaskey went to

town to have a soda and to check out the lay of the land in the girl department. When they were coming home, they hitched a ride at the bottom of the hill coming up from town.

The driver was drunk, went eighty miles an hour, and slammed into a tree. They say Spaskey will live, but his brain is damaged, a handsome Golden Gloves champion beaten by a drunk and a tree.

All my life I have been thinking about how rough it is for my father to be cooped up in some hospital, and now I am thinking about Spango, dead at fifteen years old.

Chapter Forty-one

That whole thing about Spango dying like that has been on my mind, and I see it so clearly, like the bull's-eye in the middle of the target.

I am fifteen years old, and I don't think I have even started my life yet. In fact, I am always thinking about getting my life started, and I can't imagine hitting a tree and having everything go black, every breath crushed out of you, and not even having a chance yet to get life started.

And the pain. What terrible pain they must have felt. They are just kids, both of them, who had ten or twenty years ahead of them to make something of themselves.

We are all just kids, really. I shouldn't forget that. That accident makes me think that I have a lot of years before me, and I shouldn't be wasting any of my time.

"Time," I remember Sister Alphonsus saying, "is the biggest gift that God gives you. You don't have to work for it, or pray for it, or anything. He just gives it to you free and clear, and only you can put a value on it."

I do value my time, and I want to make something of myself. I could be something important, too, something that will make people think, Holy God, Dennis did that?

I remember that I said three Hail Marys as soon as I heard about the accident. What else is there to do but pray for a guy, to hope that God won't be too hard on him? Is it too late to say that I wish I would have worked for Spango that day, giving him back the time he gave me? If he had the day off, would he have gone down to the city on a visit? Maybe then Spaskey would have done something different, too.

But thinking like that doesn't do anything for them. Spango is dead forever, and I have no power to do anything about his dying except to say a few prayers. At least God will hear me, and maybe Spango will, too, and he will know that not many people I know would have worked the whole day for me and not have asked anything in return.

After the funeral and visiting Charlie in the hospital, I practiced my basketball, set shots and layups, all summer long. I was feeling good, so good, about going to high school, about becoming more like my brother. I wanted to try to be a better student, and I wanted to work to be a sports star. I've always known I can do it, and everybody tells me I can do it. Archie and Betty down at Kips, Monsignor Ford, my mother, all of them telling me that I can recognize my famous abilities if I just pay attention.

Chapter Forty-two

I have been at Hayes for more than a month now, and I want to pay attention, too.

Or, at least, I wanted to.

It is Sunday, a crisp fall day, and I have taken a ticket at the French bakery on 54th Street. I went to the eleven o'clock Mass, and it seems that every person in the church ran directly to the bakery after the communion.

I used to wait until the priest said, *"Eta missa est,"* "Go, the Mass is ended," but lately I have been standing in the back and slipping out after the communion. I don't think much happens after the communion, anyway. The priest just washes his chalice and talks a lot to himself in Latin.

Father O'Rourke says it is insulting to God to come late or to leave early, and that if you insult God, you'll insult your mother and father and your friends, too, and what kind of a person goes around insulting everyone like that? But I don't think it is such an insult, and, anyway, God has a lot more important things to think about than me slipping out after the communion.

I thought I was the first to leave, and I don't know how so many people got so quickly to the bakery.

The rolls are six cents each, and I come here every Sunday to buy three seeded rolls. They used to be cheaper, but, no matter the price, Sunday would not be Sunday if I didn't get the rolls for my mother and Billy and me to have with our Sunday egg. Even if they cost a quarter each, I think we would still get them. The rolls and Sundays are like Mass and communion. They just go together like peanut butter and jelly.

Today, I have an extra dime my mother gave me for the collection, but Father O'Rourke was talking about how wonderful it would be if just once he could have a silent collection, where there would be just paper falling into the straw collection baskets, so that he wouldn't have to hear the annoying clinking of change. I didn't want to disappoint him by throwing a dime in the basket, and so I am going to give the dime to the French lady behind the counter for a jelly doughnut.

Most of the women in the bakery are holding wallets in their hands and wearing long dresses made of rayon. Rayon is a scientific thing, and it doesn't smell nice like cotton, like Mom's dresses when she washes them, but the dresses are pretty and in light colors, purples and greens like in Monet's *Rouen Cathedral*. The men seem all to be in brown suits with wide lapels and brown shoes. I know almost everyone who is waiting, people you see in the neighborhood, in the stores, and in church.

I am feeling dapper, too, wearing a blue shirt with a pink stripe across the chest, and my school sports coat. I am holding my chin high.

Mrs. Flanagan is here, and she smiles at me.

"How are you, Dennis?" she asks.

"I'm good, Mrs. Flanagan," I say.

I don't think she is trying to think of something else to say, and so I smile and look the other way. Anyway, my number is coming up. I would ask her about Sue, but she might think it is none of my business. I heard that Sue married a doctor in some far-off state, Illinois or somewhere. I still think about seeing Sue Flanagan in her brassiere and her silk slip.

I didn't especially want to go spying on Sue, but I guess the memory of that night on the roof will never go away, like Pop's memory of Ireland. I know I feel sorry I did it, but I can still picture the white of her skin and the shadows of her breasts as they pushed out from her brassiere. I know it is not right to take pleasure in the memory, either, but I can't help thinking what a lucky guy that doctor is to get to see her like that every day.

If I was a doctor, maybe I could get a girl like Sue Flanagan, smart and pretty. But I don't like to kid myself. I don't think I could ever be a doctor. Even if I liked school, and wanted to pay attention, I don't think I would want to pay attention that much. It takes over twenty years of schooling to be a doctor, and I have just gone through, what, maybe nine years and a couple of months counting kindergarten.

My month at Cardinal Hayes has not been a great one, and I don't think Monsignor Ford will be happy with me or my academic future.

I tried, but I just can't get my heart into it.

I made the freshman basketball team, and I went to practice for the first couple of weeks. I like basketball, and I have a not-so-bad jump shot from the foul line. I suppose I could be called a good boys' club basketball handler. But the boys on the team are much better than I am, and some are as good as Scarry. I know that no matter how much I practice I am not going to be a starter with this team. It is one of those things that you can see the first day. And if you can't see it, you'll feel it.

Some guys play basketball like poets and other guys play like newspaper delivery boys. My brother is like a poet when he plays, for the ball lands like a rhyme every time in the center of the basket, the end of every shot a two-pointer, and Billy floats through the air like he's on angel's wings when he lays the ball up. I think it's a gift that God gives you, to be able to make the basketball seem a part of your body when you dribble and jump and shoot and carry the ball. I guess I have a little gift, but when it comes to basketball, it's like God gave Billy a pair of shoes for Christmas and I got the shoelaces.

There's a Chinese boy on the freshman team who handles the ball like Bob McGuire on the Knicks, and I try to copy his style. His moves are quick and graceful, and I imagine there should be music in the background when he goes in for a layup. I must've laid the ball up a million times, and still I don't feel inside that I'm better than simply good at this. He's the first Chinese boy I have ever met, and the only one who plays basketball, too. I wonder if eating chop suey would help.

*   *   *

A pretty French girl calls my number and I give her my ticket. She checks it, because some people give any ticket hoping to get in front of the line.

"Well, what eez eet?" she asks.

"What eez what?" I answer. I don't think she likes this, and gives me a French sour puss. I could tell her that Mark Twain is always making fun of the French, but I don't think she'll care.

"Your ord-dare," she says.

"Three seeded," I say, "and a jelly doughnut."

She is about to put the jelly doughnut in a bag with the rolls, and I stop her.

"No, no," I say. "The jelly doughnut is right out of the collection basket, and I'm going to have to eat it on the way home."

She is too busy to figure anything out. I am just another pain-in-the-neck customer, and so she takes my dimes and shrugs her shoulders.

Walking home, I see Father O'Rourke still standing on the corner of 55th Street talking to some parishioners. It is not very cold, but there is a woman standing with Father O'Rourke who has a fur coat on that comes down to her ankles. She looks pretty swank, and I suppose she's from Sutton Place.

"A real howdy-do," my mother would say.

I don't think my mother will ever have a coat as nice as that. She has one coat, a red one that comes to her knees, even though most of her dresses come down below her knees. She has had it ever since I can remember.

I guess my mother will never get a chance to have nice things. My father will never come out of that hospital.

It makes me sad to think that Mom never has anyone to go out with. I don't know what happened to Artie. He just disappeared. She is always alone. Even when she is doing just ordinary things, if she's not working at the phone company, things like walking at night around the corner to 57th Street to get a newspaper. Every night at nine o'clock for as long as I can remember, she goes to get the *News* and the *Mirror*.

The *Mirror* has recently folded and is a dead newspaper now. So that gives the *News* a better chance.

Sometimes I think if my father was dead it would give my mother a better chance. I wish she could get another husband, a second one, and maybe start over.

But I know my father is not dead. They feed him every day in the hospital, so he will be around. Maybe my mother could meet some good man, and they could forget that my father is in the hospital and will never come out. Being Catholic, though, my mother could never get a divorce. Anyway, nobody ever gets a divorce. We don't know anyone who got a divorce, even Aunt Kitty, whose husband went out for milk and bread one day and never came back. People on my block get married and then they live there for life. Even Annie Dunne is still married to the guy in Sing Sing. Some things just never change for people. For some people.

I don't want to be like that, to try to be the same as the people on the block. If things are not going the way you want them to go, maybe you have to be different.

My mother, I think, is caught in this rut of having to be like everybody else, and I wish she could think she was different from the rest, better able to take care of herself without caring what anyone on the block thinks about it.

I remember lying on my mother's bed where I had gone to read a book on a lazy Sunday afternoon. I was a kid, and I could hear my mother and my Aunt Helen talking in the living room. The radio was going, and my Uncle Bob and Uncle Buddy were singing songs in the kitchen, but I could still hear my mother talking about Tommy Quigley, the man she used to go out with then. I didn't like Quigley even before he kicked the door in, and I paid extra attention to hear every word she was saying about him.

"So he asked you to marry him?" I heard my Aunt Helen say.

"He said he wants to buy a delicatessen," my mother answered, "and that he could afford to marry me and take care of the children, too."

"What did you say, Mary?"

My Uncle Buddy's voice was in the background. "Toor-a-loor-a-loor-a."

My mother took a long time to answer my Aunt Helen.

"It can't be," I heard her say finally.

It was a great relief to me, because I didn't want to see Quigley more than once a month, anyway.

"Why not, Mary?" my Aunt Helen asked. "It might be good to have a man around the house."

"It is not right," my mother said, "because I was put in this situation with two small boys for God knows what reason, and I just have to stick with it."

"You could get a divorce," Aunt Helen said.

"I never thought about it," my mother said. "My children have a father, and they don't need another one. And, until something changes, that is the way it will be."

"Things won't change, Mary," Aunt Helen said, "unless you want them to."

I remember my Aunt Helen's voice as she said this. It was like the way the priest says the last words of the sermon at Mass, winding the whole thing up.

"I suppose each of us knows that we can get whatever we want," my mother said, "depending on what we want to do to get it."

"Getting married again," Aunt Helen said, "could help you out."

"Oh, Helen," my mother said, "this man Tommy is not a bad man, but he drinks too much, and I don't see that he cares about my children. So he's not the one that makes this worth thinking about."

"Do you think any man will make it worth your while?" Aunt Helen asked.

"It is hard to say," my mother answered in a lower, much harder-to-hear voice. "I only know that Jesus, Mary, and Joseph and everyone else would tell you that it is a waste of good time to think about it until it happens."

"That's an I-Irish lulllll-a-bye," Uncle Buddy was singing over my mother's voice, and all I heard after this was my Aunt Helen laughing at something my mother said. I knew then that my mother was in no danger of getting a divorce, because she wouldn't joke about it if she was.

Father O'Rourke is now waving goodbye to the fancy woman and gives me a wave, too, as I pass by. I wonder if he will go into the rectory now and meet Monsignor Ford, and if he will tell Monsignor Ford that he saw me on First Avenue and that I did not look like I was doing too well at Cardinal Hayes High School. I am feeling that I might as well hang a sign across my chest saying, "I have not been so good for high school and high school has not been so good for me."

I want to pay attention, but maybe not to what people want me to pay attention to. If I could just study what I want to study, instead of math and science and religion. If I could just read stories by Hemingway and F. Scott Fitzgerald and O. Henry, or if someone would just pay me thirty dollars a week to go to school. But I'm not doing anything that I like to do, and I don't know why I should stay with it.

Brother Gabriel in algebra, who flung a set of keys at me the first day of class, is one of the problems. I guess I was hamming it up with some of the guys in the back of the class, and the keys, about thirty of them on a small ring, missed my nose by an inch. I knew right away that Brother Gabriel, an Irish Christian Brother, had a screw loose, and that I had to watch my step with him.

I am now walking slowly up the stairs to my house, worrying about what my mother will say when she learns what I am deciding about Hayes and working at the florist, when I tell her that I am just a boys' club basketball player and that I will never be a doctor.

I am chewing the last of my jelly doughnut as I open the door, and the brightness of the kitchen jumps out into the dark hallway. My mother and my brother are by the small green stove, and they raise their heads to look at me. Billy had gone to the midnight Mass down at St. Agnes after his basketball game last night, and my mother went to the nine o'clock this morning. Billy is in his undershirt, and my mother has the old pink robe tied tightly around her thin waist. Her hair is combed in long waves coming over her shoulders, and she is wearing a shimmering red lipstick. The bright morning light makes her look like she is all lighted up, like she is Rita Hayworth in a movie about the East Side of New York. She smiles a little when she sees me. I can always see how much she cares about me when she smiles like this. She has a spatula in her hand, turning an egg.

I kiss her cheek and punch my brother on the arm.

"You guys beat the Mount?" I ask.

"Hayes, sixty-four," Billy answers, "Mount St. Michael, fifty-nine. What are you eating?"

"The collection."

"What do you mean," my mother asks, "the collection?" She is not smiling anymore.

"Father O'Rourke," I say, "said he wanted to hear only paper in the collection basket, so I gave the money to the poor people at the French bakery."

"For what?" my mother asks.

"A jelly doughnut," I answer.

"You have a lot of nerve," she says. "Did you really go to church?"

"Yeah," I say. "I did go, and that's what he said, paper only. Did you want me to write him a note?"

"Don't be a smart aleck," she says. "What was the Gospel about?"

"The Gospel?" I say, trying to remember. "I don't know, it was about religion."

"Did you go to Mass, or didn't you?"

"I was there."

"And you don't know the Gospel?"

"I know it," I say. Then, after a long pause, I add, "Maybe."

I don't like her checking up on me this way. She never checked up on me before.

"It was about the angel Gabriel," I say, "coming to visit Mary to get her ready to have Jesus."

"Okay," my mother says, satisfied. "So you were there, but you should have put the money in the poor box."

She is now pointing her finger at me, and I think of the blue stone on that gold ring I saw, and of that woman's fur coat on First Avenue. If she had that blue stone on her finger now, she would be flashing it in the morning sunlight.

"Don't you know," she continues, "that when you give something away, even a dime, you have it forever? And where's your jelly doughnut now?"

I am thinking that I want to change the subject because an argument might interfere with the Sunday egg and the roll.

We only have eggs on Sunday, and I always get mine sunny-side up. There is nothing like dipping a buttered roll into the egg yellow on a Sunday morning, and I am not going to say anything that will put that in jeopardy.

"You're right," I say, "and I'll put a dime of my own in the poor box next time I'm in church."

Part of my deal with Monsignor Ford when he got me into Hayes was that I would quit working so much at the florist, and so now I am relying again on the money from newspaper delivery, and the folding money, too, when I can get it. Billy usually does the folding, and Scarry is always there, and I'll get some work if someone doesn't show up. We get thirty-five cents an hour for putting the papers together on Saturday nights or early Sunday mornings. There are thousands of newspapers all piled up on the sidewalk of First Avenue, and they come in sections that have to be folded together, a job that makes your fingers black. But it gives you muscles in the hands.

"How many points you score?" I ask.

"Eight," Billy says. He's reading the *New York Times* that I brought home last night.

Virginia came around last night, and we just hung around a little on the street corner until Scarry had to leave to fold the newspapers. We walked him to the newspaper stand on 57th Street. Billy wasn't there, he was off playing basketball, but a few other guys did show. There was no work for me, and so I asked Virginia to walk with me down to the 51st Street park.

She was wearing one of those black felt skirts that spread out like a tent, a pile of crinoline beneath, and a black sweater which exposed, but just a little, the white brassiere she was wearing. She had a red silk bandana around her neck. She always has a bandana around her neck.

We were looking across Welfare Island at the blinking Pepsi sign, and I was kissing her.

"Do you still like me?" I asked her as I rubbed my hand up and down her back.

What a terrible word this word *like* is. It can stand for all kinds of agreements sometimes, but other times it just means nothing more than the way you like breakfast in the morning.

She didn't answer, and I waited for a woman with four yelping dogs to pass by before I kissed her again.

"Well," I asked again, bringing my rubbing hand around to her front, "do you?"

"Yes," she said, "I still like you."

And I brought my rubbing hand across her stomach, shifting slow and then fast, trying to make my way up toward her breasts, constantly worried that she'll tell me to stop, but I find the courage inside and I slide my hand up over the outside of her sweater, in one fast movement until I get to her breast, and then suddenly my hand is fully over her breast, and for one small moment I thought I was approaching heaven.

She grabbed my hand suddenly and brought it into her other hand, and we sat there, my rubbing hand cupped in her grasp.

"But," she said, "I like somebody else, too."

Goddammit, I thought. See. This word *like*. You never know what it means.

Virginia is such a terrific girl, and I wanted so much to ask her to go with me. I wanted to say, "Let's just go together, Virginia, and the guys can talk about Virginia and Dennis the way they talk about Gail and Joey, or Maureen and Vinny, or Margaret and Dante."

But here she was in the blinking light of the Pepsi sign telling me that she also liked someone else, and I was wondering about the degree of "like" she was talking about. Was I at a fifty percent like? Or maybe the percent was more?

"Who do you like?" I asked.

"I can't say," she answered.

"It's a state secret?" I ask.

"Well," she said, "if you keep it a secret, it's Bobby Seelaw."

"But," I said in a kind of protest, "he's going out with someone."

"My cousin Maryanne," she said. "But Maryanne really likes Raymond Connors."

Oh, goddammit, I thought, Raymond Connors again.

I didn't say much after that, but I began to wonder where Marilyn Rolleri was hanging around recently. I haven't seen her around.

"Eight points," I say to Billy, still sitting at the kitchen table, "I would have done better."

"In your sleep," he says.

"Where's the Sunday *News*?"

"Behind your honor's ass, m'lord," my mother says, reaching for the newspaper that is on the floor beneath my chair.

My mother is smiling again. Good, the Sunday egg is secure.

Flipping through the newspaper after breakfast, I am thinking about the angel Gabriel from the gospel, and how misnamed Brother Gabriel from school is. They should have given Brother Gabriel a black hat and named him Simon Legree, for he never misses a chance to do something rotten to people.

I saw him take a kid and push him against a sill where there was an open window, and punch him over and over again until the kid was almost out the window, like Ameche's father, and on his way three stories down.

Last week I heard a story about an Irish Christian Brother holding a boy out of a school window by his ankles, and I am beginning to believe it.

Being in Brother Gabriel's class is like being in a torture chamber. The thing of it is that I don't know *a* to *b* about algebra, because to find *x* is as interesting to me as looking for a piece of used toilet paper in the East River. That is not Brother Gabriel's fault, I know, but I really have to watch myself with him. He's not a person you can trust in any conditions. Especially if you don't know how to make an equation.

And so every day when I go to Brother Gabriel's class, I usually get a whack across the back of the head when I am standing in front of the blackboard without a clue as to what is the next step after taking the chalk in my hand.

I know that there is something wrong with a situation where the person in control has hatred for everyone, where everyone gets whacked around except those who know how to find the cursed *x*. And I know, too, that this is something I don't have to put up with, that I can fight back.

At least, I can do things on my own terms.

"What are you going to do?" my mother asks, standing at the kitchen sink and looking at me through the medicine cabinet mirror.

What am I going to do? I repeat her question in my mind. There is only one answer. I am quitting school. It's in my mind now, solidly.

"I guess," I say to her, "I'll meet Walsh and Scarry and Jurgensen up on 61st Street and York Avenue."

I haven't told anyone, but I don't think it will be long before my mother finds out, and then I'll have to get another JAB card. She had to take me twice all the way uptown to the Juvenile Aid Bureau office, and she won't be happy going up there again.

"What's there?" she asks.

"They put up a basketball court there, in the park."

It is lucky we still haven't gotten a telephone, because when you have a telephone they can find your mother right away. But I always get the mail, and I have to make sure that my mother doesn't see any mail from Cardinal Hayes High School.

"Maybe I'll play with you," Billy says.

"We're playing two-on-two," I say.

It isn't just because of Brother Gabriel that I have decided this. I could put Brother Gabriel in my back pocket if I wanted to, learn some equations, ask for some help after class, and play his game on his territory.

"Scarry and I could play you three," Billy says, "and we could spot you eighteen points in a twenty-point game."

I just think it is all a waste of time, and I don't know why I should continue to punish myself when I can just be on my own and go to work.

"Yeah, sure," I say.

I hate it that I don't have any money for cigarettes, or to go to the movies, or to have a milk shake once in a while. But I would be kidding myself if I just wanted to earn money. It is more than that.

"Who's got a ball?" Billy asks.

I want to be in control of my own life. Every time I think about my father being locked up in that hospital I keep saying to myself that I am never going to let my life be locked up like that.

Uh-uh, I will never let that happen to me.

"Scarry," I say.

Maybe Mr. Schmidt will take me back full-time at the florist. I was fifteen years old last month, and I should be earning my way to somewhere.

"You want me to play?" Billy asks.

"Put your sneakers on," I say, "and let's go."

Chapter Forty-three

Frankie has entered his father's candy store. I am in the back of the store playing the pinball machine. It is early on a Saturday morning.

I haven't been going much to Kips lately because I began to hang around with the guys in the candy store on 55th Street. The guys here, Frankie and Nicky and Mikey, don't go to school, either, and they never think about scholarships, or taking time to do homework and research papers and that kind of thing. We just hang together, like a club, every day and night.

I like the way we're all friends. It's different from the way Scarry and Walsh and Jurgensen are friends. Here on 55th Street, all the guys have quit school, and everyone is trying to figure out what they're doing, and trying to get work here and there.

I am back working at the florist, and when I got to work this morning, Mr. Schmidt asked me if I could come back at one and then work until eight because there was a wedding or something they were doing. And so I am here to kill a couple of hours.

"Hey," Frankie says as he sees me.

"I got this machine beat," I say, banging on the side of the pinball.

"How come you're not at work?" Frankie asks.

"I don't have to be there until one or so."

I guess I could have gone home and sat around, or I could have gone to Kips to play Ping-Pong or pool. But I am feeling that I belong here, that the guys on 55th Street care more about each other than they do about themselves.

"Hey, great," Frankie says. "How'd you like to come up to 120th and score some horse with us? We'll be back way before noon."

Score some horse? I wonder what that is. But if it is on 120th Street, that is Harlem, and it must have something to do with getting high.

"I don't have any carfare," I say. "How are you getting there?"

I am thinking that going to Harlem is something I am not so hot about doing. Harlem is a dangerous place, and going there is like walking the wood on the third rail, like testing the saints and the angels. Guys carry knives up there and are pretty easy about using them. And suppose we meet a gang like those with the chains that were on the Lexington Avenue Express?

"First Avenue bus," Frankie says. "I'll give you the carfare."

One o'clock is more than three hours away. And I guess testing the saints and the angels is as good a way to pass the time as any.

"As long as you pay the bus both ways," I say to him. I can tell he just wants company.

"Great," he says. "We'll go pick up Mikey around the corner."

Mikey Fallon lives in the building next to mine on 56th Street, but he never hung with the 56th Street crowd. He was always a loner, at least until he started hanging around with Frankie on 55th Street.

I see Mikey on the front stoop of his building. He is yelling at his mother. And he is cursing like mad. A few people have stopped on the street to see what it is all about. I don't see anyone I know, and I'm glad I don't see my mother around.

"Just leave me the fuck alone," Mikey is yelling, and his mother begins to slap him across the face. But, Mikey turns his back and goes down the stoop stairs, and his mother is following him.

"You're a goddamn thief," Mikey's mother is yelling after him.

"Leave me the fuck alone," Mikey says again.

They are on the sidewalk now, his mother slapping him on the back of the head. Mikey turns to her, and you can see the veins of anger popping up at the side of his neck. I know he wants to strike out at her, but he wouldn't dare. No one I know would hit his mother.

In fact, I never heard anyone curse at his mother before now.

"You're a goddamn thief," Mrs. Fallon says again.

"Leave me the fuck alone," Mikey is saying over and over. "Leave me the fuck alone."

They are in the street now, between two parked cars. The traffic on 56th Street has stopped.

"Maybe we should come back later," I say to Frankie.

"Naw," Frankie says. "Just wait a minute."

Mrs. Fallon has her son by the shirt now, and the shirt is ripping out of his pants. Mikey now yells at the top of his voice.

"Stop it, stop it, fucking stop it!"

And he grabs his mother and pushes her hard against the parked car. She loses her balance and begins to fall over, but grabs a radio antenna. The antenna bends way back and then breaks off the car, but she has stopped herself from falling.

I am thinking that I have to run over there to help her, to try to stop Mikey from being so crazy. But, suddenly, Mikey turns and begins to run away from her, up toward First Avenue and us.

Mikey's mother is a fat woman, and she tries to run after Mikey but gives up after a few yards. She is still yelling.

"And," she yells as loud as she can, *"don't you ever come home again."*

Mikey goes past us pretty fast, and without stopping tells us to meet him around the corner.

"Did you see that?" Frankie says. "He almost beached the whale."

I don't say anything because I don't think it's so funny. I don't know how someone can push their mother like that.

We get to the bus stop just as the bus arrives.

"She caught me," Mikey is explaining, "taking a few bucks from her pockabook. I tried to get away, man, but she stuck to me like the subway to the train tracks."

He begins to laugh now, saying, "Man, did you ever see anything like it, banging away on my head. Shit, I won't be able to go home for two days."

I am thinking that my own mother would be mortified to be seen beating me in the street. Even when she was so mad at me the time I ran away from home and looked through her drawers for the welfare money. The neighbors would never get over it, just like they'll be talking about Mikey's mother for weeks. I don't know how Mikey could push his mother like that. I would get murdered if I ever tried to do that.

"You can always sleep on the roof," I say. "A lot of people sleep on the roof in the summer. You just have to push the dogshit away."

"I'm going to sleep with your mother," Mikey says.

"You don't have enough money," Frankie says.

I don't say anything. I know they think it's funny, and I suppose it is. But I just can't say anything because I don't understand how guys can talk about their mothers like that. I know they don't mean anything by it, that they are joking around, but still, I think you have to respect your mother, even if she gets on you about cleaning the floors or the windows or taking down the garbage.

Your mother is your mother. She's not your brother or sister, or a priest or nun at St. John's, or someone at Kips Bay Boys Club. She's different from all the people in the world you can make fun of.

My mother can be a real pain sometimes. And I guess everybody's mother can be. But she doesn't stop being my mother when she's a pain.

We are walking across 120th Street toward Second Avenue. It is a strange feeling being here. Everyone sitting on the stoops, walking along the street, driving cars, managing the shops, looking out the windows, is colored. We're the only whites in the neighborhood, sticking out like three snakes on an empty dance floor.

"Are we all right here?" I ask.

"They know we must be here on business," Mikey answers. "They ain't gonna mess up somebody's deal without knowing whose deal they's messing up, you know? People are cool up here."

"They know," Frankie adds, "that we just want some smack, and that nobody will see any trouble while we're here."

"How do they know?" I ask. It's like walking into the lion's den because the lion's eyes are closed and somebody tells you the lion's sleeping.

"They just know," Frankie says. "What else they gonna think, that you're the insurance man? Shit."

We are almost at Second Avenue when, suddenly, Mikey turns up a stoop and slips into a building. We follow him. The hall is dark. There are no lightbulbs in the fixtures. There is garbage in the hall, papers and crunched cigarettes. And it smells of piss and stale booze. It is a hard smell, like sulfuric acid in the jewelry shop at Kips, and it fills my nose to the brink.

If my super kept our halls like this, the neighbors would beat him up.

I am beginning to wish I stayed with the pinball machine in the back of the candy store.

It is like another world. I don't know anything about any of this. Maybe it's a little exciting, this colored world up here in Harlem, but it is also making me feel a little nervous. One brawl in this hallway and I could be down for the forever count, and there will be no one to pick me up.

Just one flight up, there are four doors in a square hall.

Mikey knocks lightly on a door. A dog barks behind a door across the hall. All of a sudden a short colored man is pulling us into his kitchen. The kitchen has a bare wooden table in it, with one chair. There is a pot on the stove and a box of breakfast cereal on the table. Nothing else. We go to the next room. There is a woman sitting in this room on another kitchen chair, and she seems to be sleeping. There are three wooden milk boxes also in the room. There are some newspapers on the floor next to a *Hollywood Confidential*. Nothing else.

"My man," the colored guy says. He is slapping Frankie's hand. "What's the word?"

"Thunderbird," Frankie says, repeating a radio commercial for wine.

"What's the price?" the guy continues.

"Sixty twice."

"Where do you cop?"

"At the neighborhood shop."

"Yeah, man," the guy says. "Let's get some money up so's we can send my mama here out for some of her fine wine, you know? Like I need two dollars. Two dollars will give us some privacy so's we can do us some busin-ness, you know?"

The room has two windows that are covered with a blanket that is hanging from a curtain rod coming down from the ceiling. The floor beneath the newspapers and magazine is covered with an old linoleum that has holes worn through it just before the kitchen door. The linoleum is a maroon color that might have once been red. It hasn't been washed, I am thinking, since it was brought into the building.

"Here," Mikey says, "I got some money."

"My man," the guy says, "you are so cool."

He pushes the woman out of the chair, saying, "Hey, Mama, here is some money for you."

The woman opens her eyes and staggers a little. She almost falls down but catches herself on the door frame.

"All right," she says, taking the wine money, "all right."

When she is gone, the man goes into the kitchen and takes a shoe box from inside the stove. I can see the roaches scurrying around inside the open oven.

"How many?" he asks as he opens the box.

There are a great many small packages wrapped up in white paper and Scotch tape.

"Just one," Mikey says.

He takes one and hands it to Mikey. It looks to me that Mikey has done this a hundred times.

What if the cops come? I am thinking. What would happen to me? This is not like playing hooky or even riding around in a stolen car. Drugs is serious business, and some judge could send me to jail for years.

Shit, what am I here for? I don't even want any drugs.

"Can I taste?" Frankie asks, taking the bag from Mikey.

"Shit no," the guy says. "You can't taste. How you expect to come to Harlem to buy some horse and taste it first, 'cause that don't sound like you think I am your friend. And I am your friend, you know that."

Frankie just nods his head and takes three dollars from Mikey. He adds this to another two dollars he has pulled from his pocket and gives the five to the colored man.

Frankie gives the package back to Mikey. We all watch now as

Mikey unbuckles his pants, pulls his drawers to his knees, bends over, reaches back, and pushes the package hard up between the cheeks of his dumper.

I am wondering why he is doing that when the colored man begins to laugh.

"Yes, my man," the guy says, "the poleece will never put their nose there if they stop you in Harlem, the land of jazz and mo' jazz."

In the street again I am glad to breathe in a chestful of air that is lighter and cleaner than that dank tenement smell. It is all done. We have scored a hit, and I am feeling a little safer now.

And, strangely, I feel like I won something. I've never done anything like this before. But I did it. Something scary. Something I was afraid of.

I like this feeling I have, this strength, knowing that I have done something that Scarry, Walsh, Jurgensen, any of those guys, have never done. Scoring horse in Harlem.

Even if all it proves is I did it.

Chapter Forty-four

I wonder how long it will be before everyone finds out.

I've been putting on a shirt and tie when I get up every morning to do the papers, and Billy and my mother think that I go straight to school when I'm finished. But, instead, I go to the greasy spoon Greek diner on 53rd Street where I read the *Daily News* and drink coffee until the florist shop opens.

I've been reading a lot about the polio epidemic that has all these kids locked up in iron lungs. They show photographs of them, and they are always smiling up in the reflection of a mirror. They are trapped in this iron tube and they can't even see the world straight on, but through the reflection of a mirror.

I guess there are worse things, to be blind and crippled, to run into a tree like Spango. I don't know how my father sees the world, but I don't think he has to look through a mirror to see it. Maybe he sees his own world, a world nobody else sees, but he sees it straight on, anyway.

I am so afraid of being trapped like these kids, of being locked in a tube, or a room, or a building. Every time I read the newspaper I take a little time out to explain to God that it's the biggest fear in my life to be trapped like that, and that's why I do all this shuffling from the papers to the florist, all this lying to my family about going to school.

I like the florist. I like the forty cents an hour. I like being on my own, controlling my own life. I wish I could get around the lies. My mother thinks I'm working only on Saturday, and that Monsignor Ford wouldn't mind if I made a few extra dollars for the family. I wish I could tell her the truth.

I told Mr. Schmidt that I had something special to do this afternoon, and he let me go early, and I am now coming back from Bloomingdale's, where I finally bought the ring with the blue stone for my mother. I guess I could wait for her birthday to give it to her, or even Mother's Day, but I want to give it to her now. This is the day I finally put the forty bucks together, and this is the day I want to give it to her, no pause, no waiting, no excuse. It's like something to celebrate, this forty bucks.

I pick up my three-ring binder from under the stairs, the same place I always hid my cigarettes before I was allowed to smoke. My mother's working the four-to-twelve at the phone company, and I catch her as she is putting on some lipstick before the mirror over the kitchen sink. I throw my binder on the top bunk in my room, and I come out to the kitchen, the little blue box deep in my pocket and burning a fast hole.

"How you doing, honey?" she asks.

I go over to the sink and I give her a kiss on the cheek. She seems surprised.

"I'm okay, I guess," I say to her, "but I have this pain in my leg." She turns quickly to look at me.

"What pain, where?" she asks.

"Up here," I say, patting the upper part of my thigh. "I don't know what it is."

And then I try to look surprised.

"It's like there is something pressing into my leg," I say, "like a sharp corner of something."

She's looking now at where I'm patting my leg, and I say, "Holy cow, there may be something here. What's this?"

I'm patting my leg like crazy, and she has no idea of what's going on. Finally, I pull the ring box out of my pocket, saying, "Look, Mom, this is the thing that I'm up against, a little box with all these sharp edges."

I give the box to her, a dark blue box with a gold stripe around the sides, and I watch as she takes it in her hands and holds it to her breast.

"What's this?" she asks.

"Just something I think you need," I say, "and it's brand-new."

She opens the box and then sits on a kitchen chair as she pulls the ring out.

"And expensive," I add. She always thinks things are better if they're expensive.

"Oh, Dennis," she says, "you're something else. This is . . ."

She can't finish the sentence right away, and she waits.

"You drive us all to the brink of despair," she says finally, "and then you do this."

I don't say anything, and I am happy to see how she likes the ring as she slips it over her finger. It fits perfectly.

"How could you afford this?" she asks. I knew she would ask.

"I just saved," I answer, "a little here, a little there."

"You know, Dennis," she says, holding the ring out in the light, "to do this shows something that's in your soul."

I don't want her to make such a splash about it. I know she has most of what she needs, like food and clothes and this apartment, and I don't guess anyone really needs a gold ring. Especially since I don't want the ring to do anything except give her something to be happy about, something out of the blue that will make her smile.

"Oh, c'mon," I say. "I just wanted to give you something."

"Yes," she says, "you have given me something. And I hope you never lose it."

"The ring?" I ask.

"No," she laughs. "Not the ring. C'mere now and give us a kiss."

I laugh, too, saying, "I already gave you a kiss, Mom, and I gotta go to meet the guys on 54th Street."

Going down the stairs to the street, I think about what I said to my mother. It was a little lie, but still it was a lie, and I wonder if I'll be able to get it out of my head. Why am I lying to my mother like this? I'm not meeting the guys on 54th Street at all. I'm meeting the guys on 55th Street, but I don't want to tell her that.

I don't want her to know.

Chapter Forty-five

It is now two weeks later, and the three of us are sitting around in the basement of number 2 Sutton Place South, on 57th Street. I come to this building a lot with the flowers, and I know the lay of the basement delivery area. So does Mikey, because his father is a janitor here. We are in the boiler room, down a deep stairwell from the basement, the deepest part of the cellar, and there is a constant background of hissing steam.

We came here straight from making a score on 120th Street.

"Nobody will ever come here," Mikey says, "unless the boiler breaks down and they run outta hot water."

It is hot, steamy. The walls are dark and shining with the sweat of the moisture. There is a water bug on the ceiling, a large one with feelers that shoot out about three inches. It doesn't move, and seems frozen by the sound of our voices.

There are no chairs, and so we are sitting on the floor. Frankie takes a set of works from under his shirt. There is a small metal cap from a medicine bottle, and he puts it between the prongs of a bobby pin, which acts as the handle. It is like a miniature cooking pot.

There is a weird sense going through me as I watch this. It is like being at a High Mass where the priests are doing things that you haven't seen before, that you don't quite understand.

Mikey wraps thread around the tip of a large eyedropper and jams a needle on it. Frankie has the junk this time, and we watch him drop his pants and pull the glassine envelope, half the size of a pack of matches, out from between the cheeks of his ass. It is almost as if he has farted it out, but no one laughs. There is nothing funny about it.

Frankie now opens the package and creases an edge of the paper to pour out the white powder.

"Careful, man," Mikey says.

"I know what I'm doing, man," Frankie says. "Don't give me this careful bullshit."

"Easy, guys," I say.

This is the first time I have said anything since we got off the Second Avenue bus. The last time I was with them we just scored the horse, but today I'm going to try it.

Frankie pours the powder in and goes to the water faucet on the side of the boiler where Mikey is washing the needle. He puts a little water into the cap and mixes the powder with the water. It looks like white mud, but when Frankie puts a match to the bottom of the cap, all of it begins to boil, and the white substance disappears. It now looks like water. Just plain unadulterated water, painless and harmless.

"Perfect cook, man," Mikey says. "Perfect cook."

"Okay, Dennis," Frankie says. "You're up."

Until this moment I was thinking that I could still be along for the ride, but now, in a split second, I am a real part of all this. I have heard so much about how taking drugs just once will make you a drug addict for life, and drug addicts are the slime and the sewer scum in any neighborhood.

"C'mon," he says.

I never think about Frankie being a drug addict, but I guess he is. He's far from being a dreg, though. He's a good friend. I can tell the difference between a good guy and a dreg.

But Mikey? Mikey pushed his mother, and being a drug addict made him do that, and so I think Mikey may be a dreg.

"C'mon, Dennis," Frankie says again.

Maybe there's still time to back out, I think. As exciting as this is to me, I know that I don't care about it so much. There's no reason for me to do this, except to try it.

"Naw," I say.

I don't know what to expect. So there's nothing wrong with being worried about it. Yet, still, there is something that makes me wonder what it is all about, what it feels like.

I think about my mother making me eat all those things I hate, like tripe and eggplant and brussels sprouts and beef liver, and I can hear her voice saying, "You have to try things, Dennis, you can't just say you don't like it if you don't try it."

"C'mon, Dennis," Mikey butts in. "You could snort some if we had some powder, but we cooked it all. You don't have to take it mainline. You could skin-pop. Takes a few minutes, but then you'll be off."

"Is it habit-forming?" I ask. I don't know why I asked, because I know the answer.

Mikey laughs.

"Yeah, man," he says, "but that's what's great about it. You're always looking forward, man, and that's where it is, you know, in looking forward. It's all there."

"You can't get a habit," Frankie says, "if you just skin-pop. Don't listen to this guy. You can only get a habit if you mainline. Like this, see?"

Frankie has filled the eyedropper with the solution and wrapped his arm with a belt, holding one end of the belt between his teeth. He is smacking his veins with two fingers, getting a vein to rise. And then he puts the needle into a vein and jabs it around a few times until he finds the hole he is looking for. Then he spits the belt out, just as he is squeezing the bubble top.

I watch the solution disappear into his body, and I watch his lips change in a second from being pursed and all business and serious to a round smile.

God, I don't know what to think as I watch him close his eyes for a long minute. He tries to talk, but I can see it is hard for him to open his mouth. Finally, he is able to say something.

"Just skin-pop, Dennis," he says. "It is okay, man, I wouldn't screw you up, you know that."

I do know that. Frankie wouldn't do anything to hurt me. I am thinking I should try. If I was ever going to try, this is the right time. Frankie won't let anything happen to me.

"All right, man," I say. "Just one time."

It is like diving into the cold water, I am thinking. Just tell yourself to do it, and you'll do it. It wipes the questions out if you just tell yourself to do it.

Frankie has his eyes closed again, and so Mikey takes the needle out of Frankie's hands and refills it. He leans over to me and pinches the skin on my upper arm, around my muscle.

"Watch, man," he says, "it's like darts."

I feel the steel going into my arm, and I flinch. But he is holding me firmly, and I don't go out of his grip. And then he lets go of my skin as he squeezes the bulb quickly, and I feel the solution going into me like a shot at the doctor's office. And then there is nothing, except that I can see a little lump on my arm where Mikey has taken the needle out.

I begin to watch Mikey load up for himself and tie the belt around his arm, and then, suddenly, out of the blue, it feels like someone has coated my eyelids with lead. They are so heavy. I am thinking, okay, I am not spinning, but everything is so heavy. My hands, my head, my fingers, all feeling like they are nailed down. I try to open my eyes, but I cannot. I think about that water bug I saw, and I begin to worry about it. I'm getting afraid. I know that the water bug on the ceiling has moved to just above my head, and that it is going to let go of the ceiling and fall through the wet air of the boiler room and land in my hair, and I try to open my eyes to see where it is, but I can't, and I am picturing the three-inch feelers coming down my face, the bug stopping high on my cheek and rubbing the feelers together, and I think I can feel it there, and I am sweating with the fear, and I can't move my hands to smack it off, and I am beginning to smell it now as it gets close to my nose.

But, then, just as suddenly I forget about being afraid, and I am not thinking about the bug. I don't care about anything except raising my hand. But my hand is made of concrete, and it is welded on my lap, and I can't raise it, but I don't care. And time begins to pass. I can't think of time. There is no time. There is just now, and the now seems to be endless, with no beginning and no end, like God Himself.

I don't know where we are, but all of a sudden, we are moving. I sense these moving shadows along the walls of the cellar, and I realize that they are our shadows. And then there is sunlight, and we're in the park on 57th Street and the East River, where my mother took me every day for all those years when I was trying to grow up in New York. I sit on a bench, and it seems like days go by as I sit there, the green strips of wood gently wrapping around me, keeping me from floating up into the trees, my body like a tub of granite floating miraculously over the trees and then down into the East River, like a concrete coffin floating on top of the water. I am so afraid. I don't know why I have done this.

My hand is now on my face, glued to my face, trying to stop the itch on the side of my nose, and the itch on my ear, but my hand doesn't move, it just stays glued there until I forget why I raised it, or how.

I can't feel my heart beating, but I sense I am sweating because of some cloudy fearfulness. I know I am afraid. And what makes me most afraid is that I don't know what to do when I'm afraid.

I just want to float in this blackness, thinking that if I had one wish in the world, I would wish that my brother and my mother knew to come get me.

Maybe then the itching would stop, and I could open my eyes.

Chapter Forty-six

I have been trying not to think about all the letters from Cardinal Hayes High School that I have been ripping up.

I guess they will send someone down to 56th Street sometime soon, but it won't get me anywhere by worrying about it. I worked a long day today at the florist, and I have a few extra dollars in my pocket besides what I spent on a case of beer.

It is a hot night now, one of those Indian summer nights just before Halloween, and I have been drinking the beer all night with the Morgan brothers down by the river. I was going to meet the guys on 55th Street, but I met Terry and Jackie Morgan just as I came out of my building. They're always a lot of laughs, and so we came down here to the Beekman Place park by the river, and we've been arguing now for more than an hour about why the Yankees lost to the Dodgers in the World Series, and how Marciano could beat Archie Moore with one hand tied behind his back. Park talk. Sports bullshit.

Terry Morgan just left us. He went to have dinner with some girl he met in a hallway when he was delivering papers down on Sutton Place. Her parents were taking him to a restaurant called the Russian Cafe, and we told him that if he got caught there, he would be arrested for being a communist.

Except for Joe's Original Restaurant and Emiliano's pizza place, I still have never been to a restaurant for a meal, and I envy Terry for finding someone to take him.

The park on 51st Street is dark, and we are alone except for a few strolling couples who pass back and forth giving us strange looks. The sound of the traffic on the East River Drive is never ending, just as the neon Pepsi-Cola sign on the other side of the river never goes out. There is a constant grind of tires against the concrete, like there is a sawmill somewhere in the distance.

"How do you get a rich girlfriend like that?" I ask, holding a can of Rheingold beer.

"Just walk the streets around Sutton Place," Jackie says. "They are desperate over there for guys like us. They go home at night and put diamond rings on their fingers to play with themselves 'cause they don't have guys like us."

"How come you don't have one," I ask, "with or without the diamond rings?"

"Because I have Annie," Jackie says, "that's why."

"Who's Annie?"

"Give me some beer," he says. "Can you keep a secret, a secret like if you tell anyone at all, I will personally cut your personals from your person?"

"I can keep anything," I say, "even a girlfriend if I could find one. A secret's easy. So who's this Annie?"

"Annie Dunne."

"Annie Dunne with the husband in Sing Sing Annie Dunne?"

"That one," he says. "I went to bed with her three times."

"Jackie," I say, trying to remember the things I heard about the Dunne family, beside the fact that most of them are a little crazy, "isn't the husband in jail for murder?"

"No," he replies, "I think for beating somebody up, but he's in jail for another ten years or something."

"Jackie," I say, swigging the beer, "you ever hear of jailbreaks?"

"This ain't the movies," Jackie says, laughing.

"But, Jackie," I say, "even in the movies they don't all get killed in the jailbreak. Some of them go on to become priests, and some others come back to kill the guy what was banging his wife."

Jackie gets up from the bench, laughing loudly now.

"Come on," he says, "let's go pay her a visit."

"It's almost midnight," I say, thinking that most of the people on 56th Street are asleep at eleven.

"C'mon, don't be such a punk," he says. "She's got some beer in the fridge, and it's something to do. Your mother waiting for you or something?"

"Don't be a pain," I say. "My mother went out to her sister's house in Queens."

"So you don't have to go home. C'mon."

"Can you call her first?"

"Yeah," Jackie says sarcastically. "Like her husband has a good job so they can get a telephone, right?"

We finish the last two cans of beer before we hit 56th Street, and we walk down to 333, the building next to mine.

Jackie has his finger to his lips as we creep down the wooden stairs that lead to the alleyway to the backyards.

"Shh," he utters in a kind of whisper. "If we wake up old Mrs. Dunne, that will be the end of it."

Old Mrs. Dunne is Annie's mother-in-law, and she is the super of the building. Her apartment is in the front, and the wooden stairs creak like an old ship. We go through the first yard and then under a tunnel passageway to the yard in the very back.

Underneath my windbreaker, I can feel my polo shirt sticking to my back. I guess it's sweat made from the heat, but maybe also because I am a little afraid. Jackie is three years older than I am, and I don't know him the way I know Walsh or Scarry or even guys like Frankie and Mikey. Jackie has a reputation for being a little wild and crazy.

Jackie Morgan once bet someone that he could steal a fifteen-foot fishing pole from Bloomingdale's up on 59th Street. A guy named Jimmy Ginty then bet that he could steal a shotgun if Jackie could steal a fifteen-foot fishing pole, the one that is used for whales or something, and doesn't come apart. It happened on a day when there was a snowstorm. Jackie shoved his jacket into a Third Avenue trash basket and walked into Bloomingdale's in his undershirt and went right to the sports department. He told them he was the new stock boy, and he had to take the fishing pole to the stockroom so they could get the numbers to order new ones.

Jackie then walked straight out the front door, dragging the fifteen feet of fishing pole behind him, asking the security guard at the front of the store to open the door because the elevator wasn't big enough to take it down to the stockroom. "The security guard told me not to catch cold as he opened the door," Jackie told us. He was back on 56th Street in less than half an hour with a fishing pole that was for sale, and sent Ginty out for the shotgun.

Ginty never got the shotgun, but Jackie made himself a neighborhood legend.

Now we're in the backyard with a canyon of windows going up either side of the alleyway, and Jackie wants to climb up the drainpipe to the second floor.

"Up the drainpipe," I say. "Why can't we go in the front door?"

"Somebody might see us," he says.

"So what?"

"I been thinking about what you said about the jailbreak," Jackie whispers, "and I gotta make sure nobody sees us."

Jackie has his hands and feet around the drainpipe like a monkey, and he is shinnying himself up. I am right behind him. I don't know Annie Dunne hardly at all, but she is a looker, and I am wondering as I am in the middle of this circus act if I will get to see her in her nightgown.

Maybe kissing Jackie.

Maybe she'll kiss me.

Finally, Jackie gets to the window above us and shoves the kitchen window open. He climbs in and pulls me in after him, all the while holding his finger to his lips. I feel a strange sensation inside my body. It's not that I am afraid, but I just know that we are doing something that is very wicked. I know they could never send you to jail for this, but if the cops came for any reason, we would have a tough time telling them we were delivering newspapers to Annie Dunne at midnight.

Jackie takes his clothes off in the small light that is shining in from the alleyway. I look over and see him right there in the middle of the kitchen, and he is as naked as the day the doctor smacked him on the ass.

"You go sleep on the couch," he whispers, pointing to the living room.

I don't like that he is telling me what to do. I thought I would get to see Annie in her nightgown, or that she would give us a drink or something, but I didn't expect to climb up a drainpipe all this way to go sleep on a couch.

In a moment, though, Jackie is gone, his clothes spread around on the kitchen floor, left there like he was a leprechaun.

I open the refrigerator door and look to see what is inside. There is no light, and I can hardly see anything. I feel around looking for a bottle of beer. I am a little bit dizzy from the beer I had in the park, and it feels funny in my stomach, too, like I ate a bad fish cake or something.

Suddenly, I hear a long scream, a woman's scream. It is like the end of a song in an opera, and like in a whirl Jackie is going through the kitchen. He's speeding like a racing car, but he stops short at the living room and comes back to the kitchen for his clothes. He is naked, searching madly for his clothes, picking them up, and then running again.

I am still standing here, holding the refrigerator door open, feeling my stomach turn over and over.

"Get going!" he yells to me.

God, I'm thinking, what's going on? I have such a pain in my stomach, and Jackie is yelling. Did he try to kill Annie Dunne? What's wrong with my stomach?

I race after him through the living room, running fast, and into the back bedroom. I can hear Jackie either laughing or crying, I am not sure which, and he is tugging at the bedroom window, the one that leads out to the fire escape. He shoves it all the way open, and, still naked and holding his clothes, he climbs out the window and runs up the fire escape stairs. The screams seem to be following us into the backyard darkness. I am following close behind Jackie, but I have to stop, because my stomach seems to be pouring out of my mouth and nose, and I lean over the fire escape railing and I heave all over the backyard below, and I hope no one is looking up, because they'll get

more than birdshit in their eye, and I know I don't have time to lally-
gag on a fire escape after midnight, and I run like crazy to the roof trying to catch up with Jackie.

I find him there, in the darkness of a corner of the roof, doubled
over, out of breath and laughing madly. He doesn't say anything at first
and begins to hop frantically on one leg as he puts the other through
his pants.

I am leaning over, trying to get hold of my own breath. My stomach is still churning, and I want to throw up again, but I can't get anything out of my throat but a belch.

"Holy God," he is saying over and over. "Holy God. Holy God.
I climbed into the bed. I saw her lying there, and I climbed into the
bed, crown jewels and ass like a jaybird, and she turned around and she
yelled like hell, and she scared the living goddamn crap outta me, and
it wasn't even Annie Dunne, Dennis, it was, Holy God, old Mrs.
Dunne herself, there in the bed, and I am in the bed with her, naked,
my underdrawers in the kitchen. And I'm there putting my arms
around old Mrs. Dunne."

"Fat Mrs. Dunne?" I say. "What's she doing there?"

"Annie must've gone away, who knows, up to Sing Sing maybe."

"With a file in her girdle," I say. "That guy is gonna escape,
Jackie."

Jackie laughs a big one and pushes me.

"Yeah," he says, "and he'll end up in bed with his fat mother, too,
and then he'll want to go back to jail."

Now I raise my finger to my lips. Jackie is making too much noise
with his laughing and carrying-on.

"The cops are sure to come," I say, whispering.

"Who cares?" Jackie says. "I'm going home anyways. Just be quiet
in your hallway."

Our buildings are all in a row, mine and Annie Dunne's, and the
Morgans'. I watch Jackie as he crosses over two roofs and goes down
the stairs in his building, and I cross just one roof in the other direction and go down the stairs in mine, thinking that this has been a crazy
thing to do, climbing into someone's window in the middle of the
night. And why do I do these things when I know that for every crazy
thing like this I do there are fifty others I've done, and fifty more that

I'll probably do tomorrow and the next day? Why am I living outside of the normal? And is it, I wonder, just on the outside of the normal? Or is it below?

I tiptoe down the stairs, feeling the sweat on my shirt sticking against my jacket. I know that if I meet a policeman in this hall, I will have to explain why I am coming down from the roof and why I am sweating so much.

I am now on the fourth floor, and I can hear someone below me running up the stairs in twos. I run quickly down the dark narrow hall to my apartment and search for the key under the ripped hall linoleum. I quickly shove the key in the door and swing it open. And then I am flabbergasted. My mother is standing right there before me.

"Where have you been?" she asks.

I am completely surprised. Here is my mother standing in the middle of the kitchen, and I am still out of breath. She told me she probably wouldn't be home, and I promised her that I would be in by eleven-thirty. She is just standing there in her pink bathrobe, her arms folded in front of her. The kitchen light is still moving from side to side, and so the shadows of her face are moving back and forth, making her seem like she is some advertisement sign.

"I thought," I answer, "that you were going out to Aunt Kitty's, that you were staying over."

"Well, young man," she says, "I came home because I want to know where you are spending your time when you go out at night. It is almost one o'clock in the morning. I just had a feeling that you wouldn't do what you said you were going to do. Where were you?"

"I was just out."

"Who were you with?"

I know she doesn't like the Morgan family, because the mother and father come out on the street drunk once in a while. My mother thinks that if you have to be drunk, you should be drunk in your own house and not share it with everyone on 56th Street.

"Walsh and Scarry and those guys," I say in a low voice.

"Did you say Walsh and Scarry," she says in an angry tone, "and those guys? Huh? Listen, Dennis, tell me who you were with."

"I was with them," I say, lying. "We went to a movie."

"Where did you get the money to go to a movie, huh?"

I can't tell her that I have this extra money from the florist, that I've been working more than just on Saturday.

"Scarry treated us all."

I know it's another lie, but I can say Scarry treated us, because she knows that Mr. Scarry has a good job as the bartender at Billy's on First Avenue, and so there is a lot of money in that family.

My mother looks very angry, and the shadows moving back and forth across her face seem like a clock ticking away, and that soon it is going to come down to zero and then she is going to explode. She throws her hands out and begins to walk into the living room, but she stops. And she turns again to me, pointing her finger.

"I don't believe you, Dennis," she says, shaking her finger at me. "You were not with Scarry and Walsh, because they would not be out at one o'clock in the morning. And you don't want to tell me who you were with."

"I was so with them," I say in one last try to get out of it.

"You weren't," she says. "And I'll say this to you. Tell me who your friends are, and I'll tell you what you are. And just as you are ashamed to tell me who you were with, you will be ashamed of who you are."

"Can I go to bed now?" I say more than ask.

"Yes," she says, now with a biting, bitter voice, and that terrible look on her face, disgusted, as if we were passing a subway toilet. "You go to bed now and think about who you are."

I turn into our room, and she is following me.

I just wish she would shut up and leave me alone. She never stops when she is complaining about something. She just keeps going at it all the time. I don't take my clothes off, but jump up fast into the top bunk and turn my body away from her and into the wall. My head is spinning, and my stomach is turning, and I know that if I can just have some quiet, I can go to sleep and get away from the spinning and the turning. But she is right behind me. She reaches me and gives me a good shove so that my whole body moves.

"And don't think," I hear her say as my body goes flat against the wall, "that I don't smell the beer along with the cigarettes."

Chapter Forty-seven

A few weeks pass, and my mother doesn't say much more than hello to me.

It is now Sunday morning. Early. My brother has just come back from a midnight-to-eight shift throwing the mail sacks for the New York Central Railroad, and he is sitting in the bathtub in the kitchen. I don't say anything to him as I go to the sink to brush my teeth. The sink is right next to the tub, and I can see the water in the tub making small waves.

I didn't get up to do the papers this morning, and I didn't do the folding last night. Instead I hung out with Frankie and Mikey, and, besides the junk, I also took a few tokes on some pot. My head aches. I am still half asleep, and I wonder since my head feels like it is the size of a watermelon if I will ever get completely awake again. I am also wondering, as I grab the toothbrush, if Billy can see the marks in my arm muscle where I have been jabbing myself, doing my own skin-popping. I should have worn a long-sleeved shirt when I got out of bed.

My mother is in her room. Thank God. I don't want to talk to anyone, especially my mother, and especially when she's not talking to me. She only has questions when she's not talking to me, and she wants answers and explanations.

Billy is quiet, which is odd. He usually has something to say, like where did you go last night, or who was that girl I saw you with yesterday, or how come you didn't get up to deliver the papers this morning? But now he's quiet.

The *New York Times* is on the kitchen table, the thick Sunday paper. Billy may tell people he just reads the sports pages, saying things like "They even tell you what the jai alai players did in Cuba last week." But I see him when he is reading it, and he reads every page front to back.

I'm not going to go to Mass today. I don't feel good. It's okay to miss Mass if you're sick.

I'm still worrying about my arm in a short-sleeved shirt, and I go into our room and throw myself into an old flannel shirt. I leave it unbuttoned as I push the paper aside with my box of corn flakes. I then pour the cereal into a chipped green bowl and look for the coffee can that is filled with the sugar. I can't find it. I look all around, but I don't see it.

"Where's the sugar?" I ask.

"Don't talk to me," Billy says.

I really don't like it that he is talking to me this way.

I open the icebox door. I know it is a refrigerator, but my mother still calls it the icebox, and lately she has started to store the sugar in the icebox. I see the can, and I pour two tablespoons over the cornflakes.

"Don't give me the bug up in your ass," I answer Billy as I sit on the chrome and plastic chair.

Billy points a finger at me. "Just watch your mouth, Dennis," he says, "or I'll take your teeth out of it."

"Yeah, yeah," I say.

I put my head down close to the cereal bowl so that I don't have to look at him. We don't argue so much, but sometimes he gets the idea that he's the boss in the house, and I don't like it. Like when he hit me with the pool stick. He just thinks he has to play the father around here.

"You know," he says, "you're not going to get away with everything."

I don't know what he is talking about, and so I keep my head down.

"Yeah, yeah," I say again.

"I played basketball up at Mount St. Vincent's yesterday," he says. "Yeah?"

"And I met Father Jabo."

He's talking about Father Jablonski, the dean of discipline at Cardinal Hayes.

"Yeah?"

"He told me you haven't been up at school for more than a month, and so I told Mom."

"Shit," I say. "Why'd you do that?"

"'Cause she should know how you're screwing up."

"Yeah, yeah, friggin' squealer."

Billy raises his voice now. "I told you to watch your mouth."

I am not going to just take it from him, and so I become a little courageous with sarcasm.

"I need," I say to him, "a mirror to watch my mouth, and goddammit, why can't you just mind your own business?"

Now he is yelling. "Because you are a little wise guy, you and the punk brizzers you hang around with."

My mother now comes running out of her bedroom, wrapping her bathrobe around her on the run, the pink one with the cotton balls and frills.

"Just stop it, you two," she says. "Stop arguing."

I put my face into the chipped bowl again as she boils the water for her tea.

"Arguing doesn't settle anything," she says.

I am always noticing how small the kitchen is, not much bigger than a dining room table in one of those houses on Sutton Place where I deliver the flowers. And, as I look at my mother, I can see she is cramped in front of the small two-burner stove, between the stove and the commode room door. The paint above her is a faded yellow, and it is flaking in peels from all the steam that has risen from the kettle since the kitchen was painted a few years ago.

I can tell she is upset because she is pursing her lips and shaking the kettle to help the water boil faster. Billy doesn't say anything, and

I am thinking that she will lay into me any minute now about playing hooky.

And so I just sit and try to chew my cornflakes quietly. Even a loud crunch might make her even madder because she hates it if we make any noise at all when we are eating. "Masticate your food," she is always saying, "masticate your food." But when we try to chew as much as we can, she says we are making too much noise.

She pours her tea and turns to me. She slams the cup on the white Formica, and the tea spills over. I jump a little at the suddenness of it.

"So what time did you come home last night?" she asks.

"You mean me?" I ask in return, looking up.

And then she lays into me.

"You are such a fast-mouth you are," she says. "You know I mean you. I don't mean your brother, who has been out at the railroad since midnight last night working to bring a few extra dollars into the house, and you are nowhere to be found."

I suddenly think that I not only do not know what time I came home, but I don't even know where I was, for I only remember the heaviness of my eyes, and the nodding, and the walking all around the neighborhood, and the sitting in the cellar of the candy store on 55th Street, and the nodding, and the walking to Riker's on 53rd Street, and the nodding, and the bite of a hamburger from someone I don't remember, and the way the food made my stomach turn like an old engine that was creaking the pistons without any oil, and then an endless stream of nodding, and I don't know where and I don't know what time.

I don't even know who was with us, except I know it was me and Frankie and Mikey and a couple of other guys, cooking up in an alleyway behind the 54th Street Gym. And now my head feels like someone has filled each ear with a grease gun, and I wish she would just lay off.

"So," she says, "what time did you come home?"

This time her voice is getting louder, and I know she is going to get into the argument she says doesn't settle anything. I don't want to be forced to lie again. It seems all I do is lie to my mother, because she's always asking questions like a detective, and, anyway, I think she can tell what's a lie before the first sentence is finished.

"I don't know what time, Mom," I say, "so just leave off, will ya?"

She pours a half-cup of milk into her tea, and a half-teaspoon of sugar.

I put my head down into my bowl and scoop up the cereal the way the Chinese eat their rice. Maybe this will get her off the subject.

"Raise your head up," she says. "Don't eat like a dog."

"C'mon, Mom."

"Don't 'c'mon Mom' me," she says. "Where were you that you don't know what time you came home?"

"I was just out."

"What were you doing?"

"Nothing, and just leave me alone, huh?"

"And what went on at the florist's shop yesterday?"

"Nothing."

"Nothing went on?" she asks. "What did you do there?"

I am thinking that it is just going to get worse for me here, and we haven't gotten to playing hooky yet. And so I don't answer.

"Answer me," she demands. "You say nothing went on?"

"No," I answer. "Nothing went on."

"You're absolutely right nothing went on," she says, opening the knot on her bathrobe and tying it again. "Because you never went there to begin with. Mr. Schmidt came here looking for you because they had weddings and dinners and you left him high and dry, and you are telling me nothing happened? So you are turning into a little rotten liar, too?"

"I didn't lie," I say. "And why can't you just let me alone? I am the one who has to talk to Mr. Schmidt, not you."

"And who were you with?"

I am now feeling the skin all over my face begin to tighten, as if a corner was being twisted like a rubber band, and I want to make one of those terrible stretching faces that will make her madder than anything. I just want to get out of the apartment before everything explodes, and I am thinking of Mrs. Fallon trying to belt Mikey all over 56th Street, and how sometimes mothers can go overboard about things.

I wish she would stop, and just drink her tea, and say nothing. But she doesn't. She is keeping it going.

"So who were you with?" she asks again. "You will not get up from this table until you tell me where you were and who you were with."

My head is now hurting worse than before, filled with grease and rocks and anything else that weighs a ton. I have got to get out of this argument, out of this house. I can feel my heart pumping like a tommy gun beneath my chest, and I close my eyes.

"Where were you?"

I feel so filled up with something, I don't know what. Maybe I am just sad, or maybe I am just mad at everybody, but I know I have to stop this, and now. And so I yell.

"MOM," I yell, "C'MON, HUH? I AM SO FUCKING TIRED OF EVERYONE BEING ON ME, YOU AND BILLY . . ."

I don't have time to finish my sentence because Billy is out of the tub in a flash and coming for me.

I know I shouldn't have cursed. And I know, too, that I have to run. But where can you run in a four-room apartment smaller than a moving truck?

My mother's room? Maybe I can lock him out.

And so I run as fast as I can and try to slam the door behind me, but my mother has so many coats and clothes hanging on the back of the door that I can't close it, and Billy has pushed the door open and is now on me, punching like a Golden Gloves contender. The room is big enough only for my mother's bed and a dresser, and I begin to fall, but I can only fall on the bed, and Billy, all naked and soapy, is on top of me, and I feel my head is heavy and sinking down into the mattress with each punch.

And now my mother is screaming.

"STOP IT!" she is screaming. "STOP IT! DON'T RUIN THIS FAMILY."

And I wonder if she is talking to me or to Billy.

She is trying to pull Billy away, but he is so wet and slippery that she keeps losing her grip and falling backward, and Billy punches me twice more, and then suddenly he stops, and he turns away and walks back to the kitchen, naked like an Indian hunter, and my mother is just standing there, tears streaming down her face, her hands clutched together, and I watch Billy disappear into our room.

I want to cry out, but I don't do anything.

I can't talk.

Here we are, all of us, the whole family in a donnybrook, and I wish I could say something that would make my mother stop crying, but there is nothing I can think of. Maybe if I said I was sorry, but I don't know what to be sorry about. Playing hooky? Staying out late? C'mon, I am fifteen years old, for Chrissakes.

It is my life, and those guys are my friends, and what else do I have but my life and my friends?

Chapter Forty-eight

It is the week before Christmas. Billy just came back from a trip through New England with the Cardinal Hayes basketball team, winning everywhere they went. They have a team of all-city players, Kevin Loughery, Don Newhook, George Gersch, all scholarship bound. He has just walked in the kitchen from a day of delivering Christmas trees for Goldfarb's Florist on 57th Street. He seems in a great mood, and is laughing.

It is seven-thirty. I have just put in a full day at the East River Florist, now that I have quit school, and I'm finishing the dinner my mother left for us before she went to the telephone company at five. It is a new shift for her, and she won't be home until one in the morning.

"Hey," Billy says, "what a day."

"There are two franks for you in the frying pan," I say, "and some potato salad in the icebox. What are you laughing about?"

"It's in the hallway," Billy says.

"What's in the hallway?" I ask as I put my dish in the sink.

"Take a look," he says, "and I'll get the saw under the bathtub."

The hallway is completely filled by a huge Christmas tree, its branches cramped against the hallway walls. The tree is lying on its side but it must be fourteen feet high.

Billy is now behind me with the saw in his hand.

"What did you do," I say, "rob it?"

I am joking. Billy would never steal anything. There are just some things Billy would never do, and stealing is one of them, and cursing. He is too busy studying his Latin and working at all the side jobs to think about getting into trouble. But a lot of Christmas trees ended up in the apartments on my block after falling off trucks or being left mysteriously under a lamppost, and I am thinking maybe someone gave Billy one of these.

"No," he says. "Mr. Goldfarb himself gave it to me because I worked all day without the truck. I had to carry everything through the streets."

"Couldn't Mr. Goldfarb give you one that fit in an apartment instead of one made for a church? And did you get the Mayflower Moving Company to get it here?"

"Michael Harris helped me," he says, "and it will be okay."

Billy jumps into the branches and makes his way to the top. He saws away about five feet of tree and stands it up. It looks pregnant, like there are two more trees inside of it. We pull and shimmy the thing through the kitchen door, move the kitchen table onto my mother's bed for a minute, and drag the thing into the living room. I take the chrome-legged chair that is in the corner and put it on the couch for another minute, as Billy shifts the tree into its place. There is hardly any room to walk into the living room now because there are branches all over the place.

"Saw some of these off," I say, "and clear a path, or we'll never get the kitchen table back from Mom's room into the kitchen."

Billy gives the tree a haircut, and then, with the kitchen table returned to the kitchen, and the chrome-legged chair shoved in front of the couch, we admire the way Christmas has taken over the apartment.

"I'm going to eat," Billy says, "and then take a bath. In an hour we'll decorate the tree together. I promised Mom it would get done."

"I'm going to go out for a while," I say.

"Right," he says. "You just better be here in an hour. I'm not going to do this alone."

"No sweat, Chet."

In the candy store on 55th Street I meet Frankie and Raymond

Connors. Frankie looks like he has already scored today. His eyelids are half down over his eyes, and his speech is a little slurred, but he is not nodding. I think when you mainline as much as he does, once a day, anyway, that the nodding wears off in a short time.

"Hey, Dennis," Frankie says. "Good to see you, man."

The candy store is long and narrow, and the front window is steamed up from the cigarette smoke and the hissing heat. Newspapers are piled high in the back of the store, and there is a musty smell everywhere. Frankie's mother is sitting behind the counter reading a *Daily News.* She is a quiet woman, and hardly says anything to anyone except a smiling hello.

Raymond Connors is laughing as he reads from a magazine.

" 'Love for Sale,' it says," Raymond says, looking up, "and I'm going to go over to Amsterdam where it says here the girls sit in the storefront windows, and you just walk up and down the street window shopping, and you can take your pick."

"Where's Amsterdam?" Frankie asks.

"Someplace over there," Raymond answers, "next to England and France and places like that. I need a new girlfriend, too, since Marilyn moved to New Jersey."

That's where Marilyn Rolleri is, I think.

"You should go out with Maryanne Maniscalco," Frankie says. "And you don't have to go over the ocean. I saw her yesterday, short skirt, crinoline slip, she bends over and you see the big planet."

"The big planet?" I say.

"Venus, man," Frankie says. "Venus, the only planet that matters, and she's not going out with anyone anymore."

Raymond is still laughing. I lean against a wall and light a cigarette, thinking that Marilyn Rolleri is probably better off in New Jersey if Raymond doesn't even care about it. All my life I have been dreaming about having a girl like her, and I never came closer than a fast hallway kiss. I would care a lot more than Raymond does about it, I know, if it was me.

"I'll talk to her," Raymond says, "maybe."

"Man, what should we do tonight?" Frankie asks.

"Where are Nicky and Mikey and those guys?" I ask.

"I'm going to meet them later, man," Frankie says. "At the Tavern Bar on 48th Street."

"I got something great," Raymond says. "C'mon with me, under my stairs in the hallway."

"I hafta go home in an hour," I say. "Maybe I'll just stick around for a little bit."

"Don't be such a queer," Raymond says. "You have all year if you want it."

Frankie's mother doesn't look up as we pass her and leave the candy store for the hallway next door. Under the stairs in the back of the hall, Raymond puts his finger to his lips as he picks up a brown paper bag and pulls a bottle from it.

"What is it?" I ask.

"Pernod," he says.

"Bernard?" I ask.

"No," Raymond says. "Pernod, like *p-e-r-n-o-d*."

"I don't think that's how you say it, man," Frankie says.

"It's like anisette," Raymond says, "but I don't know how to spell that."

"A-n-i-s-e-t-t-e," Frankie says, spelling it out.

"You go to the head of the class," Raymond says as he breaks the seal, and hands the bottle to me.

It has a sweet taste, and it doesn't make my throat hurt the way whiskey or Scotch does. I take a second swig, this time a big gulp.

Frankie drinks some, too, and then Raymond, and then it is back to me. I take two more gulps. I don't feel anything. Nothing at all.

Two hours later we are sitting in a booth in the back of the Tavern Bar down Second Avenue. We've been hanging around here, or in a bar called The Studio, for a couple of months now. You have to be eighteen to drink in New York, but most of the people I see are sixteen or seventeen. I get away with it because I use a duplicate of my brother's driver's license.

Frankie had to carry me down most of the way to 48th Street. The liquor hit me like I walked into an airplane propeller under Raymond Connors' stairs, and we just sat there trying to make words with the sounds that were coming out of our mouths.

Now I am drinking glass after glass of soda water, trying to dilute the stuff before I pass out. Raymond is still laughing. He laughs at everything everyone says, funny or not.

"Where's Nicky?" Frankie says.

Raymond laughs.

Jurgensen walks into the bar and sees us in the booth. I don't see Scarry or Walsh.

"Hey, Dennis," Jurgensen says. "Hey, Frankie, Raymond."

Jurgensen sits at the bar.

Raymond laughs.

"You got twice as much teeth as you need, Raymond," I say.

Raymond laughs.

"And your head looks like a cue ball balanced on top of a pool stick."

Raymond laughs.

I realize then that Raymond doesn't hear anything at all. He is just laughing to have some response. The Pernod has made him kind of delirious, and he can't shake that stupid smile on his face.

I know I am drunk, I am thinking, and if I could only get to the bathroom and throw it all up, I would be all right again. I am seeing two of everything. I see Jurgensen, both of him, sitting at the end of the bar by himself. There is a thin wall of a bar separation between him and me, about five feet high, and Jurgensen is watching John Conroy put a glass with an inch of water on the top of the separation.

When you sit at the end of a bar, you see everything. Jurgensen will watch that glass until somebody knocks into the separation, and he will watch the glass fall to the ground and break, and he will watch as John Conroy demands that the clumsy guy buys him another drink, a full glass of gin, or risk a broken nose. I know that Jurgensen will sit there amusing himself with Conroy and ten other neighborhood guys until he falls off the stool in another two or three hours.

I don't want to pass out like that, and if I could get to the bathroom, I could have another two or three hours of some good time here.

Suddenly, I remember that I was supposed to go home to decorate the tree for Christmas. I said I would be an hour, but that was two and a half hours ago. Maybe Billy is still there. Maybe I could still help him do the tree. If I could only get to the bathroom.

"Lemme out, Frankie," I say.

"Where ya goin', Dennis?"

"Baretroom."

Frankie gets up and I slide over the leather seat and fall right to the floor. Shit, I think. Here I am lying flat out on the floor of a bar that would serve kids from Sister Stella's third-grade class. I leave my head on my arm. I feel a bit of a comfort here, and I want to close my eyes and go to sleep, but Frankie has his arms around my waist pulling me up from the center. It would be so easy to just go to sleep, to be anything but drunk like this.

"Get up, Dennis," Frankie is saying, "before the bartender sees you and kicks us all out."

I stagger to the bathroom, and as I pass by a back booth I see Buckley sitting there with a woman. I don't pay much attention because I don't like him much, anyway, and I rock from side to side until I am before the bathroom sink, and I lean over and the Pernod comes out as I open the faucet and watch everything mix with the water, and I hear myself wretching as half my stomach goes down the drain. I take a big mouthful of water and gargle, and then I clean the sink out.

"Always try to clean the sink when you're out," my mother told us the night we were at Joe's Original Restaurant, "because there will always be somebody behind you that might want a clean sink."

I cup the water in my hand and splash it up to my face. It feels like a curtain of ocean air has swept across my skin. I am feeling less woozy now, less legless. It would be a gift from God to be home now sleeping in the top bunk.

"Sit down, Dennis," Buckley says as I begin to pass them by.

I am now in the red leather booth, next to a woman who I guess is twice as old as I am. She has a round face and full red lips, like you'd see on a billboard. I watch her figure going back and forth from being one person to being two. I guess she's pretty, but I don't like the way she has her hair, a million little crispy curls coming down over her forehead. I squint to make sure I see only one of her.

"This is Loretta," Buckley says.

"Hello, Loretta," I say, holding my hand out to shake hands.

She leans over and kisses me on the mouth.

Even in this dizziness, I am thinking that I never knew a woman could be like this, that she could just say hello, a simple hello, and then open her mouth and the full force of a hot breath mixed with alcohol and cigarette smoke could shoot into your body with a kiss.

I don't know what to say when she stops, but I am glad that I gargled. She turns fully toward me on the leather seat. I can see her legs now, and the way her polka-dotted green skirt hangs loose between her legs and over her thighs. Her clothes are clinging to her, and even in this fog I can sense the hard muscles of her thighs and the solid firmness of her breasts.

"So you're Dennis," she says.

I look at Buckley, wondering what the score is here. He's smiling.

"Loretta," Buckley says, "is a friend of mine. She's been lookin' at you and told me you remind her of James Dean."

"My mother," I say to them, "says that I look like Gabby Hayes in the morning."

"Well," Loretta says, "you look like James Dean now."

There are two shot glasses filled to the brim before her, and she lifts one to her lips and downs it like a longshoreman.

"And," she adds, "I like you."

I look at Buckley again, as I feel Loretta's hand on my leg. He is still smiling.

"Lookit," Buckley says, "I gotta meet Ray Dececci up on 54th Street. If you want, you can take Loretta to my house for a drink or something, 'cause my whole family went to Pennsylvania for Christmas. I can meet you there later."

What should I think about this invitation? I wish I was back on the floor, my head on my arm, falling into a deep rest that would take me out of this world.

I can see my brother waiting in the living room for me to help him with the decorations. He said he wouldn't do them without me, but I am also looking at Loretta, and I am wondering what is going on here.

It looks like a fix-up, but it could also be a setup. I never liked this Buckley guy too much, until now. It seems to be a generous thing if it's the real McCoy, to let me go with Loretta to his house. Real generous.

Or why didn't I think of this before? Maybe this is a prostitute, a

woman that Buckley has gone together with in some deal. He is in
with those kind of people, I know.

I better ask him straight out, I think, and I get up from the seat.

"Could I see you a second?" I say to Buckley, waving him away
from the table.

"Hey," Loretta says as he gets up and leaves.

"Look," I say to him, standing just a few feet from Jurgensen. "I
am tapped out and can't even buy a drink here, so if you're lookin' for
a few shekels to be with this Loretta, I don't know where I'll get it."

"Hey," Loretta calls again, I guess feeling abandoned. She has the
second shot glass to her mouth.

"No, no, no," Buckley says. "It's nothing like that, man. Damn,
I am giving you a hundred percent luck here, and you are breaking my
horns."

Loretta is now sitting on a worn velvet couch in Buckley's
apartment on 48th Street, just around the corner from the Tavern
Bar. She is so much older than I am, maybe thirty I am thinking,
but she has something warm about her, like she is a little girl being
quiet and polite.

She has a very nice body beneath her green skirt with the white
polka dots and her red sweater. She is like a Christmas present. Raymond would laugh now if he thought I had a Christmas present like
this.

But what do I do now that I'm here? I'm not sure how I should
act. I have never been with a girl alone like this in an apartment, where
it might lead to something. I hear guys like Jackie Morgan talk about
it, but I have never had a steady girlfriend who would even let me feel
the cloth of her brassiere.

And no one has ever talked to me about what I should do with a
girl like Loretta. She's not even a girl anymore, and if Father O'Rourke
was here, he would say that I am in the near occasion of sin, and I
should think of everything that is dear to me, to think good thoughts,
to think of everything I respect in life, like Archie, and my brother,
who is going to beat me, I know, because I didn't help him with the
Christmas tree.

This is the famous Penn Station of the Our Father. I am thinking this as Loretta puts her arms around me. And lead us not into Penn Station. Maybe I could talk to her some, get her to relax a little. I could relax, too, I feel so edgy.

"I wonder," I say to her, "why Buckley didn't go to the country with his family. My mother never goes on a trip without us."

"Maybe," she says, "they didn't want him to go. C'mon, Jimmy, loosen up, will ya?"

What is this Jimmy stuff? Does she want me to be James Dean or something?

"Why not?" I ask. "I wonder how they let him stay here alone."

I'm thinking of when my mother told me she was going to Aunt Kitty's, but then ended up back in the kitchen to catch me coming home late. What would I do here, I am thinking, if Buckley's father walked into the house?

Suddenly I can feel my eyes beginning to close. It is like I have taken a pound of horse and my eyelids weigh a hundred pounds. I know I want to keep talking to Loretta, but I am so tired.

I just want to fall into her lap, close my eyes, and sleep for a week.

"The family hates him," Loretta says. "He told me."

How could a family hate someone in their own family, even someone as pimply as Buckley? I look at Loretta, try to focus on her, but I am too dizzy to see her clearly. All that Pernod. Maybe I shouldn't have had so many club sodas. Maybe it just spread the Pernod out.

I know I could kiss her if I wanted to, but I keep my body a few inches away from her on the couch. I don't know why I am hesitating to make out with her, but I feel that it is not the normal thing, to just meet a girl or even a woman like Loretta, and then two seconds later end up on a couch with her on 48th Street.

But, still, she is a good looker, and I don't know how long it will be before I ever have this kind of a chance again. As Buckley said, he was dealing me one hundred percent luck.

Loretta takes her sweater off. Just like that, she crosses her arms and pulls her sweater right over her head, and she is sitting there in a white brassiere, again looking like a little girl waiting to be told what she should do next.

"I wish I had some whiskey," she says.

"Maybe I could find some," I say quickly, beginning to get up from the couch, happy that I could move even for a minute. I am now feeling the sweat in my hands, and I wipe my hands on my pants.

"No, no," she says. "You just sit here, and I'll look."

Loretta gets up and walks through the Buckley apartment. It is much bigger than my apartment, but it is way down here on 48th Street. I wouldn't want to live here, I am thinking as she disappears into the darkness of the kitchen. It is so far away from 56th Street.

God, if I could just rest a little, maybe I could feel better, and maybe I could talk to Loretta some more. I have never done anything like this, and if I just felt a little better now, maybe I could tell her that I have never done this.

I mean, I am still only fifteen years old, but I guess she thinks I have done this with thousands of girls. This is the 1950s, right? And in 1955 lots of guys do this, some of them almost every day. Things are changing in the world. The Korean War is over, and everybody is working hard in the neighborhoods, and they all need to have a good time on the weekends. The bars are always full, and the dances my brother goes to up at the Jaeger House on 86th Street are always packed. Everyone is drinking and making out in the corners. It's not like it used to be anymore where the girls all run home to their mothers when a guy tries to kiss them or grab them. Guys just do it whenever they get a chance, right?

But I need just a little rest here, a couple of minutes is all. She looks so pretty in her white brassiere, prettier, even, than Sue Flanagan.

I just remember a sweet darkness, and now Buckley is shaking me like a wild man.

"Come on, Dennis," he is saying. "I hafta go, and you hafta get outta here, you unnerstand?"

"What happened?" I ask. "Where is Loretta?"

"She's gone, man," Buckley says, pulling my arm, "like you are gonna be. Let's go, huh? My old man is coming home any minute, and you gotta get outta here."

I look at the clock, and realize I have to be at work in the florist in another hour, so I feel lucky that Buckley is waking me.

*   *   *

I am now inserting the key in the door of apartment 26, and my mother is standing right there as I walk in. I wonder if she doesn't stand there most of her life. She is dressed in a skirt and a sweater, and her hands are fisted and on her hips.

"Where were you?"

"I'm sorry, Mom," I say. "I fell asleep at a friend's house, I swear to God."

It is just a little lie, because Buckley really isn't a friend.

"You fell asleep?" she asks. "At whose house?"

"Buckley," I say. "At Buckley's house on 48th Street."

"Who were you with?"

"I was with Frankie and those guys from the candy store on 55th Street."

I don't know what else to say that isn't a bald-faced story.

"You were, were you?"

"Yes, Mom," I say. "I swear." I was with them, anyway.

"We'll see about that right now," she says, "and you can come or you won't, but I don't know this Frankie from a head of cabbage. I'm going around to 55th Street, and I'll find out who he is, anyway."

Goddammit, I am thinking, she is going off into one of her tirades. Why can't she just leave things alone?

"C'mon, Mom," I say, "please. Just forget about it."

Billy now appears at the door of our bedroom, rubbing the sleep out of his eyes.

"Where were you?" Billy asks.

"C'mon, Billy," I say, sitting down in a kitchen chair. "I've been through this already."

"Listen, Dennis," Billy says, now grabbing me by the sleeve of my coat, pulling hard on it, "if it wasn't Christmas Eve, I would give you something that you would never forget. Go look at the Christmas tree, and see how it doesn't have a stick of tinsel on it because you were too damned selfish to come home and be responsible."

My mother puts her hand on Billy's back.

"Leave him alone, Billy," she says. "I am going around to that candy store on 55th Street and see what kind of a person this Frankie is."

*　　*　　*

I beg my mother the whole way down First Avenue, all the way to the candy store.

"Don't do this," I beg.

I am completely embarrassed now as she opens the candy store door. I see Frankie and his father at the back of the store, shoving cases of empty soda bottles from one side of the store to the other. Frankie's mother is at the front, and she smiles at my mother. She is such a nice woman, and I hope my mother doesn't say anything to hurt her feelings.

"Where is this Frankie?" my mother says.

She looks so determined, like she is out hunting or something.

Frankie's mother is still smiling. "You mean," she says, "my son, Frankie?"

"I guess so," my mother says, "the one who my son has been hanging around with."

"He's right back there." Frankie's mother points.

She is still pointing as Frankie and his father come out of the back shadows.

"Are you Frankie?" my mother says.

I am hoping that Frankie will be polite, because I know that I can't let anybody, not even Frankie, be impolite with my mother.

"Yes, I am, Mrs. Smith," Frankie says.

"Were you with Dennis last night?" my mother asks like she is investigating a crime like Charlie Chan.

"Yeah," Frankie says, "most of the time."

"Until what time?" she asks.

Frankie's father now walks out of the shadow.

"What's the problem here?" he asks. He's a short man with a big Italian nose. I don't know him very well, because he is always on his truck delivering things like furniture for the antique dealers.

"There is no problem here," my mother says. "I just want to know what time you left him."

You can tell by his face that Frankie is being very polite. I guess he hasn't taken any drugs yet today. It is a small piece of luck, because my mother could tell with the drop of a feather if something isn't right in someone's eyes.

"It was late," Frankie says, stealing a fast glance at me. "And then I think he went to sleep over at someone's house."

"Whose house?"

I don't know why my mother thinks that Frankie should know everything about my life.

"I don't know," Frankie says. "He just left, is all."

I am mortified that my mother is here like a cop from the 17th Precinct. I just wish we could go home.

"C'mon, Mom," I say. I put my hand into her folded arm and try to edge her away. I can tell she doesn't know what else to say, and I just want to get her out of the candy store.

Her eyes are a little wet, and sparkling, and I am hoping that she doesn't start to bawl in front of everyone.

"C'mon, Mom," I say. "C'mon."

Chapter Forty-nine

It didn't take much to quit Cardinal Hayes. My mother had to go up to the Grand Concourse with me, and we sat in Monsignor Fleming's office.

"When will you be sixteen?" Monsignor asked.

"A few months," I answered.

"You won't have much of a future," the monsignor said, "when you quit school. An education is the safest thing to put between us and despair."

"Monsignor Ford is getting me a job when I turn sixteen," I said. "At Catholic Charities."

"That's something," Monsignor Fleming says. "It's good you have a friend in Monsignor Ford."

And that's all there was to it to quit high school—no fanfare, no trouble, no pledge in the rectory office. I just left Cardinal Hayes for the last time, and that was that.

Now I am one of two office boys at the Catholic Charities building on 22nd Street. It takes hardly any effort or ability to sort and deliver the mail up and down the six floors of the building, and I am getting seventy-five cents an hour, which is not bad. Thirty bucks a week. I give my mother fifteen, and I can buy whatever kind of shoes I want from now on.

I'm still working on Saturday's at the florist, and I'm glad to have the extra money. I don't know why I'm glad, though. I don't have anything special I want to do with the money. I just put it away, about ten bucks a week.

Working two jobs and being on my own is what I want. I am controlling my life, and if you don't count my mother, Mr. Schmidt at the florist, and my boss Mr. Lacy at Catholic Charities, and maybe Monsignor Ford, I don't have anybody to answer to. I can do as I want.

I am standing in the back of the church now. I've been missing Mass a lot lately, and I am making a stop-in.

"Just stop in once in a while between Sundays," I remember Sister Stella saying, "and that's the quickest way to heaven."

No matter what is going on in my life, I always try to make room for going to church. I'm an Irish Catholic, I guess, is the best way of explaining why I like to be in there. You never hear someone say, "That person is an Italian Catholic" or "That person is a Spanish Catholic." But ask someone with an Irish name in New York what religion he is and I bet he'll say, "I'm an Irish Catholic." It's as if the Irish have their own brand of religion, different from the other hundreds of millions of Catholics in the world. And I think staying close to God is the only thing that makes any sense about being separate, about being Irish Catholic.

I don't have anything to especially pray for, and so I am sitting in a back pew, sort of basking in the soft evening light, the smell of fading incense, and the wild mix of colors coming down from the saints and the angels on the ceiling and walls. It is like basking in the sun at Coney Island, when you don't think about hardly anything, but just let the warmth sink into you.

Suddenly, someone comes in my pew and sits next to me. The church is nearly empty, and I jump out of my thoughtless daydream. It's Father O'Rourke, and he gives me a big pat on the back.

"We miss you at the altar boys, Dennis," he says.

"Just getting old, Father," I say, "growing up."

"Level to level, huh?"

"Right," I say, "kid to teenager, grammar school to high school, and high school to working."

"Right," he says. "I heard you quit school and are now down with Monsignor Ford. How is it?"

"It's okay," I answer. "Okay."

"Why'd you quit school?"

"I failed everything," I say, "because I hardly went to class. And instead of going into my third year, I would have to do my first year all over again. I'd be old enough to vote by the time I graduate."

Father O'Rourke laughs.

"I know what you mean," he says. "Most days I'm trying to catch up with what I was supposed to do yesterday, but could I give you some advice?"

"Sure, Father."

"Keep reading books, and being interested in what's going on in the world around you. No matter what's going on in your life, always care about what you are putting inside your mind. It's what's up here"—he is now pointing at my head—"that will let you grow, level to level."

"I would start with Hemingway," Billy says. It's a Sunday afternoon, and we are shooting baskets up at the 61st Street park.

"I already read some Hemingway," I say.

"That's what I am doing," Billy continues. "I'm reading all of Hemingway, all of Faulkner, and all of Sinclair Lewis. You read all these books and you'll know something of how America got to be like it is."

"Which one should I start with?"

"It doesn't matter, really," he says, taking a jump shot from the sideline. "You just have to have an attitude about it, and then you'll do it."

Billy is in Hunter College now. Hunter is a free city college, but you have to pass a pretty hard test to get in there.

He got a scholarship to Oberlin College in Ohio, but first he had to get up just a little bit of money to go, to cover the book and lab fees, something like a hundred bucks.

My mother didn't have the money to give him, and so he didn't go. I wonder, though, if it was because she just didn't want him so far away from us. It was a disappointment to Billy, and I guess a setback, but he never complained about it. But lately I notice something about Billy that I never saw before. He's been spending a lot of time down at Jasper's Bar, across the street from Happy's on Second Avenue, and sometimes he doesn't come home until it closes at three A.M.

Chapter Fifty

"Last night was a close call," I say to Frankie, leaning into the velvet crunch of the backseat.

He is driving his father's car, and we are going out to Rockaway Beach. His father has gone on an all-day commercial moving job and won't be home until late tonight. I don't think he knows that Frankie took the car.

"You can do time if you get caught with a rod," Nicky the Greek says.

"That Bobby Sutton is something, huh?" Frankie says.

"I didn't know he had a zip gun," I say. "I was wondering why we went all the way almost to Queens on the 59th Street Bridge, and then he takes this gun out of his pocket and shoots it off into the sky. I'm glad there were no airplanes flying over."

"Yeah," Frankie says, swerving in and out of the traffic. "And the Keegan brothers should be happy they weren't there on 65th Street, either, or else Sutton would have let them have it. See how tough they are then, huh?"

I am wishing that Frankie would slow up a little, not only because he doesn't have a driver's license, and if the cops come he'll be in big Dutch, but because I feel like I am on a boat in an ocean storm, going back and forth like we are on the top of some drunken waves.

The Keegan brothers are boxers, Golden Gloves champs, and nobody to fool around with. But their sister Eleanor had a problem at the Kips Bay dance with someone from 55th Street. I think it was Gillespie or John-boy Daly, or someone who said the wrong thing and kept pulling her in like a vise while they were dancing, and she blew her stack. Her brothers came down to the candy store the next day and said that everyone on 55th Street was a punk unless we came up to 65th Street to fight it out with them.

It doesn't matter how these things start, because it is the end that counts and not the beginning.

The Keegan brothers are like myths up on 65th Street. No one I know has ever seen them fight, but their reputations say they are as tough as they come, as tough as Floyd Patterson. This is why Frankie said we couldn't let them get away with putting us on notice like that, and why Frankie called Bobby Sutton to come in from Astoria, Queens. Sutton had a reputation of his own, and completely dominated the Machine and Metal Trades High School when Frankie went there, the toughest guy in a tough turf.

After testing the zip gun, twenty of us marched up First Avenue to 65th Street, two abreast, like we were in St. John's grammar school. I liked being lined up with all the guys, like going into a war or something, all of us being a part of something big, bigger than any one of us alone, part of something that people would respect.

When we turned the corner there, we saw four guys standing on a stoop, and Sutton went right up to them and started punching. He was in a green quilted jacket, and the back of his jacket looked like a green wall bobbing from side to side.

I never saw anything like it, the way he charged into them like a kamikaze. These guys were just minding their own business, and then this madman suddenly, unexpectedly, began punching at them, all four of them. One, then the other, then the next. A one-on-one fight is okay, and fair unless someone pulls a knife or something, but this was something the rule books didn't cover, a madman, like a concrete truck running into these guys.

I didn't know any of them, and I don't know if I would care much about them if I knew them, but, as I watched Sutton flailing away, I couldn't help thinking about anything other than my brother Billy.

The thought came to me that these guys might come back downtown someday and see Billy standing there on 56th Street, talking to a few guys in front of Rossi's, and some wall might roll into the middle of Billy and his friends, punching away, or worse, they might have a zip gun of their own.

I guess it would be better to live without any fights in your life, and I began to realize while I was watching Sutton that I had no beef with these guys from 65th Street.

But here we were, in their territory, with Sutton punching everyone he could see, and I wish I could have stopped it, but I couldn't. It's not like the story of turning the other cheek that Sister Maureen talked about when I was a kid, the same one from the Sermon on the Mount I read in the Family Bible that my mother bought for a dollar a month for thirty-six months. We shouldn't have been there to begin with, no matter if a cheek was turned or not. I don't want anything terrible to happen to anyone, but especially I don't want anything terrible to happen to my brother, and I wanted to tell Sutton to stop it, that we defended ourselves, and maybe now we could all go home.

But then, just as unexpectedly, the cops came running up First Avenue.

"Chickie!" somebody yells. This is the word that means somebody's coming.

"Chickie the cops!" somebody is now screaming.

I ran like I was in a race in the stadium up on Randalls Island, first down to York, and, thinking that everyone would probably run back downtown, I made a left and zoomed up to 72nd Street.

I could walk then, across 72nd Street to Lexington, and down Lex until 56th Street, and then slowly, like nothing happened, around to 55th Street.

"Maybe," I say, "you could slow up a little and give us a chance to breathe, huh?"

"Relax, huh," Frankie says. "We gotta get to the Irish Riviera before all the broads are gone."

"It's amazing no one got caught," Nicky the Greek says. Nicky just started hanging around with us, and I've been seeing a lot of him since I quit the job at Catholic Charities.

It was a boring job, and I felt like I was on one of those lines in a factory where you put lids on jars, just going from floor to floor and dropping the mail off at people's desks. Also, Mr. Lacy began to yell at me all the time for being late, or not delivering the mail fast enough, or any little thing, and so I told him one day to get someone else who was willing to take his bullshit.

"Some cop got close to me," Nicky says, "and got me with a good kick in the ass, but it just made me go faster. He never got up to me."

"What are we going to do, anyway?" I ask.

"Go to McGuire's Bar on 108th Street," Frankie says, "maybe watch a little basketball in the beach court there, maybe have a couple beers, maybe shoot up."

"Maybe get some Irish girls to sit on our laps," Nicky says.

"I don't want to shoot up," I say. I like to let them know up front that I don't want to do it.

"You can skin-pop," Frankie says.

"I think I'll drink beer," I say, " 'cause I got a few bucks."

"You can keep watch for us," Frankie says, "but you hafta tell us if you want in 'cause I can only cook up once, you know. You can't change your mind."

My brother is in the fenced-in basketball court alongside the beach near McGuire's Bar. There is a fast full-court game going on, and I am thinking as I watch Billy break loose every time he gets the ball that Oberlin College lost a good opportunity to be champs with Billy.

I sit along the sidelines, watching, until Billy comes over at a time-out.

"What are you doing?" he asks.

"Looking for some broads, maybe," I say. "How you doin'?"

"I got such a hangover," he says, "I'm going to have to play fifty games to clear it all out of my system."

"Where were you?"

"Jasper's," he says, "and I was completely ossified, drinking beer out of my shoe, and I put the shoe on top of the bar, leaking all over the place, and Jasper himself was there. It was a pretty dangerous thing to do. You just don't do things like that in his joint. He threw me out, and told me that the only reason he wasn't locking me in the refrigerator was because he knew I was a neighborhood kid, and neighborhood kids always get two tries."

"Jesus, Billy," I say. "I wouldn't go back there for a while, anyway."

"Right," Billy says, "I'm banning myself."

At least Billy goes to his jobs, and he never misses college. He's getting things done.

But my life, lately, has been everything opposite to Billy's. I don't know when to stop, to ban myself from anything. But I want to try to change, and that's why I told Frankie today that I don't want any horse. I don't want to be a dope addict, I know that, and I just have to tell them I don't want it. I can still hang around with them. They are good guys, Frankie and Nicky and Mikey and those guys, friends, but I have to think about this dope stuff the way Billy thinks about Jasper's Bar. Jasper could kill Billy, and Billy knows that. And, at least, Billy is smart enough to ban himself.

I made all those faces when I was a kid. It drove my mother crazy, and she decided one day, I guess, that belting me with the strap wasn't changing anything. So she asked me to sit with her on the living room couch, and she was holding a hand mirror, which she took from the top of her bureau.

She held the mirror high in front of me.

"Now," she said, "make those faces."

I didn't want to make those faces then, not with that mirror in front of me, but my mother kept prodding me.

"Do it, do it," she kept saying. "Don't brood about it."

And she must have made me make those faces a hundred times, some with my eyebrows reaching up to my forehead, some with my lips going over to my ears, and I kept thinking that I was looking funnier and funnier, and weirder and weirder. I told my mother that

I didn't like the way I looked, but that I couldn't help it, I couldn't just stop like you stop swimming just by getting out of the water. Then she told me to cross the middle finger of my left hand over my index finger and to press down hard, and to say to myself that I won't make a face again. Never.

"Now," she said, her arms around me, the mirror on her lap, "when you make another face, just cross your fingers like that, press hard, and think about how funny you look. If you keep trying like that, sooner or later it will work for you."

She then squeezed me, saying, "Not for me, Dennis. Don't do this for me, but do it for yourself."

I am sitting in the back of the car now as Frankie and Nicky are shooting up. My fingers are one over the other, and I am looking out the back window to make sure the police are not driving by. It is a hot day. I had about five beers in McGuire's, and there were no Irish girls, not that I wouldn't take a girl from Istanbul if I could get one. I am a little dizzy, but I think as much from the heat as from the beer.

Frankie and Nicky are nodding, and I am beginning to sweat. I can't wait for the car to get going again so that we can open the windows and get some air in.

"Hey," Frankie says, "Dennis, man . . . man."

"Yeah, Frankie?"

"You got anything to eat, man, like a Yankee Doodle, man, or somethin'?"

"No, Frankie, I don't got, I mean, wait . . . I don't have any Yankee Doodles."

"Man, we gotta go to 55th Street, man, to get some Yankee Doodles, and some Coca-Cola, man."

Frankie starts the car, and I half know that Frankie cannot drive the car while he is sleeping. And nodding is a kind of sleeping. But I also half don't care.

It's hot, and I'm a little woozy. I should have gone to work at the florist today, but I asked Mr. Schmidt if I could take the day off.

I don't like delivering flowers anymore, either, and I would quit if it wasn't for my mother.

"If you quit," my mother said, "it would be the last straw, and I will kick you out of the house."

She would kick me out of the house, even though home is the place that when you go there they always have to let you in.

But poetry isn't always right. It is hard to get back in the house when you have been kicked out. I know, because Mikey Fallon and Dennis Buckley have been kicked out of their houses and they live from park to park and cellar to cellar, and I see them all the time with dirty shirts and pimply faces. And they are not the kind of guys that Archie said we respect, the guys we look up to.

I always thought I would be one of those guys, the guys people respected, but it wasn't working out that way. So if Frankie is awake or sleeping, I don't care, as long as the windows are open and some air is rushing in, and I can sleep in the dizzy whirl of five beers from McGuire's Bar.

And, I begin to think, maybe it wouldn't be so bad to get out of that cramped room with Billy and find a home somewhere on my own, somewhere I could find myself in a corner of a cold city.

We are now on Queens Boulevard at 78th Street, and we stop for a red light. A car behind doesn't stop in time and bumps us. It is not a hard bump, but enough to wake Frankie up completely.

"Hey, man," Frankie says, "my old man's car. Any dents and he'll know we took it."

Frankie looks in his rearview mirror as I look out the back window. There are six guys in the car behind us, men, maybe in their late twenties. As the light changes and we go forward, I can see that the car has a license plate from New Jersey.

"From New Jersey," I say.

"The other side of the Washington Bridge," Nicky says.

"I know where it is," I say.

"Not even America," Frankie says.

"Six guys," I say.

"If they're from New Jersey," Nicky says, "you count in halves."

"So, man," Frankie laughs, "there's only three of them?"

"Yeah," Nicky says. "In American math, anyway. In Machine and Metal Trades math, there are two of them."

Nicky goes to Machine and Metal Trades High School, too, but he hasn't quit yet like Frankie.

At 74th Street we again stop for a red light, and the same car comes behind us and bumps us again, this time a little harder.

"Oh, man," Frankie says, "they ain't gonna do that again, man, no way."

I watch Frankie as he opens the door, and I see him grab a monkey wrench from under the seat as he gets out of the car.

"I'll break their windows," Frankie says.

I am still dizzy, and I am thinking that I would love to close my eyes and fall asleep as I find myself climbing out of the car behind Nicky.

The six men from New Jersey are all out of their car, and each one seems to be bigger than we are.

Why did they bump us, not only the first time, either? What did they want? Why do people do things like this? Maybe Frankie cut them off or did something he didn't know he did. I don't know. But he was driving slowly, not like he drove out to Rockaway this morning, fast and crazy. It's hard to drive fast and crazy when you're sleeping at the wheel.

But now here I am in the middle of Queens Boulevard, punching some guy who has me around the neck and is dragging me to the street, kicking me as he pulls. It is like I entered some weird ride out in Coney Island where you never know what to expect, and this time the ride put you in the middle of a donnybrook with guys from New Jersey who should know better, and all you have to do is fight as hard as you can without knowing why.

And so I am lying on the ground, horns blaring in the middle of traffic, with some guy's hair clenched in my fist, and I won't let go, and he is screaming as he punches me, and I am punching him as I am pulling on his hair, and another guy comes and starts to kick me in the legs trying to kick me between my legs, and I am covering myself and punching and holding and pulling, and with every punch I get in I get one in return, and I feel my skin breaking apart and the blood running down my chin.

And in the middle of all of this I look over and I see Frankie on the ground and he is hitting some poor luckless fellow who made the one mistake of getting out of his car, hitting him again and again over the head with the monkey wrench, and their clothes are full of blood, and there is blood everywhere on the street, and I can hear the sirens in the distance.

Now I am in this strange place, gray stripes falling in shadow all around me, and I am feeling as if I have been let out of one ride in Coney Island only to find myself in another, a place dark in the corners except for the bare lightbulb in the hall casting the shadows within, dim stripes shooting over the bare mattress and the black-stained stainless-steel bowl, all around a deadly quiet broken by some unknown, unseen human being in the next cell, breathing heavily and cursing in whispering exhales, and I am thinking of my mother, remembering that our telephone shorted out recently and isn't working, and that Mrs. Fox upstairs will have to tell her that there is a phone call for her from Queens, and I can see my mother walking through the dark hall and up the stairs, wishing that they would come and fix our own telephone, knowing that Mrs. Fox upstairs would only be called in an emergency, and with each step worrying about who is dead and who is injured, and where were her two sons?

Oh, Mom, I think, I am sorry I am making you go through this.

And so many thoughts follow this one, the thoughts that go through the head when you are alone like this, because you know that you are powerless to change your life all by yourself, that you can only change your life if the people around you are good people and they let you make the changes, because you know you are alone with the dark, and you feel alone like Ann Kovak, or Harry Shalleski, or Spango in the coffin, where nothing will help you but a prayer, and maybe a helping hand from Blessed Maria Goretti, who was made dead for no reason of her own.

You need help because, after everything is said and done, all the prayers uttered, the Sorrowful Mysteries finished, and you're alive and in trouble like this, you know that it is all your fault. That you got here on your own, but you can't get out without somebody who cares about you.

*   *   *

The Queens County Court building looks more like a school than a courthouse, red and gray stone with two dozen charcoal-colored stone steps up to the front door.

I see Marty Trainor on the steps, his arm around my mother's shoulders. For the first time in my life, she looks frail to me, huddled there in a yellow flowered dress beneath Marty's arm.

I have no clue as to what is going on, except that I know I am in trouble, and that Marty Trainor is the guy everyone in the neighborhood calls when there is trouble. I haven't seen Frankie or Nicky or any of those guys from New Jersey since I got up from the ground on Queens Boulevard.

My mother doesn't say anything, and I can hardly look her in the eyes, those keen hazel eyes now reddened at the corners.

"Your mother and I have talked this over," Marty says, "and I think I can get you off, but you'll have to give us your word that you are willing to change your life."

Marty Trainor is an old Kips Bay Boys Club guy, and he knows that giving your word means something here. But I still don't know what he is talking about, get me off from what?

"What kind of trouble," I say in a shaking voice, "is this?"

"Pretty serious," Marty says, grabbing me by the arm, pulling me away from my mother's earshot.

"Felonious assault is pretty serious," he says, "and a lot of people go to jail for felonious assault. The guy you were fighting with has twenty-six stitches."

"Not the guy I was fighting with," I say. I was thinking that the worst thing with the guy I fought is that he could be bald.

"It doesn't matter who," Marty says. "The fact is someone has all those stitches from a fight on a public street, and the judge won't care about who actually did what."

"The guy hit me first, Marty."

I have always believed that if someone hit you first, it was not only fair to hit him back, but almost a personal responsibility. But you have to forget about Sister Maureen and the Sermon on the Mount first.

"Look, Dennis," Marty says, "we have to go in. Your mother is a wreck. This is going to cost her three hundred and fifty dollars for getting me out of bed and coming all the way out here, but I am not going to take the money from her. I want it from you, do you understand?"

"Yeah, sure," I say, "but I don't have that kind of money."

"You'll pay me ten a week until it's paid, understand?"

"Yeah, sure."

"And this is what you are going to do."

"What's that?"

My voice is not so shaky now, and I am thinking that Marty Trainor is a smart man and a good lawyer—that's what everybody says—and he belongs to the Jim Farley Democratic Club, and so he knows all the big shots in the city. I don't have to be so nervous, but still . . . still, my mother has not said a word to me.

"You have never been in this kind of trouble before," he says, "and this is the first time you've been in a courtroom. The judge will like that. But what he will really like is when we tell him that you are going to be seventeen years old in just three weeks, that it has been your lifelong ambition to join the United States Air Force, that you are making an appointment with the enlistment officer, that you will be on your way to a boot camp in a month, and that you will be far from your friends and the neighborhood that have made it possible for you to end up here in a courtroom for criminals before your weeping mother."

I don't know what to say to Marty, but I am thinking that I don't have much to say about any of it, anyway.

I guess that he has talked this over with my mother, and so I just shrug my shoulder in agreement. I look over at my mother, hoping that she will smile or say something, but she has a rock-hard look on her face, like she is worrying that the judge might yell at her for having a son like me.

It is still early morning now, and we are again at the top of the court's stone steps. Marty Trainor has just gone, and my mother and I are standing quietly for a moment, looking at one another, waiting for the right words to come.

My mother has had such a hard time of it with me, I know. I

wish she had someone to share the hard time with, maybe to soften it a little. I don't think any of this fight was my fault, but still . . .

Still . . .

Here she is in the Queens County Courthouse, prim and proper in her yellow flowered dress, but haggard, looking beaten from a sleepless night, and from being forced to stand behind her son before a ruddy-faced judge who only wants to know if her son would join the air force, and if her son would join the air force he would dismiss the charges so that her son could still be a cop or a fireman or a postal clerk or anything you could be if you aren't convicted of some crime even if the crime was something you didn't start. And so I know there is only one thing to say to my mother, only one thing she will expect.

"I'm sorry, Mom," I say to her, "I am."

She smiles for the first time and begins to walk down the courthouse steps.

"You know," she says, "you're going to have to pay Marty Trainor that money."

"I know."

"It's a lot of money."

"I'll pay him back, Mom," I say, "I promise, every last penny. If it's the last thing I do."

This is the first promise I ever remember making to my mother. I have said a lot of things with good intentions, but I have never promised before.

It's a start.

"I'll remember," she says. "And for you, remember that the road to going backwards is made out of unkept promises."

On the subway now, the train rollicking at sixty miles an hour beneath the East River, my mother puts down the *Daily News* she has been reading, and holds my hand.

I shift a little on the airy, cane-covered train seat, uncomfortable with having my hand held, not only by my mother but by anyone. She sees that she has taken a reluctant hand, and she squeezes my fingers.

"Time goes fast," she says. "It seems just yesterday you were studying to be an altar boy, and now you are going to go into the military. I know you'll look handsome in a uniform. What do those air force uniforms look like, anyway?"

"I don't know," I say. "I never saw one."

"You never saw one?"

"No."

"Then," she says, "why are you joining the air force instead of the marines or the navy?"

"I don't know," I say. "I thought you and Marty Trainor agreed about it."

"Oh, goodness," she says.

My mother is laughing now.

"I guess," she says, "when I told him that it was a great hope of mine that you would finish the Aviation High School, he just thought that the air force was the thing for you."

I am laughing now.

"Yeah," I say, "I guess so. What difference does it make, anyway? They say that the food is better in the navy, but that the beds are softer in the air force, and that there's no food and no beds in the marines. I'll be okay."

She laughs a little more, quietly to herself, and lets the train rock her back and forth. She sighs.

"I hope you'll be okay," she says. "You know, there isn't much time before you'll be away in the service."

"I'll be seventeen in three weeks," I say. "I'll go to the recruitment center on Broadway this afternoon."

"We have a lot to do."

"Yeah."

"A lot."

"Yeah," I say, and I think about it for a moment.

"Like what?"

"Well," she says, "you are leaving New York, and I don't know how long it will be before you ever come back to us. So I think it's time . . . I don't know what you'll think about it, but I think you should come with me up to see your father before you go off into the military."

There is a great silence now as the train screeches to a stop at the Grand Central Station stop on 42nd Streeet.

God, I am saying to myself, dodging in and out of the crowd as I walk up the subway stairs to Lexington Avenue. I haven't thought about going to see my father in a long time. A few years, maybe.

Chapter Fifty-one

So," I say as the New York Central Albany Special speeds up alongside the Hudson River, "I have to be there to meet the recruitment sergeant at ten o'clock on Tuesday morning. We're meeting on platform 12 at Pennsylvania Station."

I am feeling pretty good, sitting across from my mother, in one hand a roast pork sandwich from Rossi's wrapped in white paper, mayonnaise oozing out of the sides, and a bottle of Pepsi in the other. I am in a blue shirt with a long pink collar, new and sparkling from Bloomingdale's basement.

"I want you to look good," my mother had said when she gave it to me this morning.

"Sergeant Brownlee is coming with us," I continue, "three days on the overnight to San Antonio, Texas, and to the Lackland Air Force Base. Usually, he doesn't go, but this time he has eighteen recruits, and when there are so many recruits, the recruitment officer has to go along."

I wondered, when he told us he had so many recruits, if Marty Trainor has a deal going with the air force and that judge.

"I'll go to the station with you," my mother says.

She looks fresh and happy. She is sitting there, smiling, as the trees and rock walls go shooting by the train window, wearing her green two-piece suit which she has had for as long as I can remember. Her "St. Patrick's Day clothes," she calls the suit.

She has had a *Saturday Evening Post* on her lap since we sat down, but she hasn't opened it at all. She just keeps watching the passing scenery with a small, pleasant smile at her lips.

"It's okay, Mom," I say. "I can go alone."

"But," she says, "I want to go."

"Well . . ." I hesitate. "You know . . . I would want you to come if it were just . . . just me . . . But . . ."

"I get it," she says. "There will be all those soldiers there, right?"

"Airmen, Mom," I say, "and there are eighteen of us, so it is possible that seventeeen of them, these airmen, might make fun of the eighteenth, you know?"

"All right," she says, "I won't go."

"Sorry, Mom."

I am hoping that she is not too disappointed, but she makes her lips tight together and nods her head a little.

"But," I say, "maybe you can get me my last roast pork guinea hero for the trip, huh?"

She laughs at this.

"Of course," she says. "But maybe you shouldn't call it that anymore. Maybe you should just say hero sandwich, because you never know who you are going to meet down there in Texas who might take offense at words like *guinea*."

"Yeah, you're right," I say. "You never know."

"In New York, too," she adds, "they can take offense."

I have noticed that my mother has stopped using those hard and insulting words for people lately. Those words like *dago, spick,* and *guinea* are words I hear a lot around the neighborhood. But she changed her language ever since Father O'Rourke gave that sermon about the people out in the West of the United States calling Catholics *fishheads*. My mother didn't like that at all, and told Monsignor O'Rourke that those cowboys out there didn't know what was good for them, that fish on Fridays had more vitamins than canned beans around a campfire.

Archie never used these racial snarl words, and neither did Billy, and so I never had much use for them. But, I don't know what else to call this sandwich.

"I've been saying 'guinea hero' all my life," I say, "even to Mr. Rossi. But someone told me, when you comb your hair one way for so long, it's hard to comb it another way."

"Well," my mother says, smiling as she picks up the *Saturday Evening Post,* "use a brush next time."

She reads for the rest of the trip to the Poughkeepsie stop, almost two hours north of the city.

The train is much quieter than the subway, the seats softer, and there are fans on the ceiling making it comfortable enough, even on these hot, end-of-summer days. It is an easy trip, and I keep watching the endless lines of trees going past us. There are so many trees, they couldn't even all fit in Central Park.

The Poughkeepsie State Hospital is a large, brown brick building, not far from the train station, and you can see the Hudson River from here. Maybe once it was the site of one of the great river mansions with the large golden eagles in front, but now it is a fenced-in building that reminds me of all those almshouses and poorhouses and asylums that the English and the Irish writers describe in their stories, except that it is not so dark and wet like they were in Europe.

We are now walking through the main corridor, and I am looking for the reception desk. I am following my mother, who knows where she is going.

"There is no one ever on the first floor," my mother says, "and we have to take the elevator to three."

I am trying to act calm, cool, and collected. It's not easy being in an insane asylum for the first time, but it's even harder to see your father for the first time.

Except for two photographs, I have never seen my father, and I don't know what to expect. I know about these places, though, for I've been keeping up with my reading, and though I still haven't gone through all the book-bricks in my building, I have read a lot of the Dickens books, and nobody described lunatic asylums or poorhouses better.

There is a small corridor before us when we get off the elevator on the third floor, and there are two doors with wired glass on either side.

I can see a nurse reading a newspaper through the door on the left, but my mother pulls me to the right. There is no nurse there, but inside I can see about twenty beds, most with men sleeping in yellow pajamas. Some men are sitting on the floor, some walking around in circles, bumping into each other. I wonder who my father is, and watch to see how many of the men turn around as my mother raps her keys on the glass window. Hardly anyone turns.

"He was here last time I was up," my mother says, "but they keep moving him, hospital to hospital, room to room. There used to be a nurse's desk here, too. But it's gone."

She raps harder and harder, and soon the nurse unlocks the door to our left.

"That's a racket," the nurse, an older, easygoing woman, says.

"We are looking for John Smith," my mother says.

"I think he's on four," the nurse says. "He used to be here, but try four."

There is the same configuration on the fourth floor, but this time the nurse is on our right. She is in a white uniform, and ever briefly the thought of being pulled into the white starched bosom of Sue Flanagan crosses my mind. The memory surprises me, as if I suddenly fell asleep and was in some kind of dream.

The nurse unlocks the door with a key chained to her waist belt, and she seems pleasant enough as my mother asks for John Smith. We cross the hall with the nurse, and she unlocks the other door.

"If he's sleeping," the nurse says, "give him a good shake."

"Is he on medication?" my mother asks.

"No," she says, "but he sleeps easily."

I can hear her locking the door behind us as we enter the room. Like on the third floor, there are twenty or so beds, and my mother and I cruise around the room, looking for my father, but I don't know who I am looking for.

A man comes quickly up to us, almost on a run. His yellow pajamas are two sizes too big for him. Suddenly, he grabs me by the arm. I am a little alarmed, but he is not very big, and unless he has a gun I don't think I have to worry about him.

"Give me my money," the man says. His eyes are wide and seem directly connected to mine. I don't think this is my father.

"I don't have your money," I say to him, trying to be calm and matter-of-fact.

"I know you have my money."

"Tell him," my mother says, "the nurse has his money."

He doesn't look at my mother. I am thinking that my mother knows her way around here.

"The nurse has your money," I say.

"The nurse has my money?" he asks, like I told him his horse came in in the sixth race.

"Yes," I say, "the nurse."

The man turns and walks away just as quickly as he approached. He goes to the side of an empty bed and just stands there.

My mother smiles.

"They respect the nurses," she says.

There is a post in the middle of the room, and my mother begins to walk around it. But she stops and gently lifts a finger in the direction of the bed behind the post. "There he is," she says.

I see my father for the first time, lying there in a bed behind the post. He looks nothing like I imagined, and much older than his forty-five years. He is thin, but his stomach is large, as if they gave him a case of beer every night. He is clean-shaven and looks so different from how I remember him in the photographs. In one, he is in an empty lot in Brooklyn, holding a baseball glove, looking like a kid, trim and fast, trying out for the college team, maybe the Railway Express team, center field, casually leaning over to the left, his glove leaning with him, assured, knowing he'll make the cut. He is a handsome man in that photo, and a wisp of hair falls over his forehead.

In the other, he's in a big velvet chair, my mother on his lap, her legs, long and shapely, kicking out from a polka-dot dress, him, trim and good-looking in a white shirt and tie, laughing, his face a grin from ear to ear. Both photographs flash happiness like a neon sign, and I look closely now at my father and look for even the smallest sign that he is happy.

But there is no sign. There is no expression on his face, and I can think only that his nose is bigger than I thought it would be, but maybe that's because his face is so thin. He would be handsomer if he smiled.

"Hello, John," my mother says.

"Hello, hello," he says quickly, as if that is all he has to say.

His voice is not large, and quivers a little.

"It's Mary, John," my mother says, "Mary."

"Hello, hello," he says again. "Give me a cigarette."

My mother turns to me and she is whispering.

"They used to be able to smoke," she says, "but there was a fire somewhere, and they stopped allowing it."

"Do you remember me, John?" my mother asks.

"Hello, hello," he says, this time adding, "Mary."

"This is Dennis, John," she says, pulling me forward.

"Dennis," he repeats.

"How are you, John?" she asks.

He is not loooking at my mother, but staring across the room, but at nothing in particular.

"Give me a cigarette," he says.

"How have you been?" she asks again. "Are you eating anything but dessert, John?"

There is a stain on the front of his yellow pajamas, still wet, and I am guessing it is from his lunch. My mother takes a handkerchief from her pocketbook and wipes at it. He pushes her away.

"Who's this?" he asks, gesturing towards me. He doesn't look toward me at all.

"This is Dennis, John," my mother answers. "Your son."

"Give me a cigarette," he says.

I have a pack of cigarettes in my pants pocket, but, still, I have never smoked a cigarette in front of my mother. Maybe I could sneak one to him.

"Do you remember Dennis, John?" she asks. "Dennis and Billy?"

"Hello, hello," he says.

The hair at the side of his head is sticking out, and my mother pushes it back with her hand.

"You are looking pretty good, John," she says. "I bet all the nurses are after you, huh?"

"Who's this?" he asks, again indicating his thumb toward me.

"This is Dennis, John," my mother says. "Do you remember Dennis and Billy?"

"Give me a cigarette," he says in the same crispy but level voice.

"John," my mother says, her hand on my shoulder, "do you remember Dennis? Dennis is now a man, see?"

"Hello, hello," he says.

My mother goes around the bed, fluffing things up, taking the wrinkles out of the sheets. I notice that she doesn't kiss him. He has been away more than sixteen years, and I wonder how many years it is since she kissed him last.

"Okay, John," she says in the middle of a sigh. "You're looking pretty good, and so I guess we can go."

My mother reaches over and pats his hands, which are folded over his stomach.

My father doesn't say anything and doesn't look at us.

I have my hands in my pockets, and I think I should at least reach over and shake his hand. I grab a cigarette out of the pack as I pull my hands out.

I grab his hand as my mother begins to walk away.

"Goodbye, Dad," I say, something I've never before said.

"Give me a cigarette," he says.

I lean over next to his ear, and I whisper.

"I dropped one," I say. "On the sheet."

I am thinking as I walk into the main entry hall with my mother that these places are not dangerous. Things are just quirky here, and off balance.

I suppose I did know what to expect, after all. I have been thinking about my father being here ever since I heard Aunt Kitty jabbering away to Uncle Tracy that day more than five years ago, and reading everything I came across about mental disease and people who have it. And every time I think about it, I realize that there is a special kind of sadness that comes with the territory in these places. People get locked away and forgotten, and that is a desperate thing.

Maybe it is easier on the family to push mental disease into a family secret, or make up stories, like the guy fell off a truck one day and that was that.

It was hard for my mother to talk about my father, even to me. Her silence somewhere just got turned into a secret. It's easier to have a secret than to explain to people, especially the children, that he is locked up and forgotten because no one else knows what to do.

It's a very personal thing.

When I think about the attendants beating up my father and saying he fell in the shower, I get upset. I will never stop getting upset about that. But as bad as beating some defenseless person is, I guess there are worse things.

I've read about such things, what people do to defenseless young women and to children, and I wonder what kind of animal a person would have to be to abuse a young child.

Somebody like Mr. Dempsey, I guess. Mr. Dempsey should be in a place like this.

My father is a harmless person, but I know I can't ask my mother why he just can't come home with us and smoke all the cigarettes he wants.

My mother doesn't have much of a life to begin with.

That would be no life at all for her.

We are now speeding toward the city, looking at the trees and the rock walls from the other direction.

My mother is quiet.

I'm quiet, too, sad from seeing my father like that. But I'm glad I was there, finally. At least, I saw him.

In all those years when I wanted to see him, I couldn't. Then, after I found out where he really was, I didn't much care to see him at all.

It was like he let me down, being sick like that.

Being in a wheelchair or on crutches is somehow heroic, admirable, something that, like Archie would say, would make someone put their chin out for whatever is coming.

I used to dream as a kid in St. John's grammar school that one day a classroom door would open, and there would be my father on a pair of wooden crutches, and the whole class would cheer as I ran to him. But his being in an asylum was such a letdown to me, an embarrassment, maybe, something to become a secret that was to be kept at any price.

And, today, to see him remembering just that one thing, how much he liked cigarettes, and not being able to remember anything else, was pretty rotten, especially since he never has the chance to smoke any.

Maybe he'll find the cigarette I left, and a match, too, and put back into his life the one pleasure he craves.

But I hope he doesn't burn the place down.

All my life, I guess, I've been wishing that things would get better for us, for Billy and me, that my mother would be happier.

And that my father would get better.

But I can see now that my father will never get any better, and that is a hard and a bitter thing to know for sure. Before, when I thought about it, I thought it could get better for him if I prayed enough, but now I have seen it with my own eyes.

I'll still say those same prayers, but I know it won't make much difference, not for my father. God has kept him alive, anyway. And instead of asking Him to make my father better, I'll just thank Him for that.

My mother pats my gabardine covered leg and breaks the silence.

"I'm glad," she says, "that you came with me."

"I'm glad, too, Mom," I answer. "Even though it was pretty strange, like looking at someone in a movie or something."

"He loved being around you and Billy," she says. "His memory is completely shot now. Those shock treatments, you know. But he used to have a good, long-term memory of you and your brother. He would always ask about you."

My mother looks away now, and I can't tell if she is laughing or crying. She turns back to me and has a soft, resigned look on her face.

"He would remember you," she says, "and forget me, because the wires for his short-term memory were completely cut somehow."

"How did that happen, Mom?" I ask. "How did you find out?"

"I don't know," she says, holding her palms out, "nobody knows, really. They call it catatonic."

"How . . ." I say, "how . . . I mean, how did it actually happen, how did you know?"

"I had no idea anything was wrong," she says, looking down at her hands. "Everything was so normal. We were living in Sterling Place in Brooklyn. You had just been born in the Jewish Hospital and christened in St. Theresa's. Billy was just a little over two."

She stops now and looks at me, smiling.

"I remember," she continues, "you and Billy were both in the same carriage, and we were out for a walk. I had you stuffed in that carriage like socks in a sock drawer, and when I got home I rang the bell for your father to come down to help me, and I rang and rang.

"It was his day off from the Railway Express, and I was hopping mad that he never came down, and so I asked some man on the street, a passerby, to help me up the two flights, and I took you boys one in each arm and carried you up the stairs, and the man carried the carriage. He left the carriage in the hall, and I opened the door. I saw your father's legs in the living room as I thanked the man for helping."

Her expression became serious as she talked, but now it becomes animated, like she is telling an old joke that she has learned to tell really well.

"I guess it was a funny scene," she says, "because I saw him sitting in the big, blue velvet chair, and I began right away to complain about him not coming down to help me. 'Here I am,' I was saying to him, 'all alone with these boys, and here are you sitting on your lordship's ass and giving me no help at all.'"

As she is talking I can see a tear in the corner of each of her eyes, but she is laughing as she talks.

"And then I started to raise my voice a little," she goes on, "because he wasn't answering. 'Well, say something,' I said, 'and don't sit there like a wrapped package.'

"And then I went into the living room from the kitchen and saw him sitting there, his hands grabbing the arms of the chair as if he was falling off a cliff, and his eyes staring out in front of him like he saw a ghost or an army of bad angels. Oh, Dennis, I was so frightened."

"What happened?" I ask.

"I have never seen a person like that," she says, "just completely frozen to that chair, unable to speak or utter a sound. 'What's the matter, John?' I kept asking over and over. 'What's the matter?'

"But he couldn't move even his mouth. And so I went to a neighbor and asked him to run to the bar where your Uncle Bob worked, so that I could get some help. Uncle Bob came, and then the doctors and the police, and then the ambulance came. He was, completely, a different person forever after that, never knowing where he was or what was wrong."

"God, Mom," I say, putting my hand on her arm. "That was pretty hard on you, huh?"

She takes the handkerchief again from her pocketbook and dabs at her eyes.

"Well, I would say," she says, "it was harder on your father."

Her voice now is cracked and small, and she breaks into a laugh.

"Yeah," I say quietly, not knowing if I should laugh, too.

I wish I had something to drink, for suddenly my throat has become dry and sticky. It feels as if a two-by-four is going through it when I swallow.

"So," she says calmly, "it was just the three of us after that."

"What about the relatives?" I ask.

"Kitty and Helen had families of their own," she says, "and your Uncle Buddy was working three jobs so that he could get married."

"How about Grandma Hogan," I say, "and your father?"

"They were around," she says, "but being emigrants from Ireland, they believed that everyone had to take care of themselves. You lived what you were born into. Anyway, they lived on the other side of Brooklyn, and my mother was sick, dying really."

She pauses for what seems like an hour.

"So," she says finally, "it was just me and you two little guys."

"Well," I say, trying to make her feel good, "you did okay."

"Did I, Dennis?" she asks.

I'm not sure she wants me to answer, but I answer, anyway.

"I mean," I say, "Billy is in college, and I am going into the air force, and we both know how to read and write. This all came from you."

*   *   *

There are just a few people, maybe a dozen, on the train going down to New York. It is late in the afternoon. I have been clearing my throat and coughing, because my mouth is still dry. My mother gets up and walks to the end of the car where she fills up a paper cup with water from the spigot. Everybody watches her as she moves past them. She takes a sip and brings the cup to me.

"This will make you feel better," she says.

She sits again and puts her pocketbook on her lap. I know I am not going to spend much more time with her alone like this before I go off to Texas, and there are so many things I would like to ask her, about how she grew up next to a firehouse in Brooklyn, about graduating from high school, about what boyfriends she might have had, about how she and her brother and two sisters lived in a two-bedroom apartment, about how she met my father, about her wedding day.

But she seems so relaxed now that I don't want to bother her. She has settled back and closed her eyes and seems to be keeping some inner rhythm in tune with the clacking of the wheels against the tracks.

I think she is sleeping, but without opening her eyes she begins to whisper.

"Dennis," she says, "would you do me a favor?"

"Sure, Mom," I answer, "anything."

"Would you sing me," she asks, "'The Rose of Tralee'?"

God, I'm thinking, I don't want to be singing on a train in front of the whole world. Maybe if I just don't answer her, she'll fall asleep, and forget all about asking me to sing in the middle of a crowd, even if it is just a dozen.

"'The Rose of Tralee,'" she whispers.

She must be thinking about all those Sunday afternoons sitting around a keg of beer on 56th Street.

It's funny how people are, and what makes them happy.

I am looking at my mother now, and thinking that the only time I saw her being really happy was when I sang that song for her one day, and then again on that night she took us to Joe's Original Restaurant. And it seemed she was pretty happy when I gave her that ring.

Three times is not many in a life.

I felt so close to her those times, like she knew her life was safe with me and she trusted me completely.

I never gave her much reason to trust me after that.

But she brought me here with her today. She could have forgotten all about it. But she didn't. She told my father that I was a man now. She wanted me in that hospital with her. She trusted me to be there with her.

And so here I am, seventeen years old and about to leave home for God knows how close to forever, and I take a deep breath to sing this song for my mother.

I strain my voice to be above the clacking of the train, and I know that the whole train is looking at me. But I look over at my mother as I sing the first verse of "The Rose of Tralee."

> The pale moon was rising
> Above the green mountains
> The sun was declining
> Beneath the green sea
> As I strayed with my love
> O'er the pure crystal fountain
> That stood in the beautiful
> Vale of Tralee.

Her eyes are still closed, and I believe she is happy behind the smile on her face. She seems, for the moment anyway, to have forgotten all those tenement tears I caused her over the years, and her smile makes me sing louder as I enter the refrain.

I don't care what the people on this train are thinking.

Fifty-two

It is now three years since I rode that train to New York with my mother, and the air force came and went.

And I am talking to a horse.

It seems the time has sped by so quickly, and I still haven't made anything of myself. In fact, I think I've gone backward a little.

I'll be twenty years old soon, and as sure as I can feel the Nevada wind pushing against my face, I know that I have to make a change somewhere.

It's a clear day, and before me I can see forever over generations of mountain peaks. And I am talking to this horse.

It's not just any horse.

It's my horse, and it's funny how life can shift you onto roads you never expected to be.

"Easy, Patches," I am whispering as I pull back on the reins.

We both heard that unmistakable hollow rattle. We both know that it is there, a rattlesnake in the shale rocks somewhere. Patches can sense where it is, but I don't see it, and the horse is shifting like crazy beneath me.

"Whoa, big fella," I say, kicking out the tapaderas hanging from the stirrups, trying to control him, but he's completely going the other way from where I am heading. I grab onto the cantle behind me, a three-inch cantle where the back of the saddle comes up, and it gives me a better balance. I don't want to get thrown and end up eye-to-eye with a rattler.

But I also don't want to give Patches an inch, because if you let them have an inch, horses will take the whole north forty. And so I'm now bouncing off the saddle shoulder and trying to be more determined than he is. I throw my spurs back and dig into his hindquarter, and I begin to pull back on the reins with both glove-covered hands.

"Whoa, you son of a . . ."

And now I see the snake, a four-footer, dart off down the mountainside, and I think all three of us will begin to breathe a little smoother, anyway.

I bought Patches about a year ago, and I've been working as a cowboy whenever I get the chance. He's a gelding, and because he's a little wind-broke, he's not as easy to handle as a well-trained cow pony. Every noise to him, even the wind pushing the grasses together, is like an opening gate to a thoroughbred, and he just wants to run flat out. Loping is a skill we are still working on, but I have come to love this impatient horse, every brown and white patch that runs through his coat.

I'm now working as a per diem ranch hand, riding through the open range in these northern Nevada hills about twelve miles from the town of Gerlach. There is no feeling I know of, inspired anywhere else in the world, like what I am now feeling on this high, shale-rock-covered mountain. I can't see anyone before or behind for ten, maybe twenty miles, and so I'm as alone as I've ever been.

I see some cows and calves ahead, about thirty or so, grazing on a flat about a mile or so distant. Patches and I will just amble pretty easylike in that direction, because I don't want to scare them off. It's hard enough to rope them when they are corralled, and here they have half a state to roam. So you can see why I don't want them running.

I have an old and torn straw hat pulled down low over my eyes to protect my Irish skin from the sun. It's desert-hot up here close to the sun, and I was sure to pack a couple of long-sleeved shirts for the week, along with a change of underwear and a toothbrush.

"You don't need a toothbrush," is what Dave Iverson said as we packed our things in the truck, "as long as there is some grazing grass in the hills. Just chew a little grass, and it's goddamn better than Dentyne gum, you bet."

People on 56th Street never talked like this, but people on 56th Street don't have a thousand head grazing on open range, either.

We drove as far as we could in the truck, an old government-surplus weapons carrier, the kind that ranchers up here buy for the hills. Dave is the boss, and there are four of us who have packed into the hills for a week. Even with a four-wheel-drive vehicle, though, we could drive just so far, and then we had to ride into the hills for about three hours before we found the high corral, made about twenty years ago of sticks and rope, where we could put the horses.

I don't know how much Dave will be paying us, but I guess it'll be ten dollars a day or so, which isn't so bad if you're spending most of the time lazing in a saddle.

There is not much to do but think, and, until we get to those animals, I have a lot to think about.

There's nothing and nowhere in life that can be as free and easygoing as this life in Nevada. I've come to like it here, and feel relaxed like a native. I've had good times, especially during rodeo season, when the girls are all skinny and in jeans that seem painted on the skin of their backsides and their fronts, when there is endless two-stepping dances, interrupted just occasionally by a drunken cowboy who feels an inner need to start a community brawl, and everybody, men and women alike, is wearing a silver belt buckle as big as a bumper on a Lincoln Continental.

People work the full daylight hours every day of the week except Sunday, and on every Saturday night they have to remember what is expected of them in mixed company, and some forget completely. Some go stallion-wild, and some sit on a dance-hall bench, speechless, tapping their feet to the music and waiting for something unusual to happen.

There is a party going on in Nevada every Saturday night, born and planned of a week's lonely labor. There are always lots of whiskey and beer, and pretty girls who like to kiss and dance and no more than that. And I have had amusing times and learning times here, seven days a week for almost three years.

But now I have to think.

The air force made me a radar operator at the Fallon Naval Air Station, just sixty miles east of Reno, and I liked the job well enough. But the hours were not great, and I had to work the midnight-to-eight shift for one week a month. Our country's distant early warning system never sleeps, and I dutifully watched out through the nights for enemy planes from Quemoy and Matsu and other communist hotbeds, each revolution on the radar screen going out five hundred miles and taking sixty seconds to go around.

It was monotonous work, but you are not given many choices in the military. You fall into an empty slot when you graduate basic training, and that is that, and my empty slot was in this desert aircraft control and warning squad.

Who knows how things would've turned out if I fell into a Boston, a Los Angeles, or an Italy slot, or if the bus from Las Vegas had not been exactly on time?

I had been to an Indian powwow in Carson City. Paiute Indians from all over the state came to dance, meet each other, and trade, a colorful event with more feathers than on a chicken farm. And more energy than a prison riot. Dancing, singing, and those constant tom-toms always in the air. It was thoroughly enjoyable, and it was hard leaving the spectacle, especially since the daylong festivities would go well into the morning hours.

But I knew I had to be back at the base in Fallon at midnight, and the nine-thirty bus from Las Vegas would have done it for me.

There is no excuse that I got to the bus depot five minutes late. It doesn't matter that I was told that this was the only day in decades that the bus was on time. Now I remember simply a regret, and I chalk it up to a bit of bad luck.

I was more than an hour late for the midnight shift at the radar operations building, and here is where the bad luck comes in. This was the same night that orders came in for me to transfer to the United States Air Force Base in Bermuda.

I had not been home in two years because I could not afford the transportation. This transfer would not only have taken me into one of the world's greatest playgrounds, but it would have paid my way to New York to see my family and friends.

The captain on duty that night was someone I hardly knew, a hardnose who did not care about some Indian jamboree in Carson City or a bus that I missed by just minutes. He redlined the transfer order and submitted a request for company discipline to the company commander, something called an Article 15.

That was a year ago, and up until then I was a pretty good airman, did my job, and had no difficulties with anyone or anything.

But now, sitting here on top of Patches, the rest of America stretched out before me in a thousand colors, I am thinking that I have failed again, that the rest of my life looks to be in dark colors and shadows and has none of this clear excitement I see in this vista before me.

I have no skills, I'm almost twenty years old, and I'm living from hand to mouth with a dollar here and a dollar there, bucking bales of hay or milking cows or riding the hills looking for sucking calves, living with friends a week here and a week there.

The only thing I have working for me is that I still have a lot of freedom in my life. I'm still free to make choices for myself. But what's the point of having the freedom to make choices if there are no choices lined up?

The military system was not for me. It had such unappealable control over my life. And that captain who redlined my transfer orders, I don't know how I should think about him. He was just doing his job, but maybe he didn't have to do it so well. Maybe he could have found even the smallest excuse if he looked at my whole record, and not just that one night.

I had great good fortune presented to me in one hour, the possibility of going home and then on to Bermuda, which was replaced by a furnace of bad luck in the next hour. If only the bus had been a little late. If only there had been another captain on duty that night. If only my transfer order had come in the day before.

All these ifs that turned my life around from being an ordinary live-by-the-rules airman to being a guy from the streets of New York who would go back to living by his own rule, the rule that says I am always right and everyone else is always wrong.

So have as good a time as you possibly can and the hell with everything else.

And I did have a good time. It seemed there was a party every night in the town of Fallon with wild cowboys and great-looking women. I still have never had a permanent, go-steady girlfriend, but there is always someone to dance with, and hug when the moon is up. Maybe it is the times, and maybe it is Nevada women, but I can never seem to get past the hugging part out here.

Having sex, like getting transferred, is something that other guys seem to do. There have been times when I thought the stars in the sky would rattle with sex, and the moon would fall climaxing into the desert, but it never quite happened, and I find myself in the morning with a lingering disappointment and a memory that doesn't explain why.

There is one girl, a doctor's daughter, who I like, but she hasn't given me a tumble so far.

I have heard guys, whether speaking in cut New York accents, barracks drawl, or cowboy twang, all speak the same thing, of their times with their imaginations, of the rooms and women behind their eyes in the night-black, moving their bodies with the rhythms of their appetites and sweating with the fever of their wishfulness, dancing with Mary Palm until they can sigh within that made-up picture of some delicious girl, on some luscious bed in some plush room, and then smile until sleep comes.

But the lessons of Sister Stella still stay with me most of the time.

When she wasn't knuckling us under the chin, she told us that there is little difference between the thought and the deed.

I suppose we can't hide anything from God. But even if I could, I would want to apply all this sexual thinking to someone I really care about, someone I love, and so far I just haven't met anyone like that.

The hugging part isn't bad, though, and I keep hoping.

I have come close to actual sex out here in the Nevada desert.

There is a place called the Sally J Mustang Ranch, about forty miles from Fallon, where my friend Bub Williams says you can get anything you want for fifteen dollars. I have done a lot of work for Bub's dad, who has a small ranch, and I stay with them from time to time.

I am laughing now as I am getting closer and closer to the cows, because, not long ago, Bub, Ike Hiibel, a few of the fellas, and I drank a couple of cases of beer out in the boondocks, and then, legless, we went to a town hall dance, where the sailors and airmen were out to have a good time, the cowboys were hootin' it up good, and both groups were eyeing each other like the farmers and the cowboys in *Oklahoma!*

I was with the cowboy group.

I danced a few two-steps, and when we went back to the car for a few more beers, Bub began talking about driving down to Sally J's place in Fernley. I know that this is famous for being the only legalized whorehouse in America. Guys even drive up from Las Vegas to go to it.

"It's like heaven," Bub said. "The women come out in under-clothes. They line up, and they tell you their names. And you go up to one you like. Right there in her bra and panties she holds out her hand for a shake and says, 'Hi, my name is Blossom.' And if you like her, you just wink, and she takes you to her room and washes you with warm water before you just lie there like a stud horse and you try to make a ribbon-winning colt."

"Let's do it," I said. Except for that time with Loretta, I never before thought about getting passionately close to a woman without taking her out, or getting to know her and her family, or spending all your money on movies and hamburgers, or riding out to the boondocks where you can be alone under the stars. One, two, three and you are in bed with a woman. It sounds like something you can only do when the lights are out and you are alone in your bed before sleep, and you can make anyone and everyone do anything you want.

But this was no daydream, no fantasy. I was ready to go to Sally J's and see if I could just do it, just lie there and try to make a ribbon-winning colt.

"You go get the guys in the dance," Bub said, "and I'll get some more beer from the trunk."

I staggered a little when I got out of the car and bumped into a swabbie I had seen once or twice at the navy base, a big guy with a mustache from sideburn to sideburn. He was just coming out of the dance, and I think he just saw the cowboy shirt I was wearing. "Sorry," I said to him. He didn't care about my apology. He just swung a roundhouse at me and ripped open the top of my lip, just beneath my nose.

I got up and ran at him, but all of a sudden there were ten sailors in the parking lot, and five guys were holding me.

The next thing I knew I was on an operating table at the base hospital, and the doctor was stiching me closed with a half-moon needle. I remember sitting there, feeling the needle go through my skin, wincing at the pain, thinking that I have never started a fight in my life, and yet I seem to have been in more of them than is natural. But in this one I barely had a chance to even raise my dukes. So I can't call it a fight so much as a testament to sailors' impatience.

What great heaps of anger must get filled up in people's minds that they can lash out so unpredictably like this? It makes me think that when we are driving down the Nevada highways at seventy miles an hour, there are guys as angry as this swabbie on the other side of the road, and there is nothing but a painted white line on the ground that is separating us.

I never met that guy again, but I see his punch every time I shave around the scar on my lip, and it reminds me of how close I came to visiting the only legalized whorehouse in the United States.

Just another if, and I will never know what it was like.

But, still, maybe I should count my blessings.

Patches begins to shift in his steps as we get closer to the calves because he knows he will have to start running as soon as we get them riled.

"Whoa," I say, and I pat his neck, which calms him a little. But not much. Horses are too excitable to calm completely. If a cow got caught in a roll of barbed wire, she will just stand there until some providence sets her free, but a horse will tear its leg off to get free. I think that is why I like Patches so much, because he won't just settle into anything I want him to do. I have to work at it.

This thought makes me think of my mother because I would not own Patches if she didn't come through a year ago.

"How much do you need?" she asked, and I could imagine her looking for a place to sit down as she carried the big black phone around the living room, the phone the telephone company gave her as an employee benefit after a year of working.

"It's a lot of money, Mom, but I really need it."

"What do you need it for?"

"I want to buy a horse."

There was a long pause. She must have been laughing, with her hand over the phone, or else she was trying to put part of a puzzle together.

"Dennis," she said, "people from 56th Street don't buy horses. They buy tickets to the circus if they want to see a horse."

"C'mon, Mom," I answered her. "I really want it, and I can pay you back, honest."

"How much?"

"Two hundred for the horse."

"*What?*"

"And another fifty for the saddle."

"A saddle? Do you really need a saddle?"

"I need the saddle, Mom."

"The Indians never use a saddle. Don't you go to the movies?"

"Well," I answered, trying to contain my joy, because I know she would never joke unless she was willing. "I just found out that the Irish from 56th Street always use saddles. That's the way it is. I read it in a book."

I heard her begin to cough as she laughed, a deep cough that I knew was cutting into her chest.

"Are you okay, Mom?" I know she smokes too much, and no one gets colds as hard to live with as she does. And she is now near fifty and never gets any exercise.

"I'm okay," she said. "It's the stairs. I just came up and I need to rest a little, is all. So did you pay Marty off?"

"Completely, Mom. I sent the last ten dollars a few months ago."

Marty Trainor was very good about the late payments, too, I

thought. They should make every lawyer memorize the pages of that guy's life.

The cows are beginning to sense us walking toward them, and they begin to shuffle some. I see a veal calf sucking at a cow, but I can't make out the brand on her side. I'll have to get a little closer to see if it's Dave Iverson's double crossed bars, which looks something like a drunken tic-tac-toe drawing.

I miss my mother and brother, and being part of a family, and lately I have been thinking about going home. I can always sell Patches and my saddle to raise the airplane fare to New York, and maybe there will be a little left over to pay my mother the rest of what I owe her.

If I stay here, I will just, well, get by, from day to day, without any plan. But in New York maybe I can get my old job at Catholic Charities back, or even at the florist. Something will work out.

And since I passed all the GED tests, maybe I can get into a college and learn something that might give me a leg up on things.

Sure, I've been reading tons, like my brother said, and Father O'Rourke, too. All the works of Sinclair Lewis, J. P. Marquand, Eugene O'Neill, James T. Farrell, Hemingway, and Fitzgerald, and anyone whose style of writing appeals to me. If I like one book, I try to read everything that author wrote, so that I get to remember how the writing flows from one voice to another.

But that and fifteen cents will get me on the subway, something my mother used to say.

Literature will not help me when I am trying to get a job. It doesn't matter how many books you have under your belt if you don't have that diploma.

Anyway, there are no jobs in Fallon, Nevada, except what I am doing. In New York, maybe I can become a teacher, or a cop or a fireman.

Or, as Sister Stella used to say to the class, "You can all become president of the United States, but you need to get in a good high school."

None of the girls in the class ever told her that all the presidents seem to be men.

I came pretty close to serious, lifelong trouble when I was hanging around with the guys on 55th Street. But I also know I have been drinking too much beer out here, and I am beginning to feel about beer what I feel about drugs. It comes with trouble, and trouble comes with it.

There are only three streets in Fallon, and one of them is filled with gambling casinos, where, like the bars, you have to be twenty-one to get in. Because it is a navy town, there are SPs, who are like MPs, on shore patrol at all hours on the streets, and one thing about them is that they think all the airmen have it too easy and are easy prey in an idle night's work.

I got picked up twice by the same SPs, was put in the back of the patrol wagon and taken to my barracks. Each time, they said I was drinking alcohol as a minor, and drunk. And they filed a complaint with my commander.

Maybe I was drunk, but I thought you had to be disorderly, too, to get charged. I was certainly having a good time in town, and they may have seen me walking in a crooked line, but I know I never started any trouble. Those SPs just saw me as trouble, like I was wearing a banner on my sleeve. Another New York City kid.

The commander filed the complaints under "Airman drinking under age" and confined me to the barracks for a week each time. It was a kind of fine. You're out having a good time, the SPs nab you, you pay the dues.

But the third time was like they were picking on me. It was like Shalleski was punching me on First Avenue again. I just wasn't going to let them pick me up every time they saw me on the street.

I was always drinking beer.

And when you drink beer, you usually get drunk. That is what guys in the military do on their time off. I guess I would have done the same thing if I got transferred to Bermuda.

For some reason, I just wasn't growing up.

Maybe I could have cared more about my job, or not been late for every single thing I was scheduled for, or been more snappy in my salutes to the commander, but drinking beer in my time off was my business, and I wasn't going to let these SPs pick me up again without giving them a hard time.

They said I punched them, but I didn't. I just twisted myself out of their grip, one on each side of me, by flailing my arms and moving faster than my brother Billy, faster than they could comprehend, the way I did as a kid when I got into a problem. They couldn't hold me, and they pushed me to the ground and sat on me until the patrol wagon came.

This time my commander did not settle for a complaint. Resisting a direct order by a Shore Patrol was punishable by another Article 15 discipline, and the commander sent me to Hamilton Air Force Base for an evaluation.

The officers there looked at my two Article 15s and my other two altercations with the SPs, and decided that while I was not an undesirable person in the military, neither was I filling the ideals of the air force, and so they gave me an honorable discharge. It was like they were saying, "No hard feelings, but we have eight hundred thousand other guys who can do your job."

The air force wasn't happy with me, no doubt about it, and if they didn't want me around anymore, at least they were giving me the benefit of the doubt by laying me off and giving me a good discharge. This is fair, and it is also a little bit of good luck.

And so here I am without any more excuses.

No more ifs. It was me who didn't make the bus. It was me who was late for work. It was me who became a slacker after my transfer was redlined. It was me who drank all that beer. It was me who resisted the direct order of the SPs.

If I have a black and a bleak future, the fault is all mine. I cannot any longer believe that I am a lone figure, like a dolmen on a plain, fighting the elements.

I have to believe that I have been running after the good times and blaming the bad times.

But there is a difference between admitting your fault and trying to rectify it. I have to do something. I can't just live like a trail bum in the Nevada hills. If I go back to New York, at least, I will have my mother, and Monsignor Ford, and Archie, and people who have been "interested" in me, to use Archie's word. The air force is giving me a clean slate, and now I have to look for a new opportunity to make something of myself.

I don't know how many second chances a man can get in this world, but I know I have to ask God for one more.

I can tell now that Patches has his eye on the calf as well. The calf turns and runs, and I can see the double crossed bars of the cow as she also bolts.

We are pretty close to them, and I take my rope from over the horn. I grab the honda, my hand firmly over the knot, and swing about six feet of rope out while I throw my spurs into Patches' rear shanks. He doesn't need much kicking or encouragement, for he loves to do this, run for a calf across the sandy grass flats. I keep the calf on my right. The little guy runs about half as fast as Patches, and I now have my right hand about two feet down from the knot, holding firm onto the reins and the rest of the rope in my left hand. Patches is running full gallop, and I am yelling "giddap, giddap, yippee" to frighten the calf, to keep it from thinking too much. Yelling and galloping, I am now swinging the rope in moderate, graceful circles until I am five or six feet from the calf, and I let the rope loose, and it flies in circles over the calf's head and falls onto its shoulder blades, and I pull back fast before he runs through the loop, and the rope falls down and secures around his neck, and I take what rope is left in my right hand and make two fast turns around the saddle horn as I pull back on the reins with all my strength. Patches doesn't want to stop, which is his biggest problem, and I pull back harder and harder, hoping the reins won't break, because if a rein breaks, I'll lose the calf and the rope, and it will take me forever to stop Patches.

Finally, Patches stops, and the calf gets pulled to the ground by its own momentum.

I am now patting the horse's neck, saying "Good boy, good boy," pulling back gently on the reins so that Patches is keeping the rope taut. I get off the horse and follow the rope down to the calf. It's a real little guy, maybe two months old. I pick him up, plop him easily onto the grass-patched sand, and pull the knife from my jeans pocket. Two small triangles is all I have to cut from his right ear. People can remove and replace a metal tag, but no one can change an ear mark like that. It is a registered cut, along with Dave's brand. Now if a federal inspector rides these hills and sees this calf sucking on Dave's cow, he will also see that the ear mark is Dave's, too, because no cow will let some strange calf at her teats.

I take the cuts. The calf does not feel them, for it is dead skin I am cutting. There is a lot of whining, but the calf lies easily on the ground until I take the rope from around his neck. I can see the cow not far off, and so can the calf. He has a bouncy spring to his gait as he runs to his mother.

These cows and bulls and calves are closely controlled in this great open and fenceless space. It has been like this for more than a hunded years, and the system works.

Patches is standing still, my rope hanging limply from the saddle horn alongside him. I grab his reins, pat his neck a few times, and kiss the sweaty top of his nose.

"Good boy, Patches," I say as I pull myself back into the saddle and wind the rope in curls over the saddle horn. "There is a calf that won't get waylaid, anyway. It's a good system for the cows."

Patches seems to nod his head as we continue to walk the hills looking for more of Dave Iverson's calves.

I laugh a little. I don't usually carry on a conversation with Patches, but now I just laugh a little more and say, "If there was a system like this for people, maybe none of us would get lost, huh?"

Chapter Fifty-three

My mother was right. There are no good times in a person's life, like in historical periods. Just different times. Or maybe all time is just a series of little difficulties and challenges wedged between big ones, and if you're lucky, you are able to squeeze as much happiness as is possible between the beginning and the end. The key is to know when you are happy, and I have recently come to think that I know when I am happy.

It is hard to put into words, but I know.

When things are going right, I can feel it inside.

I can feel my soul dancing.

This is my first week working as a mechanic's helper in the pipe-fitting shop of the New York Central Railroad, and it is Friday afternoon. I just received my first paycheck, $94 for forty hours' work, which, when you consider I was making $180 a month in the air force, you can understand why my soul was dancing.

I have no great interest in being money hungry or in the accumulation of things, but I don't know of any other way to make a judgment about how I'm doing. I suppose I could measure my happiness, but somehow that often seems to be directly tied into the amount of cash in the pocket.

I know that money can't buy happiness, but without it you can't buy anything.

I was flat broke after I bought that little gold ring for my mother, and she was flat broke when I gave it to her. Sure, she would have been just as happy if I gave her a little pencil drawing I made, but I was made happier by having the forty bucks to buy her the ring. The thing about true happiness, I guess, is to recognize that both of us would have been just as happy if we put the money for the ring in the poor box, for the thought of doing something generous for another is what carries the day. If you can find a scale to weigh the value, you'll find that a generous thought is always heavier than gold.

I've just cashed my railroad check and my pockets are flush with money. I'll be able to pay my mother back for Patches in just a couple of months, and everything seems to be going great.

My mother is still working for Ma Bell, and still doing the ironing for neighbors.

Billy left Hunter College, but he started up again at New York University. He's working full-time at Kips Bay as the gym instructor, but I have the best-paying job in the family.

"The Irish are getting up in the world," my mother said at breakfast this morning, folding over the pages of the *News*.

"You bet," I said.

My mother laughed. "I'm talking about Senator Kennedy," she said. "He's running for president."

"He's no Al Smith," Billy said.

"But he is Irish," my mother said.

"So was Al Smith," my brother answered.

"If he can get me on the police department or the fire department," I said, "I'll vote for him."

There is enough money in the family now to buy all the clothes we need and go to a movie whenever we want. Everyone is working, and, so to speak, there is a chicken in every pot.

Billy told me recently that New York University is trying out a special program for people like me who have no high school, but who have a General Education Development certificate from the military. I'm going down to Washington Square tomorrow to see about it.

*   *   *

There is just an hour or so until quitting time.

People who work for the railroad, I have found, have developed a lot of sloppy attitudes about work.

At least, I have never seen anything like the shirking that goes on in Grand Central Station, where every afternoon like clockwork the whole working corps slips into the dark train cars, sitting idle in the terminal, for a lazybones nap. Some mechanics and their helpers even lay themselves out in nice clean sheets in the Pullman cars, the sleeper cars, for the last two hours every day.

It is all pretty boring to me, and since there is nothing for me to do, I have been carrying around a paperback book so that I can sit under a light on the back tracks to read until the workers come out of the railroad cars at ten to four.

It is like a retreating army at ten to four every afternoon as the plumbers, electricians, steamfitters, carpenters, the railroad cops, pipe coverers, and maintenance men pile out of the Pullmans. I know that this kind of nesting can get you fired, and I don't want any part of it.

But today, my mechanic, Jimmy Niven, doesn't go to the Pullmans, and he takes me to the north end of track 16. He hands me his flashlight and gives me an order.

"Go down under the track," he says, "and find my tool bag, a canvas one. It should be right beneath us."

A helper has to do what his mechanic says, and I don't think much of it.

I jump down on the tracks and look for one of the small entrances beneath the platform, squares cut into the concrete walls of the platform above. The steam and water pipes and the electrical conduit run beneath these platforms in Grand Central Station, and I guess Niven was working there before I came on the job.

I put the flashlight on and crawl into the hole. There is just room enough for a man to get around on his hands and knees. It is tropical-jungle damp because of the heat of the steam pipes, and I suddenly begin to sweat. I aim the flashlight quickly left to right, and I see a tool bag about twenty-five feet down the long and narrow chamber, on its side on the dusty, brick-strewn floor of hard-compacted earth.

I am more than ten feet into this crawl space when I realize I am hearing a strange noise, a sort of fluttering sound. It is a weird sound, something I have never before heard, and I throw my light beam upward, and I am stopped like glue in my crawl by what I see.

The walls and the ceiling above are covered with water bugs, not a clear inch of concrete shows through, and they are vibrating and crawling over one another like ants. Not one is less than two inches long, and many have antennae which go another two inches. I have never seen anything like this, and I am frozen.

There could be a pot of gold next to that tool bag, I am thinking, and I would give it up in a second. I just have to get out of here because I know that this shaking ceiling, like the walls full of roaches I used to think about as a boy in my top bunk, is going to fall down right on top of me, and they will carry me away the way ants can carry a dead fly.

I have to get out of here, I am thinking, before it crumbles and it is raining water bugs.

God.

I remember picking up that beer bottle when I was a kid, putting it to my mouth for the last drop of beer left by the aunts and uncles who had been singing Irish songs, and that scurrying roach falling into my mouth, spitting it out, thinking that I would die in a minute, the roach germs running rampant through my body. I know I have to get out of this scourge, this plague, before I pass out, and tell Jimmy Niven that he will have to crawl for his own tool bag, that he can stick this job in with his dirty laundry, that I don't care what he does, but I'm not going in this torture chamber to get a bag of tools someone forgot.

God.

The sound is like a purring interrupted by coughing from a consumptive cat. I am still frozen.

I can't tell Niven that I won't do it. I can't risk my job. I am making all this money, I am paying back my mother, and this is the first real shaft of light I have had over my life in New York, the first job I have found since I came home from Nevada. These jobs are hard to get, and I wouldn't have gotten this one if Denny Reade hadn't knocked on the door to say that he heard I was home and looking for a job. "A messenger from the angels," my mother called him.

Denny Reade isn't more than a few years older than me, and I don't even know him that well, but he got me this job because people on 56th Street help each other out, like the Pennsylvania Dutch who put up each other's barns. If I back out of this corridor, I will disappoint my mother, and Denny Reade will think that I'm a loser, and everybody on 56th Street, the whole neighborhood, will think me a yellow-striped loser.

I can't back out.

But I'm frozen here. I can't go in, either.

I remember now what my mother said when she had me make an hour's worth of stretched faces. "Cross your finger, one on the other, and press down as hard as you can. And say 'stop,' over and over."

But now I want to say "go," and not "stop."

Now I have one finger crossed onto the other, pressing down like a vise, my eyes closed.

"Go, go, go, go, go," I am saying out loud as I inch nearer and nearer to the tool bag, feeling out before me, not wanting to open my eyes, knowing that to see a water bug on me is going to be harder to take than thinking one is on me. I can live with the thought as long as I keep my eyes closed.

I am not thinking at all now of the vibrations above and around me. I am wondering if the builders put the water bugs under these tracks because they knew the Irish would be working for the railroad.

Finally, I feel the tool bag, and I turn quickly, dragging it behind me. Finally, I open my eyes, and I see the light at the opening door, and scurry as fast as I can, feeling my insides fluttering now like there are a million winged things in my stomach, flapping their two million wings trying to fly out.

Now I am out on the track again, and I look to see if there are any trains coming. The third rail is across from me, and I have to remember that even if I am covered with water bugs, I will have to keep watching that rail. I drop the tool bag and wipe my hands all over my body like I am wet and have fallen into a sand pit. I look all around, and I do not see a single bug. Not one. I take three deep breaths to bring my blood pressure down as I throw the heavy canvas tool bag up on the track.

Jimmy is lighting a cigarette, and he watches me climb up on the platform out of the corner of his eye. I know that he knows there are millions of water bugs down below us, and he is just waiting for me to say something.

But I don't say anything.

I just carry his bag up the track because that's my job. We are silent until we enter the great open space of the Grand Central Terminal.

"Well?" Jimmy says, a little grin on either side of the cigarette hanging from his mouth.

"Well, what?" I answer.

"Any trouble finding the bag?"

"No," I say, "no trouble at all."

I am laughing to myself as we walk, thinking that the consequence of a bad experience can be beneficial beyond understanding or explanation. Maybe I had to go in there with the water bugs, but nowhere does it say that I have to give him the satisfaction of knowing I almost pissed in my pants.

I am now driving a cab, stopped at a light at the corner of 134th Street and Lenox Avenue. Most cabdrivers pass blacks by if they are trying to hail a cab, even in the rain and snow, but I don't think that is right.

I remember something Billy said to me when we were both boys. I was thirteen, maybe fourteen. We were walking down to a game we had planned at the basketball courts just below the United Nations building, and a bum came up to me with a ditched cigarette in his hand. The guy had not bathed in months, was a little drunk, and had an open sore over his eye.

"Gimme a light," the bum said, stopping us in the middle of the sidewalk in front of the General Assembly Building.

"Get lost," I said, and I continued walking around him.

But my brother stopped.

"Dennis," he said, "do you have matches in your pocket?"

He knew I had matches in my pocket because I just started smoking in front of him and I had a butt going down First Avenue.

"Yeah," I said.

"Give the guy a light," Billy demanded.

I shrugged my shoulders and lit the bum's ditcher.

My brother was silent then, for the next two blocks, until we got to the basketball court. He dribbled the ball twice before he spoke.

"You have to give everyone the benefit of the doubt," he said, "if you don't know any more than you see."

I never said anything to my brother in return then, but I think of that now when I see people like these two guys in the back of my cab. It is my last fare of the night. I picked them up down on 14th Street, and they have taken me way up here in the heart of Harlem. They look pretty tough, but for all I know they could be scientists working on the cure for cancer.

Not likely, but I don't know any more than I see.

I hear the back door opening and I turn around.

"Wait here," one of the men says, " 'cause we have to be in this place to get us some money, some cab fare."

They don't stop to look back as I watch them go into a crowded bar on the avenue. I have the meter running, and it is already almost ten dollars. I wait, and I wait, and it is now almost twelve dollars. I will only make a dollar of this twelve dollars, but the cab company is going to want the whole twelve first.

They won't care if I get beat for the fare.

"It's your problem, pally," the dispatcher will say. "You should have got a cop."

I stop the meter and press one finger on top of the other to concentrate. This is a lot of money to lose.

I lock the cab and walk into the bar.

Jazzy music is playing loud and people are yelling at one another to be heard above the noise. People turn to look at me as I go down the aisle past the bar, looking for my fares. I don't care what anyone says or does, because I know that I cannot afford to lose a night's wage like this. I have to make a stab at trying to get my money, even if, I am thinking, somebody makes a stab at me.

I see my fare, deep in conversation with another man. I don't see the other guy who was also in the cab.

But a scone on the dish, as my mother used to say, is always better than one in the oven.

"I'm sorry," I say, interrupting the man in his conversation, "but I guess you forgot about me."

"What you want?" the man says.

"What you want?" the other man says.

"I want my cab fare," I answer, trying hard to keep my chin up. "Twelve bucks."

"Man," the one I don't know says to my fare, "you owe this man for a taxi ride?"

"I don't know," my fare says, "maybe Horace owes him."

"Man, Horace is gone, and now you pay this man his money, hear."

My fare now looks at me, up and down.

"How much?" he asks.

"Twelve."

He takes twelve dollars from the bar and hands it to me.

I shove the money in my pocket and skip out of the bar like I had a winning sweeps ticket.

Then, back in the cab, driving down Lenox Avenue with my off-duty light on, I had a thought.

You should've, I scolded myself, asked for a tip.

I am now in the street watching Donald Doran fold the moving blankets. He is sweating heavily, and I am feeling guilty that I am so cool and collected. All the furniture is in and up, including the big Magnavox TV that Uncle Andy gave us when Aunt Kitty got him to buy her a new one. It's the third TV Uncle Andy has given us. It's as big as a jukebox, but the screen is just ten inches across. Not that it matters, for I watch TV even less than my mother, and I have never seen Billy watch anything other than a game, any kind of game.

It was the only day Billy could organize the move, and I had a final examination at New York University. I felt I was letting my brother down, but he understood. He is turning out to be a professional student himself, and no one knows the importance of a final examination better than Billy. If you fail a course, the loss will put you in the hole for almost a hundred and fifty bucks. You could get a moving company to move a palace for that kind of money.

But now a neighborhood moving job like this one costs just a case of beer and a half dozen heroes from Rossi's. All you have to do is round up the guys on their downtime.

Billy, I knew, wasn't going to rearrange it because of my final exam schedule. He already had Mike Harris, Vinny Gaezo, and Tommy Henderson rounded up, and Donald Doran was bringing his father's truck.

We have moved just two blocks away, to 54th Street off Second Avenue. It is still up three flights. I was hoping my mother would find something on a lower floor, but she told me it was a good deal, "a classy apartment" for fifty-six dollars a month, and rent-controlled 'til death do you part.

My mother is under the sink as I enter the apartment for the first time. She is scrubbing away as Billy and the others are moving the furniture around to make everything fit. It's another railroad apartment, and a little smaller than apartment 26 on 56th Street. I am wandering around, looking to see what happened to the bunk beds, so at least I will have somewhere to throw my books.

"Not a roach in the place," my mother says, popping out from under the sink, "and if you look out the back window, you will see a tree, green leaves and all."

Sure enough, out the kitchen window there is a tall backyard tree.

I know a sagebrush from a cactus, but I am uncertain as to what this tree is. It could be a sycamore or an oak for all I know, but in New York they are called backyard trees, which is easy to remember, and this one is full and waving slightly in a breeze. It adds something bright and fresh to the apartment, and I can almost smell its fragrance. My mother is smiling from ear to ear. She is drying her hands with the bottom of her apron.

"How," she asks, "did you do on the test?"

"A hundred."

"You got a hundred?"

"No," I laugh, "that's how many questions there were."

"C'mon," she says, "how did you do?"

"Flying colors, Mom, is all I know." I raised a finger and continued, "The professor asked the one question with which I was thoroughly acquainted."

"What's that, big shot?" Billy breaks in.

" 'What is the difference between truth and beauty?' the professor asked, and you know what I wrote?"

"What did you write?" my mother asks.

"I wrote that the truth is I don't know any of the answers, and the beauty is I don't give a damn."

"You didn't?" my mother says.

I laugh. It's always so easy to pull my mother into a joke.

"I didn't, Mom," I say. "It was all Greek to me, but I knew about the wine-dark sea and poor Mrs. Oedipus, so I guess I got a B."

"Oh, I am so proud of you," my mother says. "But I'd be prouder if there was an A."

"Well," Billy says, "it's okay to get out of a moving job for a B, I guess."

These are salad days for me, even though I got caught in the lay-off by the railroad and have to drive a cab when I can get one in the shape-up, or work as a chauffeur for the limousine company if they have a job when I call them.

I am not making a decent salary by a long shot, but I am reading everything in and about literature I can get my hands on, and sensing that I am changing with every page I read.

It is now a September morning, and I have read that the City of New York is accepting filings to take the police and the fire depatment examinations. I am in the middle of breakfast, and I have an early morning class, but the news sparks an enthusiasm inside me that I have hardly known. I am going to the department of personnel first thing today. I dress fast, and then I do something I haven't been doing much lately. I grab my mother around her slender shoulders and give her a kiss on the cheek.

"Mom," I say, "the Irish are really going to get up in the world this time."

She gives me a welt on the rear end as I head out the door, and says, "Good luck to you now, Dennis."

Chapter Fifty-four

Four years later I am twenty-five years old, and it is 1966. The war in Vietnam is beginning to boil over, there is something called Black Power that is taking over the civil rights movement, Muhammad Ali is beating everyone, and Bobby Hull has scored fifty-four goals for the Rangers.

My mother's good-luck wish seems to have worked, because I got the fire department job.

This is the job that has saved my life.

I could go on from here and make a million dollars, but that wouldn't be such a great leap. It wouldn't mean half as much as having gotten through all the trouble of my young years on the East Side of New York, and still being able to take the oath of office for the New York City Fire Department.

I am now crossing the wide, dirt-strewn, cobblestoned surface of Intervale Avenue. I look up at the front entrance of Engine Company 82, at the high, red-painted doors. The red is so vibrant it makes me think that a flashbulb has gone off.

I look around the area.

The corner of Intervale Avenue and 169th Street is filled with action. There is loud Latin music blowing out of a loudspeaker in front of a bodega across the street from the firehouse. In the distance I can hear a couple of bongo drums coming from another block. There is such a different culture in this neighborhood from the one on East 56th Street. There is garbage at the curbs, and the buildings are stained with roughly painted initials and symbols of one kind or another. The street itself is cobblestoned, like from a bygone era. It is everything you expect to find in a neighborhood the newspapers refer to as a ghetto.

This is my first day here, and I am scheduled to work the night tour, from six in the evening to nine in the morning, fifteen hours straight. I am not a "johnny" firefighter anymore, but neither am I a seasoned vet. I've only been in a few fires these last three years, but up here in the South Bronx it's a different fire-fighting story, and miles from the quiet firehouse in Queens where I have been working the last few years.

Here the firehouse is like an island surrounded by a sea of fire. Engine Company 82 responds to forty alarms a day, and there is nothing like this alarm rate anywhere else on the face of the earth.

I am feeling good, real good, because this is my firehouse now. I had gotten my feet wet in fire fighting out in Queens, but it just wasn't active enough there for me.

Engine Company 82 is on the top of the list of the busiest fire companies in New York, and I asked a friend of mine who is driving a deputy mayor to put the fix in for me to get me transferred here. He is also the manager of the department bagpipe band, and since I started to play the bagpipes I have been introduced to people like him who are "heavy" in the politics of the department.

So here I am, just assigned to the busiest engine company in the city, in the world, and I have no idea of what to expect. I was only told that if there is anything easy in this company, it has been hidden away for years.

I remember the day I became a firefighter as clearly as any president remembers the day he was elected. It was a day of pride and exuberance. I passed a firehouse on the way to the subway that day, the one on 51st Street, ecstatic that I would soon be a part of the whining sirens and clanging bells. I felt both reverence and the excitement of a new beginning when I was finally presented the three-inch silver Maltese cross, which is the firefighter's badge.

My wife, Pat, was there, and my mother, too, one prouder than the other that I had made it through the mental and the physical tests and the character investigation.

That badge to me was the shield of the diligent, for I was now in a job that was a fulfillment of a goal, a job that I loved in the same way patriots love America. There is so much good about it, particularly the way it makes me feel good about myself.

Maybe that comes with putting yourself on the line for other people.

This job will not make any of us rich, but I can't help thinking, after three years of fire fighting, a fabulous wife, two kids, four years of college, and a healthy mother, it would be hard to be much richer than this.

Still, I am working to lay up the stores of tomorrow.

I have become what all in my neighborhood respect—a cop or a fireman.

If I could go off to war, or perform surgical miracles, or nurse the dying, or give out soup on the Bowery, or teach in a paint-worn classroom in the South Bronx, I would have a job that would let me look in the mirror and say that the people need me. I think that's true for a fireman, too.

Not that I expect people to think of me in this way, or that anyone will be better off because of me. No. I just know that because of the nature of my work, I am needed, for fire is a thing that doesn't happen just to the other guy.

And when the alarm gets pulled, I'll do my best.

Fire fighting is a good job. I mean good, like in regular-paycheck, pay-the-rent-every-month, twenty-year-pension good.

I know I didn't have much success as a kid in school, and I didn't make such a good job of it in the air force, either.

But I was given another second chance, and a great chance it was.

It got me into college. It got me married to a wonderful woman. It got me appointed to the fire department. And it got me here to the front doors of the busiest fire company in the world, just where I want to be.

And the funny thing is, I don't know where that another second chance came from if it didn't come from God.

I had applied for the police officer job and the fireman job, and passed both tests. The police department called me, and I was being investigated, but I knew that I wanted to wait for the fire department.

I heard that the cop's job is harder to take day-to-day. People are not always supportive of cops. Except in those situations when you are being murdered or mugged, people don't like to think about cops, especially if you are double-parked, spitting, littering, loitering, making a U-turn, or fighting with the landlord or the bookie. The last person in the world you want is a cop, and when a cop shows up, you are never happy to see him.

Not the firefighter, though.

I remember that firefighter who came when I was sleeping on the fire escape so many years ago.

He was there when Mr. Sorenson needed him, because they carried Mr. Sorenson out and he just spent a day or two in the hospital after being knocked cold by the smoke. The firefighters seem to come when you need them. Even in the middle of some great tragedy, where you think no one can help you, the firefighter is going to do something that helps.

I guess I've always wanted to be like that fireman that night on the fire escape. "Hey, kid," he said, "how about that DiMaggio?" I will never forget what a great way that is to keep a youngster from being frightened.

There is no doubt that I got off to a few good starts with some disappointing finishes. I am not sure what interfered with a steady upward progress for me, and I don't think I will spend much time thinking about it.

All of us carry around some psychological baggage—if only my mother had done this, or if Father O'Rourke had done that, or if only people did not exploit or abuse children, or if only my father hadn't gotten sick, or if my mother had remarried.

None of it matters now.

What matters is that I am a part of the New York Fire Department, and the rest is all behind me.

I think being a fireman made all the difference to Pat, too. No smart girl would marry someone without a future, without the ability to provide. And now I am becoming a man with definable abilities.

My famous abilities. All my life people have been telling me that I have to recognize my abilities, and now I'm beginning to waltz in the cloak of those abilities.

I met Pat the year before I went on the fire department. Walsh and Scarry and I were in East Durham, a resort village upstate they call the Irish Alps, not far from places like Grossinger's, which they call the Jewish Alps. It was a wild, youthful weekend.

Pat was with friends, and we danced a hundred dances in some Irish ginmill a hundred miles away from the city, and had the best time. She knows all the Irish dances, and we did the Stack of Barley and the Siege of Ennis, and then we did the New York Savoy, and since I didn't know anyone with a car, we walked what seemed a hundred miles under the moonlight to where she was staying.

We dated steadily after that, the first truly steady girlfriend I ever had, and it went straight down the road called serious. So serious that we just had our second son, Dennis, who will probably wrestle his brother Brendan for a good seat at the table for the next decade.

My wife is from Queens, the daughter of a roofer like my grandfather, but her family is from county Kilkenny and mine from county Cork. Meeting Pat was also part of the good luck my mother wished me, like a good-luck prediction of a seventh son of a seventh son.

Maybe someday God will bless Pat and me with a girl to sweeten the pot. I've always wanted a Deirdre, or maybe an Aislinn, to join our Brendan and Dennis. But, if we have another boy, we'll call him Sean and maybe Sean will be the first up in the morning, and the best dressed in the family.

We are building our future together, and little by little we are doing more than getting by. We even bought a new car, a Volkswagen Bug, and we go to a play off-Broadway once in a while. I have the good city job, and I have the twenty-year pension that goes with it.

*   *   *

"If they knew about the twenty-year pension," I can remember my Uncle Buddy saying, "they'd be swimming like dolphins across the Atlantic, leaping and dancing with the joy." He wasn't talking about whatever relatives we had still working the land in Cork and Monaghan, but the whole of the Irish *publicht* from Dublin to Galway, people who we remembered as those we left behind.

When I was growing up, we always thought of the Irish we knew in Ireland as the poor relations. I never realized the history then, that they were just newly relieved of the suffering handicap of British government.

There were no "good jobs" in Ireland then, and not many now, either. If there are good jobs, we do not know anyone who has one. I never heard of a civil servant in Ireland, and while I'm sure there are some, they are not anyone we know. The good jobs are here in America.

I think of people in Ireland as heroic legions, battering rams who are there in our name denting the doors of British history. Maybe someday, like my father and all four of my grandparents, they might leave their homes and come to America to escape the English and to secure a bountiful future.

My four grandparents came from different parts of Ireland to the borough of Brooklyn, America's city of churches, land of Pee Wee Reese and one end of the Brooklyn Bridge.

They worked at laboring jobs and raised their families. There may not have been fistfuls of dollars, but there were pocketfuls of morality tales, and they all had to do with hard work and clean shirts and being on time.

My Grandfather Smith traveled, with his five children, including my father and my Uncle Tommy, whose plaque is in the back of the church, from county Monaghan, Ireland, where he owned a pub, to Glasgow in Scotland, where he owned another pub, to Detroit, Michigan, where he had hoped to work for Henry Ford, and, finally, to Brooklyn, to work in the shipyards. He did all this, like most immigrants of the time, to search out a better future for his wife, who was Ellen Cosgrove, and his children.

My mother's father, John Hogan, worked on the fishing boats out of Kinsale Harbour, county Cork. None of us knows how he came here. He just somehow walked out of the shadows of Ireland, without a history, a story, or an explanation, and ended up in Brooklyn, where one day he met my grandmother, Elizabeth Harrigan, who was born in county Clare.

"He was a solid man," my mother says, "and he always had a job—until he fell off the roof anyways."

None of my grandparents were ever on the inside of anything out of the ordinary, but they had families they loved, and they provided for them, probably better than they would have in the old sod.

And so, what does it matter if my grandparents were on the outside looking in on establishment America? They probably didn't think about it or know that once the Irish got inside of anything, politics, business, education, or sports, they always found a way to get to the top.

That kind of observation would not have helped my grandparents, or my mother or father, either. They were too busy getting by.

It doesn't matter what the top is, it could be anywhere you want it to be.

I know about the "No Irish Need Apply" signs that were in New York and Boston, and I hope my own children remember this, too. But we must also remember that America is such a different country now. We even have a civil rights law to protect against prejudice.

I don't feel put upon in any way for being of Irish parentage. Prejudice is something I worry about in our country, which still has plenty of inequities, but not for the Irish. I have always felt that I could do anything anyone else could do, could climb to any top that I wanted to climb to. I think it is good to think this. People are not like paintings where you can say that a Leonardo da Vinci is worth more than, say, a Modigliani, or like cars, where a Rolls-Royce might be better made than a Caddy. This is America after all. A car is just a car, unless you worry too much about it. And every person has a shot at going wherever they want to go.

Look at my brother Billy.

Billy's become a schoolteacher in Harlem, 127th Street and Lenox Avenue. He's read more books than anyone I know, and hasn't disappointed anyone in meeting the potential of his intellect. Things could've been a lot easier for him, but he's not the complaining type. He didn't go to Exeter, and he didn't go to Oberlin, and he never had a year in college when he didn't work two jobs. But if you asked him, he'd tell you that he got a good deal, and the deal paid off.

I can hardly ask a question about literature, philosophy, history, art, or music that he doesn't know the answer. And he cares about everything. He leaves the humanitarian talk to the civic theorists and do-gooders, and commits himself to the education of Negro children.

Billy was offered an assignment in a softer school out in Queens, or in midtown Manhattan, but he wanted to go where he would be challenged by the toughest kids in New York.

And who knows how many da Vincis or Thurgood Marshalls may evolve out of his classroom?

Sometimes I think about the impoverished childhood so many of us lived on East 56th Street. If Billy and I grew up poor, so did my mother and her brother and sisters. But that shouldn't make any difference in a person's life, good or bad, positive or negative. It didn't in ours. Billy and I never missed a meal, and we sang songs around a keg of beer on Sundays. It was never a life of hardship for us. We may have been on the welfare rolls, but we always saw and understood how much better it is for people when they are working.

Working, as my mother tried to teach us, is the key to tomorrow and the definition of life.

Such is the nostalgia of the tribe—my tribe, anyway.

My earliest memory is of my mother taking in a big pile of shirts from a neighbor down the hall on 56th Street.

"Work," she said, plopping the shirts into the kitchen bathtub, "is the thing that supports the neck."

It was a long time before I knew what she was talking about, and it might be her greatest lesson. Whether it is ironing shirts or being a firefighter, twenty-year pension or not, caring about your work is the thing that supports the neck in keeping the head high.

If there is anyone to thank for getting me through to where I am, it is my mother. She is having a tough time with the stairs now, and I know that she will have to move from the tenement on 54th Street pretty soon, by the time she retires from the telephone company, anyway.

I try to see her once a week. She comes to our house mostly, to see the kids, to baby-sit while Pat and I go out to a movie.

I wish she would stop smoking. If she stopped smoking, she could do another few years of climbing the stairs. But she has been combing her hair one way for most of her life, and I know that she would not take the advice she once gave me to use a brush.

"I'm going to have to put a carton of Old Golds in your coffin the day they bury you, Mom," I said to her recently, when we were sitting across from each other, having a cup of coffee.

"Don't forget the matches," she returned quickly, with a wink of her eye.

I like being with my mother. She has humor. She might have some prejudices and periods of short temper also, but they are a consequence of a longtime loneliness, I think, and a small price to pay for giving up any chance of a normal social life to care for her two sons.

I believe she has earned the right to tons of happiness, but it doesn't look like much will come her way. I suppose she is like a million other women who were left alone with a few kids by a husband who became absent for whatever reason. They are like the fifth estate in America, and what they do is every bit as consequential for America's future as anything that gets written in a newspaper or done in Congress, a church, or a synagogue.

I am sure it is not easy to be alone now, but my mother does it with her chin held high, anyway. She works six days a week at the telephone company. She comes home after work, makes a small dinner, gets into bed, reads the *Daily News,* and sips a small glass of port. She does this every night without fail.

It may not be much of a life, but it's a respectable one, I think. I make sure I call her every day, to let her know that she is being thought of, to thank her in my own way.

But there are others to thank as well. My mother always reminded me that I had to say thank you for any little good that came into my life. Who do I thank now for getting me through? I haven't asked my mother, but I am certain she would say that I should start with God.

And then?

A city that paid the rent and put an egg on the table for us when we needed it?

A church?

A boys' club on 52nd Street?

I met a lot of caring people on the concrete streets of New York, and I guess they will never know that I sensed that they cared. I never said thank you to any of them.

They were just good and decent New Yorkers doing their jobs, and I don't think they expected thank yous at the end of the day.

Now I am thinking of summing up the twenty-five years I've lived through, and the first thing that comes to mind is the face of my mother, and I can see all those tenement tears rolling down the soft, sculpted cheeks of her face.

It is the only real regret I carry with me.

I know that a good life can change on a dime, and it does for many people. An accident, an illness, or a death can change everything in the life of a family. My family and I have been lucky, and I have been especially lucky. I guess all those prayers my mother said were heard, because the tomorrows, without a doubt, are a lot brighter than the yesterdays.

I'm an Irish Catholic kid from the tenements, and I learned a lot with the help of people like Archie and Father O'Rourke and Monsignor Ford. I learned that in America you just have to have a sense of what's fair, and to keep your chin up as you try to make a life. Here a gas station attendant is as good as a banker. We have Jacksonian democracy on our side, and our pants are donned one leg at a time like anyone else, popes or presidents.

I guess I learned from Archie in the Kips Bay Boys Club that we must believe that we all start from a playing field that is level enough for us to build something on. And, on that field, you just have to believe in yourself.

"Get out there and do something with yourself," Archie would scold. "Blow a trumpet. Yell, if you have to. Make yourself known."

There is not a moment that I think I didn't get a fair shot at every opportunity.

Look, I have a mother who never took her eyes off me. She gave us the liturgy of work, and she taught us the litany of learning without thinking twice about it.

And I was lucky to be born in this country.

The long-range possibilities that come with these facts are more than enough to build a future.

I remember reading Benjamin Franklin's autobiography and *The Diary of Anne Frank* and thinking that somewhere within the thoughts and passions of these two books can be found all a person needs to know about life.

For myself, I think there are three things about living a life that make sense to remember.

The first is the proverbial adage about working hard, which is so entrenched in American mythology that it hardly needs mentioning, yet it's the undeniable foundation to build anything.

The second is to believe passionately that everything is possible if you follow the advice of the first.

The third is spiritual, something that comes with time, thinking about people and our relationship to each and every person we have met, what that means to us, and how it affects our day-to-day living. This is the thing that brings quality to a life.

Like any father, I hope my children will figure it all out better than I have. At least they will know that I thought it important to try to figure it out.

They might ask me, "What is this 'it' you are always talking about?"

"Life," I will say, "just life."

I guess it's not worth much if it's not worth the time to take a look at it.

I know my life was hanging for too many years by a very thin thread, like the sword of Damocles, threatening to crash into and destroy the thin structure of my future.

But I know that I am not living so precariously now, the dangers of fire fighting notwithstanding. My feet have become planted into the concrete of New York, and I have a newfound stability I trust.

You can always tell how much someone cares about his future by how much he cares about his present. In the same way my mother used to smile at me, that smile of regard and confidence, I am now smiling at myself, and giving myself a wink in the mirror once in a while.

I am doing what I want to do, and I realize how important that is and how lucky I am that I can do this. I have changed, and I am changing. There is no one right system of behavior in the world, and there shouldn't be, but what is the point of talking about literature or history or religion if we don't believe we should get a little better in all things as we go through our years? Our lives, like our morality, our sense of fairness, and the quality of our love, should improve measurably from decade to decade, and I am thinking that if I don't sense this about myself, I am missing out on the real excitement of it all.

So here I am looking up at the towering, yellow-bricked building of Engine Company 82.

And I'm hoping I have whatever I need to fight the fires that I know will be before me. I guess that is mostly courage, which is not a personality trait you can train for in a few months at a training school.

Courage is like character, something you build up in small degrees from the day you are born.

There are a hundred things I might think of, but I'm now seeing my mother's face, in her apartment, probably reading the paper and having a cup of tea, and I wish she was here, even for a moment, as a smile slides across my lips and as the blood begins to gush through my veins, to see how happy I am.

Suddenly, as I am thinking these things, the huge red doors of Engine Company 82 and Ladder Company 31 fly open, and the trucks come out like drag racers, big and powerful, careening around the corner, speeding up 169th Street, air horns and sirens blaring all the way. All around, the bongos are beating out their quick rhythms, the crowds are snapping their fingers and feet to the music or rushing about from one side of a litter-strewn street to another. I watch the trucks until they disappear from view, off to some unknown emergency in our country's most forgotten, falling-apart, crime-ridden neighborhood. It is like the doors have been opened to a new world, one I have not seen before.

God.

This is going to be exciting.

Reading Group Guide

On Reading
by Dennis Smith

When I think of the thousands of reading groups now meeting regularly, not only in America, but throughout the world, I think back to those multitudinous hours I spent with my fellow firefighters between alarms in the kitchen of the firehouse watching TV, drinking coffee, talking city and department politics, joking, and just hanging out. If only I'd been sagacious enough to create a reading club within that group of active and quick-thinking firefighters. Oh, how much more fun and productive that down time would have been!

You probably noticed in *A Song for Mary* how often I made reference to the books I read at various periods in my early life. I loved books in the way I loved ice cream, for nothing compares to the youthful vitality and yearning that a youngster brings to the act of picking up a book. The love of reading is not a natural phenomenon, but a learned behavior that develops in substance and measure as time and books go by.

Surely by that definition, the love of reading grows as one gets older, but I'm not so sure if the enthusiasm I brought to reading when I was a boy can ever be matched. Such was the influence of my mother, who never sat down without a book or a magazine in her hands. I'm certain I watched her reading even before I was able to describe what I saw, and that image has stayed with me these many years.

An early love of books brought me to an early love of writing. With every book I read came the demand of inquiry, and I remember on some days I spent as much time with the dictionary as with the book I was reading. I don't know exactly when it was, but sometime in my teenage years I realized that I had a larger vocabulary than just about all of my friends, and I intuited that the ability to say what you mean was enhanced by the amount of words you could call upon. I also knew this ability would be useful in my life, but I wasn't sure how.

When I was growing up on East 56th Street, getting along with others didn't require language skills so much as the ability to bring a man home in stickball or to handle your dukes should the need arise.

School was not central to our lives, and few kids on the block ever made it all the way through college. To finish high school was quite an accomplishment, something that made your family proud indeed.

At sixteen, though, I had already quit school and was working at a florist shop. Somehow I knew that my education wasn't over, that I still had more to learn if I was to get along in this world. I didn't want to deliver flowers for the rest of my life, but I had no idea what I wanted to be. Like many people I knew, I just wanted a well-paying job and the freedom to enjoy myself as I pleased. We never talked of succeeding, for it was enough to get by. Success was something that was accidental, and happened to other people. There was no misery as long as there was a job.

I bought a notebook while I was working for the florist. I had an idea for a story that would satirize our local politicians, and that's all I remember of it. What I remember more clearly is the *act* of buying the notebook. I was just sixteen years old, and I suppose it was then that I decided I wanted to be a writer. I don't remember a specific story inscribed in that notebook, nor what became of the notebook itself. It remains curious to me that I thought to buy a notebook, a positive act in itself, while the rest of my life was in turmoil.

Yet still, during this time that I'd abandoned schooling and was working at the most menial job, reading a book was as natural to me as a luncheon sandwich in a brown paper bag. I read every day, and would occasionally scurry off to the library to consult cited books or the almanac or encyclopedia. I became interested in, well, just about everything. This is the first, and perhaps only, requisite for a person who wants to be a writer. Looking back, I feel privileged that I was so motivated at such a young age. I'm certain I have my mother to thank for that, along with the nuns who taught the skills of sentence construction and the librarian down at Kips Bay Boys Club, who made books so accessible.

If we go through our libraries we'll find that all books can be separated into two groups: those that provide data and those that provide joy. All books provide information of one kind or another, and usually we can find the information easily arranged in our libraries. To learn that Rome is in Italy we can look in the geography section; that all roads lead to Rome sends us to the history section; to see the influence of modern-day Rome in the world we might look under the Roman

Catholic Church in the religion section; and to learn how to make Spaghetti la Romano we will go to the food section. In all of these books we will find data that will help us in understanding the world.

And then, there are the books, happy or sad, that provide pure joy in the reading.

Brendan Behan once said that most people have nationalities but the Irish and the Jews seem to have psychoses. I often think of this in relation to my own writing, for it's not enough to have just a cursory understanding of the character I might be writing about. I have to know his or her educational and social background and family's history. In my novels, most of my characters are Irish-American, and since the Irish had been a subjugated and mistreated people for 800 years I can see what Brendan Behan meant by psychosis, how the Irish might share a social and psychological affinity with the Jews, and how any or all of this information might shape my character's view of the world.

To me, the understanding of characters is at once the challenge and the excitement of literature. Can any of us ever forget, in *Moby Dick*, Ishmael's alarmed first sighting of Queequeg in New Bedford's Spouter Inn? Or, in *Crime and Punishment*, the rambling of Raskolnikov's thoughts as he crept those 730 steps to the pawnbroker's apartment? It is a skillful writer who creates characters—even historical characters—with issues that relate to you and me, and to apply those issues to the here and now.

Oh, the joy I continue to get from reading—there is nothing like learning about the world's people, and to learn about myself.

I've published ten books thus far, every one originating in some idea I found in my wanderings, some of those wanderings literary. From the wellsprings of experience and reading, I've managed to craft fictional stories, vignettes, memoirs, even some data-sharing nonfiction books—all of which, I hope, have been helpful to readers. I also hope I've provided some joy.

If I had the opportunity to do it all over again, I don't think I'd change a comma, except, perhaps, that I'd start a reading club in my firehouse on that dingy cobblestone street in the South Bronx. I'd find some way to get those firefighters away from the cards and the television and into a group discussion about something we've all read. And what book would we start with? I know the book *I'd* vote for, but I'll leave it up to you, dear reader, to determine which book it should be.

Questions for Discussion

1. In the prologue, Dennis talks about finding the memory that "resides in the swelling of the heart" and "speeds the blood." Which memory seemed to have the most positive effect on Dennis? The most negative? Which memory affected *you* the most?

2. The subtitle is "An Irish-American Memory." In what ways is this a particularly Irish book? How is it distinctly American?

3. Dennis had strong role models in his life: his mother, his priest, Billy, Archie at the Kips Bay Boys Club. How did each of these role models affect his behavior? How did their effect on him change as he grew older? How would their influence be different if Dennis had grown up in the 1990s, not the 1950s?

4. The Catholic church plays a large role early on in Dennis' life, especially being an altar boy and the story of Saint Maria Goretti. What was the significance of the Saint Maria story? How did being an altar boy affect him? What are the positive and negative aspects of his experiences with the church?

5. At one point, Dennis is rescued from a fire escape by a fireman. Later we find out his life is changed when he joins the NYFD. How did the incident on the fire escape influence his choice? Tell about a moment in your own life that, although it seemed insignificant at the time, altered your future in a meaningful way.

6. The absence of Dennis' father is a recurring theme in the book. What actions were a direct result of his father's absence? How did he try to fill the void in his life with other male role models? How was his relationship with Billy affected? How did it influence how he saw his mother, as a single mother and as a woman? How did it affect her over the years, in her relationship with other men and with her sons?

7. New York City is its own character in this book: the welfare it

provides the Smiths, Dennis' travels through Kips Bay, into Harlem, to St. Patrick's Cathedral, to the public library, etc. How would his life have been different had he grown up in a rural, instead of urban, area? What do you think they would have done if the welfare system had not helped them? How did his mother try to get Dennis to make the most of the city? At what point did he finally understand the meaning of her "tenement tears"? Do you think life in a small town would have been easier or more difficult for Dennis and his family?

8. Dennis' relationship with his mother is the central theme of the memoir. Which scenes are the most representative of her guidance? What does the ring symbolize? What does the song "Rose of Tralee" symbolize for Dennis and his mother? How did her purchase of the aviator jacket make you feel? What do you think that meant to Dennis? Why was she so adamant about not telling anyone they were poor? How do you think she felt when she saw Dennis spiraling into crime as a teenager? When her husband went to the hospital?

9. Dennis' life changes when he gets in a street brawl and is ordered to join the Air Force. What do you think would have happened to him had he not gotten into the fight? Would he have turned his life around eventually? What other things in his life would have helped to turn him around?

10. When Dennis joins the fire department, he has a moment to reflect on what has brought him to Engine Co. 82. What lesson was the most important that he learned? Who helped bring him to that point in his life? Share a moment in your own life when you knew you could achieve your dream, no matter what transpired before then.